건강보건관련
국제기구 지식정보원

국제기구 지식정보원 시리즈 ❽

건강보건관련 국제기구 지식정보원

International Organizations ㅣ홍현진 · 노영희ㅣ

ICSi 한국학술정보㈜

머리말

 건강이란 단순히 질병이 없고 허약하지 않은 상태만을 의미하는 것이 아니라 육체적·정신적 및 사회적으로 완전한 상태를 말한다. 일반적으로 'health'를 '건강' 혹은 '보건'으로 번역하여 사용하고 있으며, 전문학문 분야에서는 이를 보건학, 보건의료, 보건복지 등 건강이 아닌 보건으로 사용하고 있다. 그러므로 보건이란 지역사회 대중을 대상으로 건강을 해치는 원인이 되는 사회적 요소를 제거함으로써 각 개인의 질병을 예방하여 건강을 증진하고 생활구조를 개선(환경위생)하는 것이라 할 수 있다.

 공중보건학이란 환경위생의 향상, 전염병의 관리, 개인위생의 개별교육, 질병의 조기진단과 예방을 위한 의료서비스의 개별교육, 질병의 조기진단과 예방을 위한 의료서비스의 조직, 건강을 적절하게 유지하는 데 필요한 삶의 표준을 보장하기 위해 사회적 목표로 조직화된 지역사회의 공동노력을 통하여 질병 예방과 생명 연장, 그리고 신체적·정신적 효율을 증진시키는 기술이며 과학이다.

 한편, 보건에 대해 국제적인 차원에서 접근한 국제기구 중 대표적인 기구는 WHO(World Health Organization)이다. "세계 모든 국민이 가능한 최상의 건강수준에 도달하도록 한다."는 유엔헌장의 원칙에 따라 모든 지구촌 식구들의 행복, 조화로운 인간관계와 안정을 위해 WHO는 유엔헌장을 선언했다. 그 외 인류의 건강, 복지와 보건에 관련된 사업을 하는 국제기구들은 식량 및 농업기구(FAO), 국제노동기구(ILO), 국제연합교육과학문화기구(UNESCO),

유엔개발계획(UNDP), 유엔인구활동기금(UNFPA)과 유엔환경계획(UNEP) 등의 보건 관련 국제기구들이 있다.

이러한 건강보건 관련 국제기구들은 정부 간·지역 간 연합에 의해 설립되고, 그 각 국제기구들은 개발원조와 관련한 세계적인 현안들을 협력하여 해결해 나가면서, 그 과정에서 발생하는 모든 활동과 정책을 문서화하고 있다. 각 기구의 활동에서 생산된 각종 법률과 수천 종의 간행물은 다양한 정보를 수록하고 있으므로 지식정보자원으로서 중요한 의미를 지닌다고 할 수 있다. 본 저서에서는 이러한 정보를 체계적으로 수집하고 유통시킬 수 있는 방안을 강구하고자 하였고, 이를 위해 각 국제기구가 생산 및 관리하고 있는 지식정보원에 대한 정보를 최대한 수집하여 정리하였다.

첫째, 조사대상 국제기구를 선정하였다. 현재 건강보건 관련 국제기구 중에서 비교적 규모가 큰 국제기구만을 선정하되 기구 활동의 결과를 문서로 생산하거나 기구 내에 도서관·정보센터를 두고 있는 기구들을 중심으로 조사하였다.

둘째, 선정된 국제기구 자체에 대한 조사를 함으로써 국제기구 정보원에 대한 자료를 제공할 뿐만 아니라 그러한 정보원을 제공하는 각 국제기구에 대한 이용자들의 이해를 돕고자 하였다. 각 국제기구의 소재지, 설립연혁, 설립목적, 국제기구의 회원, 주요 사업, 한국과의 관계 등에 관한 정보를 조사하였으며, 주요 사업이나 국제기구 회원에 대한 정보는 국제기구 사이트나 관련 문헌에서 정보를 찾을 수 없는 경우 생략하였다.

셋째, 선정된 각 국제기구가 제공하고 있는 정보서비스 및 그 특징에 대해서 구체적으로 조사하였다.

■ 각 국제기구의 정보배포정책에 대해 조사함으로써 향후 국내

특정 기관이 건강보건 관련 국제기구 정보원을 수집하고자
할 경우 본 저서를 통해서 그 정보배포정책에 대한 정보를 얻
을 수 있도록 하였다. 즉, 각 국제기구별 온·오프라인 정보배
포정책을 조사하였다.

■ 각 국제기구가 보유하고 있는 데이터베이스에 대해 조사하였
  다. 각 국제기구는 기구에 따라 약간의 차이가 있으나 각 기
  관이 소장하고 있는 데이터를 데이터베이스로 구축하여 서비
  스하고 있는 경우가 있으며, 본 저서에서는 이러한 각 국제
  기구가 제공하고 있는 데이터베이스 및 각 데이터베이스의
  서비스 방법에 대해서 조사하였다.

■ 각 국제기구가 보유하고 있는 다양한 종류의 간행물에 대해
  서도 조사하였다. 대부분의 국제기구는 각 국제기구의 활동
  을 관련 국가 또는 관련 분야 사람들에게 알리고자 하는 목
  적에서 정보 자료를 생산하여 제공한다. 따라서 국제기구의
  활동 결과는 회의보고서, 보고서, 단행본, 뉴스레터, 연속간
  행물 등 매우 다양한 정보 자료 형태로 생산된다. 본 저서에
  서는 이러한 다양한 종류의 정보원이 관련 분야 전문가 및
  이용자에게 매우 유익한 지식정보원이 될 수 있기 때문에
  모두 조사하였다.

본 저서는 2006년에 출판된 『국제기구 지식정보원의 이해와 활용』
에서 출발한다. 즉, 세계적으로 국제기구는 2만여 개가 넘는 것으로
알려지고 있으나 지면상의 한계로 위 책에는 비교적 규모가 큰 국제
기구만을 선별하여 주제 구분 없이 수록하고 있다. 그러나 각 주제
분야별로 수많은 국제기구가 있고, 각 기구에서는 관련 분야 연구자
및 행정가에게 매우 유용할 것으로 판단되는 지식정보원이 계속적으

로 발간되고 있어 주제 분야별 지식정보원 시리즈를 발간하게 되었다. 지금까지 발간된 '국제기구 지식정보원 시리즈'는 다음과 같다.

제1권: 『해사(海事)관련 국제기구 지식정보원』
제2권: 『경제관련 국제기구 지식정보원』
제3권: 『환경관련 국제기구 지식정보원』
제4권: 『인권관련 국제기구 지식정보원』
제5권: 『개발원조관련 국제기구 지식정보원』
제6권: 『문화·스포츠관련 국제기구 지식정보원』
제7권: 『정보통신관련 국제기구 지식정보원』

이번에는 제8권으로 『건강보건관련 국제기구 지식정보원』을 발간하게 되었으며, 앞으로 예술, 의료, 법률, 교육 등 다양한 주제 분야의 국제기구 지식정보원을 시리즈로 발간함으로써 국제기구 지식정보원의 국내 유통을 활성화하는 데 기여하고자 한다.

끝으로 이 책을 출판하기까지 정보 자료 수집 및 교정과 색인 작성 등 정성과 노고를 아끼지 않은 Manchester University의 임소진 연구원, 건국대학교 송영림, 이은미 연구원, 그리고 구로초등학교 사서교사 정미숙 연구원에게 깊은 감사를 드린다.

2009년 1월
홍현진·노영희

일러두기

1. 발간 목적

이 자료의 발간 목적은 세계적으로 유명한 건강보건관련 국제기구에서 생산되는 정보 자료를 국내 정보망을 통해 공식적으로 유통시키기 위함이며, 이를 위해 각 국제기구에서 생산되는 데이터베이스, 연속간행물 및 단행본에 대한 정보를 수록하고 있다.

2. 자료 수집

건강보건관련 국제기구 및 단체에서 발행한 안내서, 홈페이지, 연감 및 각종 보고서에 실린 자료들을 기초로 국제기구에 대한 간략한 정보와 각 기관에서 생산되는 자료에 대한 정보를 수집하였다. 추가적으로 보완이 필요한 경우 전화나 이메일을 이용하여 보다 구체적이고 정확한 정보를 수집하고자 하였다.

3. 기구 선정

현재 세계적으로 건강보건관련 국제기구 및 단체는 3천여 개가 넘는 것으로 나타나고 있으며, 본 저서에는 비교적 규모가 크고 정보생산량이 많은 기구를 중심으로 선정하였으며, 총 44개의 기관을 선정하여 수록하였다.

4. 수록 내용

본 저서는 건강보건관련 국제기구에서 생산되는 지식정보원을 주로 소개하는 자료이지만, 각 국제기구에 대한 일반적인 내용도 포함하고 있다. 즉, 국제기구의 소재지, 설립연혁, 설립목적 및 기능, 회원국, 한국과의 관계 등에 대한 정보를 포함하였다. 또한 정보 자료에 대한 내용을 주로 수록하고 있는데, 각 국제기구의 정보배포정책, 정보원의 주제 분야, 정보원의 종류, 서비스의 특징, 소장하고 있는 데이터베이스, 산하 도서관의 유무, 그리고 정보획득방법에 관한 정보까지도 최대한 수록하고자 하였다.

5. 약어표 및 색인

본 저서에는 독자의 이해를 돕기 위해 약어표를 첨부하되, 약어, 완전기구명, 한국어 국제기구명을 약어의 알파벳순으로 수록하였다. 또한 본 자료에 실린 국제기구를 보다 신속하게 접근할 수 있도록 국제기구명 국문·영문색인을 수록하였다.

목 차

Ⅰ. 건강보건 및 건강보건관련
국제기구의 이해

1. 건강·보건의 개요

1.1 건강의 정의

건강(Health)은 생존의 조건일 뿐 아니라 행복의 조건이기도 하다. 건강하지 않으면 어떤 호조건에서도 쾌적한 생활을 할 수 없으며, 건강하다고 하는 최대의 조건은 사회생활에서의 활동능력이 충분히 있다는 것이다. 생명의 유지에 불안감이 없는 것은 물론, 사회생활에서의 왕성한 활동능력, 여러 가지 외부 환경에 잘 적응할 수 있는 능력 등을 건강의 특성으로 보아야 할 것이다(한명규 2003).

건강이란 무엇인가에 대해 여러 가지 논의가 있을 수 있으나 이에 대한 객관적이고 폭넓은 의미로 세계보건기구(WHO: World Health Organization)가 다음과 같이 정의를 내리고 있다.

> 건강이란 단순히 질병이 없고 허약하지 않은 상태만을 의미하는 것이 아니라 육체적·정신적 및 사회적으로 완전한 상태를 말한다(Health is a complete state of physical, mental and social wellbeing and not merely the absense of disease or infirmity).

위의 정의는 1948년 4월 7일에 발표한 보건헌장(A Magna Carta for World Health)에 나타난 개념이므로 건강의 개념이 19세기 중엽 이전까지는 몸이 건강한 자가 사회를 지배하고 신체가 허약한 사람은 무시를 당하는 신체개념이 주를 이루었음을 알 수 있다. 이후 건강한 육체에 건강한 정신이 깃든다는 심신개념이 뒤를 이었으며, 20세기 중반부터는 일, 운동, 식사, 휴식, 수면 등의 일상적인 생활을 영위하는 데 아무런 지장이나 고통이 없는 상태를 말하는 생활개념으로 바뀌게 되었다.

그 후 1998년 1월 101차 세계보건기구 집행이사회에서 결의하고 5월에 열린 세계보건기구 본회의에서 승인하여 건강의 정의에 영적인 개념을 추가하게 되어 "건강이란 질병이 없거나 허약하지 않을 뿐만 아니라 육체적·정신적·사회적 및 영적 안녕이 역동적이며 완전한 상태이다."라고 정의하였다.

1.2 건강의 수준 및 유지

개인의 건강상태는 유전적 및 환경적 요인과 보건시설 혜택, 그리고 생활양식 등에 의하여 좌우되므로 건강수준 역시 각 개인의 사회적 혹은 문화적 환경에 따라 차이가 날 수밖에 없다. 따라서 건강의 척도를 간단히 나타낼 수는 없으나, 일반적으로 병이 없고 신체기능이 정상이며, 신체의 존재에 대하여 무의식 상태로서 일상생활에 보람을 느끼며 활기에 차 있고, 좋은 식욕과 안정된 몸무게를 유지하며, 충분한 수면과 심신의 안락감을 유지하고, 정서적으로 안정되고 사회생활의 조화를 이룰 수 있을 때 건강하다고 할 수 있다.

건강을 유지하기 위한 조건으로 크게 신체의 항상성설(homeostasis)과 욕구설(need)을 들 수 있다. 항상성설을 주장한 버나드(Claude bernard)는 "건강이란 외부 환경의 변화에 대하여 신체 내부의 환경의 항상성이 유지되는 상태이고, 질병에 감염된다는 것은 항상성이 파괴되어 외부 환경에 적응치 못하는 상태"라고 하였고, 욕구설을 옹호하는 학자들은 건강은 육체적·정신적 및 사회적으로 개인의 생활에 대한 욕구, 즉 1차 욕구인 본능적 욕구, 2차 욕구인 문화·

문명적 욕구, 그리고 3차 욕구인 취미와 봉사 등의 적극적 만족 추구가 어느 정도 충족이 되어야 이루어진다고 주장하였다.

1.3 보건의 정의

보건이란 영어단어인 'health'의 'hal'에서 온 것으로 몸의 건강을 의미하고 있다. 일반적으로 'health'를 '건강' 혹은 '보건'으로 번역하여 사용하고 있으며, 전문 학문분야에서는 이를 보건학, 보건의료, 보건복지 등 '건강'이 아닌 '보건'으로 사용하고 있다. 그러므로 보건이란 지역사회 대중을 대상으로 건강을 해치는 원인이 되는 사회적 요소를 제거함으로써 각 개인의 질병을 예방하여 건강을 증진하고 생활구조를 개선(환경위생)하는 것이다.

2. 공중보건학의 개요

2.1 어원

공중보건학(public health)과 같은 의미로 사용되고 있는 용어로는 위생학(hygiene, sanitation), 예방의학(preventive medicine), 사회의학(social medicine), 지역사회보건(community health) 등이 있는데, 일본이나 독일에서는 위생학이라는 표현을 애용하고 있는 반면, 영국이나 미국에서는 공중보건학이나 예방의학, 사회의학, 그리고 국내에서는 공중보건학이라는 용어를 주로 사용하고 있다

(한명규 2003).

위생학(hygiene)이란 용어는 희랍신화에 등장하는 Apollo의 아들이며 의학의 신인 Aesculapius의 딸 중에서 건강을 상징하는 여신으로 불렸던 Hygeia에서 유래하였는데, 이탈리아의 의학자인 Galenus (A. D. 130~200)가 처음으로 'hygiene'이라는 용어를 사용하였다.

2.2 정의

위생학은 환경위생을 중심으로 하는 개인위생이 주가 되었으며, 예방의학은 학문 위주로 개인의 질병 예방이 중심이 된 반면, 공중보건학은 일반 대중의 건강을 증진시키는 실천 위주의 학문이며 예방의학적 내용을 기초로 한다.

미국의 윈슬로 박사(E. A. Winslow, 1877~1957)는 "공중보건학이란 환경위생의 향상, 전염병의 관리, 개인위생의 개별교육, 질병의 조기진단과 예방을 위한 의료서비스의 개별교육, 질병의 조기진단과 예방을 위한 의료서비스의 조직, 건강을 적절하게 유지하는 데 필요한 삶의 표준을 보장하기 위한 사회적 목표로 조직화된 지역사회의 공동노력을 통하여 질병 예방과 생명 연장, 그리고 신체적·정신적 효율을 증진시키는 기술이며 과학이다."라고 정의하였다.

따라서 공중보건학의 최소 단위는 지역사회이며 대상은 개인이 아니고 지역주민 전체가 대상이 되며, 목적은 질병 예방, 수명 연장, 신체적·정신적 건강 및 효율의 증진이라고 할 수 있다.

위와 같이 공중보건학은 한 개인의 건강문제를 다루는 학문이 아니고 인간집단, 즉 지역사회 전 주민 혹은 한 나라 전체 국민의 건강을 증진시키고 향상시킬 목적으로 연구하는 학문이라 할 수 있어서 사회의학(social medicine) 또는 지역사회의학(community health)이라고도 한다.

2.3 공중보건학의 내용

공중보건학은 사회 집단을 대상으로 하므로 그 범위는 매우 다양하다 할 수 있다. 즉 사회 집단의 불건강한 상태들을 배제하는 것을 다루어야 하므로 그 범위의 내용으로는 질병 관리, 환경위생, 역학, 사회보건, 보건교육, 보건영양, 보건기획, 환경오염, 가족계획, 국민의료보험, 노인보건, 보건사회사업 등 매우 폭넓다고 할 수 있다. 이를 좀 더 세분하여 분류하면 다음과 같다(이인모, 2001).

1) 기초 분야의 내용

보건행정학, 보건교육, 보건통계학, 환경위생학, 식품위생학, 역학, 보건, 영양학, 전염병 관리, 기생충 관리, 소독, 정신보건, 위생학, 인구학, 국민의료보험, 사회보장 등이다.

2) 응용 분야의 내용

환경오염 및 공해, 도시 및 농어촌 보건, 산업보건 등이다.

3) 임상 분야의 내용

가족계획, 모자보건, 학교보건, 성인보건, 비만관리 등으로 사회가 주체가 되어 건강의 위해를 방지하는 분야를 그 대상으로 한다.

3. 건강보험과 사회보장제도

3.1 건강보험시스템

1) 건강보험제도

질병 및 부상에 대한 발생과 아기의 질병, 사망으로 인한 일시적인 의료비에 대한 개인의 경제적인 부담을 줄이기 위한 제도이면서, 국민의 건강 증진과 유지를 위한 제도이다.

2) 의약분업제도

환자치료에 사용되는 의약품을 의사가 환자의 증상을 진단한 후 처방하면 그 처방전에 의해 약국에 가서 의약품을 구입해 환자가 복용하는 제도가 의약분업제도이다. 의약분업으로 환자가 약물의 오용 및 남용을 억제해 건강을 증진시킬 수 있다.

3.2 사회보장제도

1) 산업재해보상보험

산재보험이라고도 하며, 목적은 근로자의 업무상 재해 발생에 대한 예방사업과 근로자의 복지 증진을 위한 사업을 전담하고, 업무재해에 대한 공정한 보상을 제공하는 데 있다.

2) 국민연금제도

가족의 생계를 꾸려 가는 한국의 국민이 사고나 질병으로부터 소득활동이 중단되거나 가족생계가 막막해졌을 때를 대비하여 소득 중 일부를 보험료로 납부했다가 사상이나 장애로 인한 소득생활이 중단될 경우 본인이나 유족에게 연금을 지급해 기본 생활을 유지할 수 있도록 하며, 정부가 직접 운영하는 소득보장 제도이다.

3) 고용보험제도

사회 전반적으로 감원조치 등에 의해서 직장을 잃게 된 실업자에게 실업 보험금을 지급하고 직업훈련 등을 위한 장려금을 기업에서 지급하는 4대 보험 중 하나이다. 사업주와 근로자가 월정급여액의 0.3%를 보험료로 납부하며, 고용보험전산망을 이용해 구직정보를 제공받는다. 고용보험을 통해 실업예방, 고용촉진과 근로자 직업능력 개발을 도모해서 국가의 직업지도나 소재기능 강화로 실업자의 생활안정을 위하여 구직을 장려해 사회발전에 기여하고 있다.

4) 국민기초생활보장제도

국민의 기초생활 보호대상을 확대하고 급여수준을 높여서 보상지급기준을 다양화하여 부양능력 및 부양의사가 없어 의무를 다하지 않는 경우에 이를 정부가 최저생활 보장비용을 징수할 수 있게 하는 데 있다.

4. 국제보건기구와 국제협력

4.1 세계보건기구(WHO)

1) WHO와 유엔헌장

"세계 모든 국민이 가능한 최상의 건강수준에 도달하도록 한다."는 유엔헌장의 원칙에 따라 모든 지구촌 식구들의 행복, 조화로운 인간관계와 안정을 위해 WHO(World Health Organization)는 유엔헌장을 선언했다. 건강은 질병에 걸리지 않거나 허약하지 않은 상태뿐만 아니라 육체·정신·사회적으로 온전하며, 행복한 상태이다. 유엔헌장은 인종, 종교, 정치적 신념, 경제나 사회적인 조건에 차별 없이 최상의 건강수준을 유지하는 것이 인간이 누려야 할 기본권의 하나이다.

2) WHO의 조직

① 세계보건총회(World Health Assembly)

매년 5월에 회원국 대표들이 스위스 제네바에 모여서 회의하는 최고 의사결정기구이며 주요 공중보건의 정책과 예산(약 90~100억 달러 정도)을 승인하는 회의를 한다.

② 집행이사회(Executive Board)

총 32명의 보건 분야 전문가들이 매년 1월과 5월에 모여서 총회에 상정될 의안과 결의문 등을 사전에 의결하고 총회에서 위임

된 사항을 처리한다.

③ 사무국(Secretariat)

보건과 전반적인 의료 분야의 전문가 3,700여 명이 모여서 보건
사업에 대해 의논한다. 사무총장의 임기는 5년이고 예산은 2년마
다 편성한다.

3) WHO의 주요 기능

- 국제적인 보건사업과 보건문제의 협의, 규제와 권고안을 제정
- 보건서비스 강화를 위한 각국 정부의 요청에 대해 환경위생,
  산업보건의 개선사업을 지원
- 각국 정부의 요청 시 적정한 보건시술 지원과 응급상황 발생
  시 필요한 서비스 제공
- 전염병 및 질병의 예방과 검역관리 지원
- 필요시 식품위생, 주택, 위생, 오락, 경제, 환경위생 및 직업
  등의 기술자, 전문가와의 협력 지원
- 보건 향상, 재해 예방과 모자보건 향상을 위한 기술협력사업
  개발
- 보건, 의학과 사회보장 향상을 위한 교육, 통계자료 수집과 의
  학적인 조사연구사업을 추진

4) 우리나라와 WHO

가입국의 의무로 WHO에 대한 기술상의 협력과 분담금의 지불
이 있으며, 기술상의 협력은 WHO의 요청에 따른 전문가의 파견

이나 연수생의 교육, WHO협력센터를 통한 협력을 행한다.

우리나라는 1949년 8월 17일 65번째로 가입하였으며, 북한은 1973년 5월 19일 138번째로 가입하였다.

4.2 기타 국제보건기구

인류의 건강, 복지와 보건에 관련된 사업을 하는 국제기구들은 식량및농업기구(FAO), 국제노동기구(ILO), 국제연합교육과학문화기구(UNESCO), 유엔개발계획(UNDP), 유엔인구활동기금(UNFPA)과 유엔환경계획(UNEP) 등의 보건관련 국제기구들이 있다(방두언 외 2008).

국제공중보건처(IOPH: International Office of Public Health)는 1851년 파리의 지중해 연안에서 최초로 12개국이 모여 국제위생과 역학에 대해 논의했다. 1907년에는 40개국으로 늘려 국제적인 전염병 예방과 보건문제로 급성 전염병 등의 질병에 관한 정보, 방역 조치에 관한 기록을 수집해 통보하는 국제공중보건처가 창설되어 1909년부터 파리에 설치되었다가 1950년에 WHO에 흡수되었다.

범미보건기구(PAHO: Pan - American Health Organization)는 1889년 워싱턴에서 국제회의로 개최되었는데 전염병 관리와 방역 등의 의견교환을 위해서 1901년 멕시코 회의 때 창설되었다. 1924년 국제연맹 보건부의 지역사무처로 되었다가 1946년부터는 WHO의 지역사무소가 되었다.

유엔국제아동긴급기금(UNICEF: United Nations International Children's Emergency Fund)은 1946년 UN총회의 직속기구로 설립되어 WHO와 함께 모자보건사업인 어린이의 기아문제와 보건·

복지·건강 증진을 위한 원조사업과 보건사업을 지원하고 있다.

4.3 국제협력

최근 우리나라는 급속한 경제성장과 함께 국제적 위상도 매우 높아져 국제사회에의 책무 차원으로 원조와 협력을 요청받게 되었다. 보건 분야에서도 단순히 국내의 보건문제뿐 아니라 국제적 시야에서 취급해야 할 과제가 해마다 증가하고 있다.

1) 국제협력 구성

국제협력은 행정상의 조정, 기술·정보의 교환, 인적 교류 등을 행함으로써 자국의 향상을 꾀하는 국제교류와 개발도상국에 대하여 인적·물적·기술적 자원을 제공함으로써 그 나라의 향상을 꾀하는 국제협력(협의)으로 대별된다. 또 각각 다국 간 교류(협력)와 2국 간 교류(협력)로 세분된다(이용성 외, 2005).

2) 국제교류와 국제협력

우리나라의 국제보건의료협력의 상황은 <표 1>에 나타나고 있다. 정부 차원의 보건의료협력과 별도로 다수의 민간 차원의 국제보건의료협력단체가 있다. 정부 간 국제협력과 비교하여 재정액은 적으나 민간이기 때문에 상대국의 필요에 유연하게 대응하고 있다.

<표 1> 국제보건의료협력 현황

구분	교류	협력내용
국제교류	다국 간 교류	UN(국제연합: 인구위원회, 마약위원회 등)
		WHO(세계보건기구)
		IARC(국제암연구센터)
		UNEP(UN환경계획)
		FAO(UN식량농업기구)
		ILO(국제노동기구)
		OECD(경제협력개발기구)
		ESCAP(아시아태평양지역경제사회위원회)
	2국 간 교류	한미의학협력계획
		한미보건통계회의
		한미환경보호협력
		한미과학기술협력협정
		한미암연구협력
		한일과학기술협력
		한독과학기술협력
		한불과학기술협력
		한중과학기술협력
		한호과학기술협력
		한가과학기술협력
국제협력	다국 간 교류	WHO(세계보건기구)
		UNDP(UN개발계획)
		UNICEF(국제아동기금)
		UNFRA(UN인구기금)
	2국 간 교류	JICA(국제협력사업단) 의료협력부, 연수사업부, 파견사업부, 무상자금협력부
		OECD(해외경제협력기금)

Ⅱ. 건강보건관련
국제기구 소개 및 정보원

ACQUIRE Project

Access, Quality, and Use in Reproductive Health Project
모자보건프로젝트

1 기구

1) 소재지

주　　소	the ACQUIRE Project c/o EngenderHealth, 440 Ninth Avenue New York, NY 10001
전　　화	＋1 212 561 8000
팩　　스	＋1 212 561 8067
전자우편	info－acquire@acquireproject.org
홈페이지	http://www.acquireproject.org/index.php?id＝245

2) 설립연혁

모자보건프로젝트(ACQUIRE Project)는 모자보건 양질 및 이용(Access, Quality, and Use in Reproductive Health)을 뜻한다. ACQUIRE Project는 모자보건(RH: Reproductive Health)과 가족계획(FP: Family Planning) 서비스를 지원하기 위해 시작되었다.

ACQUIRE Project는 전체적인 접근법을 이용한다. 임상적 치료에 관한 기술적 리더십을 제공하고 의료서비스를 발전시킴으로써 모자보건 서비스의 질을 향상시키고자 한다. 동시에 ACQUIRE Project는 커뮤니티의 참여가 모자보건과 가족계획의 활용을 증가시킨다는 점을 강조한다.

ACQUIRE Project는 지역단계에서의 파트너십과 협조를 바탕으로 모자보건 및 가족계획의 문제점들에 맞서고자 한다. 세계적 리더십과 현장 활동을 통해 ACQUIRE Project는 HIV/AIDS 예방을 포함한 가족계획에 대한 문제를 다룬다.

3) 설립목적

① 양질의 모자보건/가족계획 서비스 이용 증가
② 서비스 제공자들의 활동 향상
③ 모자보건/가족계획 서비스 제공자를 위한 환경 강화

4) 파트너 기관

ACQUIRE Project는 Engender Health에 의해 운영되며, 아드라(ADRA: Adventist Development and Relief Agency International), 케어(CARE), 국제인트라헬스(IntraHealth International, Inc.), 국제메리디안그룹(Meridian Group International, Inc.), 아프리카에이즈와여성을위한 사회(SWAA: Society for Women and AIDS in Africa)와의 파트너십을 맺고 있다.

5) 주요 사업

ACQUIRE Project는 가족계획, 모자보건관리, 모자보건서비스, 중절이후관리, HIV/AIDS를 포함한 성병 예방에 대한 이용자 증가를 위한 노력에 참여하고 있다. ACQUIRE Project가 활동 중인 국가는 다음과 같다.

아제르바이잔(Azerbaijan), 방글라데시(Bangladesh), 캄보디아(Cambodia), 네팔(Nepal), 에티오피아(Ethiopia), 케냐(Kenya), 남아프리카(South Africa), 탄자니아(Tanzania), 우간다(Uganda), 베닌(Benin), 카메룬(Cameroon), 콩고민주공화국(Democratic Republic of Congo), 가나(Ghana), 기니(Guinea), 말리(Mali), 나이지리아(Nigeria), 르완다(Rwanda), 세네갈(Senegal), 시에라리온(Sierra Leone), 볼리비아(Bolivia), 온두라스(Honduras) ACQUIRE Project는 또한 영구적 방법(Long-Acting and Permanent Methods), 통합(Integration), 파트너로서의 젠더/남성(Gender/Men As Partners), 누관(Fistula), 피임보안(Contraceptive Security) 영역을 중심으로 활동한다.

② 정보원

1) 정보배포정책

ACQUIRE Project의 정보원은 'Publications'와 'Resources/ Links', 'Publications'에서 찾을 수 있다. 모든 자료는 온라인 무료열람이 가능하며, 출판물이나 보고서는 PDF로 제공된다.

2) 정보 자료

① 출판물(Publications)

다음과 같은 분류별로 출판물을 찾아볼 수 있다.

[연구조사보고서(Evaluation and Research Study Reports)]

- *Improving the Use of Long-Term and Permanent Methods of Contraception in Guinea: A Performance Needs Assessment*
- *Bolivia Baseline Survey, 2005: Technical Report*
- *Bangladesh Baseline Survey, 2004: Technical Report*
- *Tanzania Baseline Survey, 2004-2005: Technical Report*
- *Factors Affecting Vasectomy Acceptability in the Kigoma Region of Tanzania*
- *Reproductive Health and Services in Azerbaijan, 2005: Results of a Baseline Survey in Five Districts*
- *Community Awareness of and Attitudes towards Long-acting and Permament Contraception in Guinea*

[프로그램보고서(Program Reports)]

- *ACQUIRE Project Final Report: Obstetric Fistula in Amhara Regional State, Ethiopia, January 2006 - March 2007*
- *'Get a Permanent Smile' - Increasing Awareness of, Access to, and Utilization of Vasectomy Services in Ghana*
- *Repositioning Family Planning Case Study Reports:*

Ghana Case Study, Malawi Case Study, Zambia Case Study, Synthesis Report, Senegal Case Study, Tanzania Case Study

- *Traumatic Gynecologic Fistula as a Consequence of Sexual Violence in Conflict Settings: A Literature Review*
- *Integrating Best Practices for Performance Improvement, Quality Improvement, and Participatory Learning and Action to Improve Health Services*
- *Performance Needs Assessment on Revitalization of the IUD: Bamako, Mali*

[프로젝트개요(Project Briefs)]
- *ACQUIRING KNOWLEDGE: Integrating Family Planning with Antiretroviral Therapy Services in Uganda*
- *ACQUIRING KNOWLEDGE: The AMKENI Model – Learning Global Lessons from Improving Family Planning, Reproductive Health, and Child Survival in Kenya*
- *ACQUIRING KNOWLEDGE: A Focus on the Fundamentals of Care*
- *ACQUIRING KNOWLEDGE: Revitalizing the IUD in Kenya*
- *ACQUIRING KNOWLEDGE: 'Get a Permanent Smile'*

－*Increasing Awareness of, Access to, and Utilization of Vasectomy Services in Ghana*

[회의보고서(Meeting Reports)]
- *Traumatic Gynecologic Fistula: A Consequence of Sexual Violence in Conflict Settings*
- *Consultation on Improving Contraceptive Continuation: Meeting Proceedings*
- *Report of Fistula Counseling Experts' Meeting*
- *Expert Consultation on Vasectomy: Meeting Report*

② 정보 및 링크(Resources/Links)
- *Medical Eligibility Criteria for Contraceptive Use,* WHO, 2004 － Third Edition
- *Selected Practice Recommendations for Contraceptive Use,* WHO, 2004 － Second Edition
- *MAQ IUD Toolkit*
- *Contraception for Women and Couples with HIV,* CD － ROM
- *Obstetric Fistula: Guiding Principles for Clinical Management and Programme Development,* WHO, 2006

AED – SATELLIFE

Center for Health Information and Technology

의료정보기술센터

① 기구

1) 소재지

주　　소　30 California Street Watertown, MA 02472 USA
전　　화　+1 617 926 9400
팩　　스　+1 617 926 1212
홈페이지　http://www.healthnet.org/index.php

2) 설립연혁

의료정보기술센터(AED – SATELLIFE)는 1980년대 중반 버나
드 라운 박사(Dr. bernard Lown)에 의해 고안되었다. AED –
SATELLIFE 창립에 앞서 1985년 라운 박사는 그가 공동 지원한
기구인 핵전쟁방지를위한국제의사기구(International Physicians for
the Prevention of Nuclear War)를 대표하여 노벨평화상을 수
여받은 적이 있다. 라운 박사는 우주를 대량살상무기가 아닌
생명을 살릴 수 있는 정보를 교환하는 의료전문가들의 기반으
로 보았다. 미국 가정에 개인컴퓨터가 보급되기 오래전, AED

- SATELLIFE는 이미 전 세계 개발도상국들의 건강관리를 위한 정보의 힘을 인식하였다. 지난 19년 동안 AED - SATELLIFE는 에이즈나 말라리아 등이 심각한 지역 커뮤니티를 위해 활동하면서 저널이나 인터넷의 사용이 힘든 곳에 위치한 의료전문가들을 위한 정보로의 솔루션 개발의 선두를 달려왔다. 정보통신기술의 혁신적인 애플리케이션을 통해 AED - SATELLIFE는 정보이용의 장벽을 뛰어넘었다. AED - SATELLIFE 활동의 결과로 인해 주요도시뿐 아니라 지방마을에 이르기까지 더 나은 건강을 위한 지식이 보급되었다. 2006년 7월, SATELLIFE가 비영리 국제개발기구인 교육개발아카데미(Academy for Educational Development)에 합류하면서 현재의 이름인 의료정보기술센터(Center for Health Information and Technology)의 AED - SATELLIFE라는 명칭을 사용하게 되었다.

3) 설립목적

① 올바른 의사결정을 위한 최근 정보 배포
② 다방면의 기술 분배와 이러한 기술을 효과적으로 사용할 수 있는 의료 종사자의 능력 구축
③ 정보를 공유하고 서로를 지원할 수 있는 지방, 지역, 글로벌 커뮤니티 형성

4) 조직 - 건강네트(HealthNet)

건강네트(HealthNet)는 AED-SATELLIFE의 글로벌 커뮤니케이션 네트워크의 이름이다. HealthNet는 이메일을 통해 전 세계 의료업 종사자들을 연결하는 역할을 한다. 아프리카의 최초이메일 네트워크 중 하나로서 HealthNet는 개발도상국의 의료전문가들 간의 정보의 빈곤을 위한 솔루션을 제공하는 개척자역할을 하였다. 이 새로운 망을 통해 의사, 간호사, 연구원, 의대생 및 그 외 의료관리 제공자들은 마침내 서로 간의 커뮤니케이션과 경험 공유, 정보로의 접근이 가능하게 되었다. 오늘날 AED-SATELLIFE는 기구의 의료정보자원이 HealthNet를 통한 이메일 소통이 가능하지 않더라도 개발도상국의 모든 의료전문가들에게 가능하도록 제공하고 있다. 그런 의미에서 HealthNet라는 의미는 AED-SATELLIFE의 이메일 기술뿐 아니라 AED-SATELLIFE의 정보자원의 한 종류로 이해되고 있다. AED-SATELLIFE는 지역적으로 조직되고 운영되는 HealthNet 네트워크를 구축하기 위해 보건복지부, 의학대학, 의학도서관과 함께 활동한다. 각각의 HealthNet는 지역의 필요성에 의해 발전되었다. 모든 HealthNet는 HealthNet 정보서비스의 이용을 위한 무료 또는 저가의 이메일 서비스를 제공한다. 지역별로 때로는 정보자원, 정보기술(IT)교육, 전자콘퍼런스, 웹전화 또는 웹사이트 호스팅과 같은 웹기반의 서비스를 제공하기도 한다. AED-SATELLIFE는 하드웨어 및 소프트웨어, 시스템 운영자를 위한 기술교육, 기술적 지원, 프로그램 개발 및 사업계획에 대한 자문 서비스 제공을 통해 HealthNet 파트너들을 지원한다.

5) 관련 기관

HealthNet 파트너 기관은 다음과 같다.
- HealthNet 에리트레아(Eritrea)
- HealthNet 에티오피아(Ethiopia)
- HealthNet 네팔(Nepal)
- HealthNet 우간다(Uganda)
- HealthNet 짐바브웨(Zimbabwe)
- HealthNet 남아프리카공화국(South Africa)

6) 주요 사업

AED-SATELLIFE는 세계적으로 가장 시급한 건강주제에 관한 대화 촉진과 관련 자료 배포를 통해 글로벌 건강커뮤니티를 강화한다. 자원이 부족한 국가에서 강력한 의료관리 전달시스템을 구축하는 데에는 믿을 만한 데이터와 지식관리 방법이 필요하다. 정책입안가, 계획담당자, 프로그램 및 자원관리자, 의료업 종사자들은 최신 관련 자료가 필요하며, 그것을 바탕으로 올바른 결정을 내릴 수 있다. 본 기구에서 행하는 사업은 모두 무료로 이루어지며, 기술이 빈약한 지역의 특정 주제를 기본으로 이루어진다. 이메일 및 인터넷을 이용한 AED-SATELLIFE는 의사결정을 위한 정보의 교환이 가능하도록 한다.

② 정보원

1) 정보배포정책

AED-SATELLIFE의 정보원은 '정보자원(Information Resources)'에서 찾아볼 수 있다. 토의그룹(Discussion Group), 출판물, 그리고 링크로 분류되어 정보를 열람할 수 있다. 토의그룹이란 관심 분야를 다루는 토의그룹에 회원으로 등록하여 전 세계 사람들과 의견을 나눌 수 있도록 하고 있다. 출판물은 뉴스레터를 포함한 소식지 등의 정기간행물이 해당되며, 열람을 위해서는 구독신청을 해야 한다.

2) 정보 자료

① 링크

AED-SATELLIFE에서 제공하는 관련 기관의 링크목록은 다음과 같다.

[심장질환 및 당뇨병(Cardiovascular Disease and Diabetes)]

- Academy for Educational Development
- American Diabetes Association
- Global Cardiovascular Infobase
- Heartfile
- InterAmerican Heart Foundation(IAHF)
- International Diabetes Foundation
- Lown Cardiovascular Center
- ProCOR: Global Electronic Conference on Cardiovascular

Health in the Developing World
- World Heart Federation(WHF)

[필수의약품(Essential Drugs)]
- Essential Drugs: Global Discussion Groups in English, French, Spanish, and Russian
- Free Peer Reviewed Pharmaceutical Reference
- The Global Alliance for Vaccines and Immunization(GAVI)
- International Network for Rational Use of Drugs(INRUD)
- MSF: Campaign for Access to Essential Medicines
- South African Drug Action Programme(SADAP)

[건강관리(Health Management)]
- WHO's Website for Health Service Managers

[HIV/AIDS]
- AEGis, the Largest HIV/AIDS Web Site in the World; Updated Hourly
- The Body
- Global Network of People Living with HIV/AIDS
- Harvard AIDS Institute
- HIV InSite
- HIV/AIDS Education and Resource Center
- ProCAARE: Program for the Collaboration against AIDS and Related Epidemics

- Women, Children and HIV
- Reuters Alertnet News Services

[산모와 자녀건강(Maternal and Child Health)]

- Engender Health
- Family Health International
- The Maternal and Neonatal Health(MNH) Program
- PREME - EU Pregnancy and Malaria
- Reproductive Health Outlook

[정신건강(Mental Health)]

- American Psychological Association
- National Institute of Mental Health

[영양(Nutrition)]

- Academy for Educational Development
- Frequently Asked Questions about HIV/AIDS and Nutrition
- International Food Information Council Foundation
- LANIC: Food and Nutrition in Latin America
- Nutrition in Pediatric HIV Infection
- PronUT - HIV: Nutrition and HIV/AIDS
- Save the Children: School Health and Nutrition
- Rehydration Project

[열대질병(Tropical and Infectious Diseases)]

- CDC Major Tuberculosis Guidelines
- Columbia University: What You Need to Know about Tuberculosis
- Environmental Health Project
- Global Health Council
- Malaria Foundation International
- ProMED
- Special Programme for Research and Training in Tropical Diseases
- Tuberculosis.net, Tuberculosis Teaching Materials

[숙소정보(Hospice Information)]

- International Hospice Information

[실사병(Diarrhca)]

- Enhanced Diarrheal Disease Control Resource Center

FCTC

Framework Convention Alliance for Tobacco Control

흡연규제협약연합

① 기구

1) 소재지

소재국가	미국
주　소	Framework Convention Alliance c/o ASH Int'l 701 4th Street NW, 3rd floor Washington, DC 20001, USA
전　화	+1 202 289 7155
팩　스	+1 202 289 7166
전자우편	fca@fctc.org
홈페이지	http://www.fctc.org/index.php

2) 성격

흡연규제협약연합(FCTC)은 흡연규제 프로토콜을 실행에 옮기고자 하는 100개 이상의 국가를 대표하는 약 300개의 기구들로 구성되었다.

3) 설립연혁

FCTC는 2005년 2월 27일부터 시작되었다. 당시 168개국이 조약에 서명하였고, 그중 157개국이 협약 회원국이 되었으며, 2008년 6월 3일자로 러시아도 협약 회원국이 되었다.

4) 비전 및 임무

FCTC의 비전은 '흡연에 의한 사망 및 질병이 없는 세상'이다. 본 연합의 임무는 협동적인 흡연반대 국제캠페인을 위한 글로벌 네트워크의 촉진 및 지원, 특히 개발도상국에서의 흡연규제 역량 강화, FCTC의 효과적인 감시인(watchdog) 기능수행에서 찾아볼 수 있다.

5) 조직

FCTC는 지역별 사무소로 구성되어 있다. 각 지역별 담당자는 다음과 같다.

(1) 아시아(Asia)
　① 동남아시아 대륙(Mainland Southeast Asia)
　　• Yel Daravuth − DRA(Cambodia)
　　　전자우편: yeldaravuth.toh@bigpond.com.kh
　② 동남아시아 섬 지역(island Southeast Asia)
　　• Edgardo Ulysses Dorotheo − FCTC Alliance, Philippines
　　　전자우편: dorotheo@globalink.org

③ 동아시아(East Asia)

- Marcus Yu – Hong Kong Council on Smoking and Health(China)

  전자우편: hkcosh@hkstar.com

④ 남아시아(South Asia)

- Olcott Gunasekera – IOGT Regional Council for South and South East Asia(Sri Lanka)

  전자우편: iogt_arc@sltnet.lk

- Shoba John – Programme for Appropriate Technology for Health(PATH Canada)(India Office)

  전자우편: sjohn_pathcan@vsnl.net

⑤ 중앙아시아(Central Asia)

- Erdene – Ochir Uranchimeg – Adventist Development and Relief Agency(ADRA) Mongolia

  전자우편: urnaae@yahoo.com

(2) 오세아니아 – 호주 및 태평양 섬 국가들(Oceania – Australasia and Pacific island Nations)

- Shane Kawenata Bradbrook – Apaarangi Tautoko Auahi Kore – Maori Smokefree Coalition(Aotearoa/New Zealand)

  전자우편: atak@clear.net.nz

(3) 유럽(Europe)

　① 서유럽(Western Europe)

　　• Andrew Hayes－UICC and European Cancer League
　　　전자우편: hayes@globalink.org

　　• Francis Grogna－European Network for Smoking Pre-
　　　vention
　　　전자우편: francis.grogna@ensp.org

　② 동유럽(Eastern Europe)

　　• Tibor Szilagyi－Hungarian National Tobacco Control
　　　forum
　　　전자우편: tibors@health.usyd.edu.au

(4) 서부지중해(Eastern Mediterranean)

　• Ehsan Latif－Coalition against Tobacco, Society for
　　Aletrnative Mcdia and Reaserach Pakistan
　　전자우편: ehsan_latif@hotmail.com

(5) 아프리카(Africa)

　① 남아프리카(South Africa)

　　• Yussuf Salooje－International Non Government Coalition
　　　against Tobacco(South Africa)
　　　전자우편: ysalooje@iafrica.com

② 동아프리카(East Africa)

- Philip Karugaba - The Environmental Action Network (TEAN)(Uganda)

  전자우편: karugaba@globalink.org

③ 서아프리카(Wast Africa)

- Akinbode Olufemi - Environmental Rights Action (Nigeria)

  전자우편: bodufemi@hotmail.com

④ 프랑스어권아프리카(Francophone Africa)

- Inoussa Saouna - SOS Tabagisme(Niger)

  전자우편: sos_tabagisme - niger@caramail.com

(6) 미대륙(America)

① 남미(South America)

- Eduardo Bianco - Sindicato Médico del Uruguay(Medical Syndicate of Uruguay)

  전자우편: biamau@adinet.com.uy

② 카리브 해(Caribbean)

- David Bristol - St. Lucia Cancer Society

  전자우편: bristold@candw.lc

③ 북미(North America)

- Mele Smith - San Francisco Tobacco Free Coalition
  전자우편: mjsmith@igc.apc.org
- Susana Hennessey - San Francisco Tobacco Free Coalition
  전자우편: susanht@igc.apc.org

6) 회원

회원은 크게 활동회원(Active Member)과 후원회원(Support Member)으로 나뉜다. 활동회원은 본 기구의 목표를 지지하는 기관들로 구성되었으며, 후원회원은 본 기구의 목표를 지지하는 실제적인 개인으로 이루어진다. 다음은 FCTC의 회원기관이다.

① WHO 아프리카 지역(WHO African Region)

- 알제리(Algeria)
  - Association Club Scientifique de la Faculté des Sciences Médicales
  - Association Oxygène Algérie
- 베닌(benin)
  - Potential 2000
- 카메룬(Cameroon)
  - Health Promotion Watch
  - Mutuelle Sociale de Sante(MSS)(Cameroon)
  - onG LIFE
- 차드(Chad)

- Association Pour la Défence des Droits des
  Consommateurs(Chad)
- 콩고민주공화국(Democratic Republic of the Congo)
  - Agir Ensemble
  - Bons Templiers Congolais
  - Croix Bleue
  - Croix Bleue de la Republique Democratique Du Congo
  - Lutte Contre le Tabagisme en Afrique
- 감비아(Gambia)
  - Africa Network for Information and Action against
    Drugs(RAID)
  - I.O.G.T. of Gambia
- 가나(Ghana)
  - Action for Integrated Development(AID)
  - Consumer Concerns Initiative(CCI)
  - Ghanaians for Tobacco Free Society
  - Vision for Alternative Development(VALD)
- 케냐(Kenya)
  - African Centre for Empowerment and Gender Advocacy
    (Kenya)
  - African Network for Health Knowledge Management
    and Communication
  - Campaign against Drug Abuse(NACADA)
  - Centre for Tobacco Education and Development(CTFED)
    (Kenya)

- Consumer Watch(Kenya)
- Den of Hope
- Kenya Anti－Tobacco Growing Association
- Social Needs Network－Kenya
- 라이베리아(Liberia)
  - Community Development Outreach(CDO)
- 말라위(Malawi)
  - Consumers Association of Malawi
- 말리(Mali)
  - Mouvement National des Consommateurs(MNC)
  - SOS Tabagisme(Mali)
- 모리셔스(Mauritius)
  - Association Visa(Mauritius)
- 모잠비크(Mozambique)
  - Mozambican Public Health Association/Associação
    Moçambicana de Saúde Pública(AMOSAPU)
- 니제르(Niger)
  - OTAF
- 나이지리아(Nigeria)
  - All Nigerian Consumer Movements' Union(ANCOMU)
  - Campaign for Tobacco－Free Youths
  - Citizens Assistance Center
  - Educare Trust
  - Environmental Rights Action－Nigeria
  - Journalists Action on Tobacco & Health(JATH)(Nigeria)

- Nigeria Tobacco Control Alliance(NTCA)
- People against Drug Dependence and Ignorance(PADD) (Nigeria)
- Youth Action on Tobacco Control and Health(YATCH)
- 콩고공화국(Republic of the Congo)
  - l'Association Congolaise Pour la Santé Publique et Communautaire(ACSPC)
- 세네갈(Senegal)
  - ASPAT(Senegalese Organization for Peace, against Tobacco, Alcohol and toxicomania)
  - Reseau Sante Sida Population/Conseil des onG d'Appuiau Development(Senegal)
  - Senegal Anti‐Tobacco Movement
- 시에라리온(Sierra Leone)
  - Community Action Development Programmes and Services(CADEPS‐SL)
  - National Council for the Prevention of Alcoholism and Drugs Dependency
- 남아프리카공화국(South Africa)
  - National Council against Smoking‐South Africa
  - Soul City‐South Africa
  - Tobacco Control Board
- 토고(Togo)
  - Association‐PonT toGO
  - Association Togolaise Pour la Défense du Consummateur/

Togolaise Consumers Association(AStoDEC)(Togo)
- Togolese Association of Campaign against Alcoholism and other Drugs/Association Togolaise de Lutte Contre L'Alcoolisme et les Autres toxicomanies(ATLAT)
- Togolese Youth Association for Development(Togo)/ Association Togolaise des Jeunes Pour le DÈveloppement (togo)

• 우간다(Uganda)
- Big Change Ministries
- Caritas Uganda
- Environmental Action Network(Uganda)
- Family Talk Initiative
- Fetters of Smoke Association
- Health and Environmental Rights Organization(HERO) (Uganda)

• 탄자니아(United Republic of Tanzania)
- Center for Substance Prevention
- Tanzania Public Health Association

• 잠비아(Zambia)
- Zambia Consumers Association

• 짐바브웨(Zimbabwe)
- Zuna Women's Operation Green - Zimbabwe

② WHO 미대륙지역(WHO Region of the Americas)
• 아르헨티나(Argentina)

- Against‒Tobacco Group of Hospital Italiano of Buenos Aires(GRANTAHI)
- Argentine Union against Tobacco
- Asociación Argentina de Prevención y Educación del Cancer
- Instituto de Ciencia y Tecnologia Regional(ICTER)
- 바베이도스(Barbados)
  - Heart and Stroke Foundation of Barbados
- 브라질(Brazil)
  - ACT‒Alliance for the Control of Tobacco Use
- 캐나다(Canada)
  - Airspace Action on Smoking and Health(Canada)
  - Canadian Cancer Society
  - Canadian Global Tobacco Control forum
  - Canadian Public Health Association
  - Health Bridge Foundation of Canada
  - Heart and Stroke Foundation(Canada)
  - International Tobacco Control(ITC)
  - Non‒Smokers' Rights Association(Canada)
  - Ontario Tobacco Research Unit
  - Physicians for a Smoke Free Canada
  - Saskatchewan Coalition for Tobacco Reduction
  - University of Waterloo
- 칠레(Chile)
  - CIPRESS

- Fundación Educación Popular en Salud(EPES)
- 코스타리카(Costa Rica)
  - Fundcion Pro Derechos de Los No Fumadores
- 에콰도르(Ecuador)
  - Cruz Roja Ecuatoriana
- 온두라스(Honduras)
  - Accion Para la Promocion de Ambientes Libres de Tabaco(APALTA)
  - Alianza Hondurena Antitabaco
  - Instituto Hondureño de Psicoterapia(IHPSTE)
- 자메이카(Jamaica)
  - Heart Foundation of Jamaica
  - Jamaica Coalition for Tobacco Control(Jamaica)
- 멕시코(Mexico)
  - Alianza Contra el Tabaco, A.C.
  - Asociacion Mexicana de Estudios Para la Defensa del Consumidor
- 파나마(Panama)
  - Coalicion Panamena Contra El Tabaquismo
  - Fundacion Cardiologica de Panama
- 파라과이(Paraguay)
  - FEDAPAR — Federación de Associaciones de Padres del Paraguay
  - onG Vida Saludable
- 페루(Peru)

- Centre of Information and Education for Drug Abuse Prevention(Peru)
- Comision Nacional Permanente de Lucha Antitabaquica (COLAT)
- Peruvian American Medical Society(PAMS)

- 세인트루시아(Saint Lucia)
  - St. Lucia Cancer Society

- 트리니다드토바고(Trinidad & tobago)
  - Coalition for Tobacco-Free Trinidad and Tobago

- 미국(United States of America)
  - Action on Smoking and Health(USA)
  - Advocacy Institute(USA)
  - American Cancer Society
  - American Heart Association
  - American Lung Association
  - American Public Health Association
  - American Society of Clinical oncology
  - American Thoracic Society
  - Americans for Nonsmokers' Rights
  - Campaign for Tobacco Free Kids(USA)
  - Chinese Progressive Association(USA)
  - Corporate Accountability International
  - Corp Watch(USA)
  - Essential Action(USA)
  - Institute for Global Tobacco Control(Johns Hopkins

Bloomberg School of Public Health)
- Interfaith Center on Corporate Responsibility
- Islamic Medical Association of North America
- National African American Tobacco Prevention Network
- Robert Wood Johnson Foundation(USA)
- San Francisco Tobacco Free Coalition(USA)
- Smokefree Air for Everyone(SAFE)
- Society for Research on Nicotine and Tobacco(USA)
- Tobacco Free Coalition(USA)
- Tobacco Law Center(USA)
- Tobacco – Free Las Cruces Coalition(USA)
- Transnational Resource & Action Center
- 우루과이(Uruguay)
  - Asociacion Civil Fumadores Pasivos Uruguayos
  - Federacion Medica del Interior
  - Grupo Universitario Anti – Tabáquico(Uruguay)
  - Sindicato Médico del Uruguay(Medical Syndicate of Uruguay)
  - Uruguay AntiTobacco Commission

③ WHO 동부지중해 지역(WHO Eastern Mediterranean Region)
- 바레인(Bahrain)
  - Bahrain Anti – Smoking Society
- 이집트(Egypt)
  - Asdekaa Elkheir – Al Hyah Team

- Youth Association for Population and Development (Egypt)
- 이란(Iran, Islamic Republic of)
  - Iranian Anti-Tobacco Association
  - Iranian Heart Foundation
  - Isfahan Cardiovascular Research Center
  - National Research Institute of Tuberculosis and Lung Disease(Iran)
  - Tobacco Prevention and Control Research Centre
- 요르단(Jordan)
  - I Quit Smoking-Jordan
  - Jordanian Anti-Smoking Society
  - Land and Human to Advocate Progress
  - Libyan Arab Jamahiriya
  - Libyan Anti-Tobacco Society
- 모로코(Morocco)
  - Association Marocaine de Prévention & Education Pour la Santé AMAPES-Stop Tabac
- 파키스탄(Pakistan)
  - Network for Consumer Protection(Pakistan)
  - Pakistan Society for Cancer Prevention
  - Society for Alternative Media and Research
- 카타르(Qatar)
  - Childhood Cultural Center
- 사우디아라비아(Saudi Arabia)

- Jamaitul Khairiyah Anti‐Smoking Anti‐Drugs Charitable Organization
- Saudi Charitable Anti‐Smoking Society
• 수단(Sudan)
- Sudan Committee for the Control of Tobacco Consumption
- Sudanese Cancer Society(SCS)
- Toombak and Smoking Research Centre(Sudan)
• 시리아(Syrian Arab Republic)
- Syrian Center for Tobacco Studies
• 튀니지(Tunisia)
- Association Tunisienne de Lutte Contre le Cancer (ATCC)
• 예맨(Yemen)
- Hadramawt Cancer Control

④ WHO 유럽지역(WHO European Region)
• 아르메니아(Armenia)
- Coalition for Tobacco Free Armenia(CTFA)
- International Center for Human Development(Armenia)
• 아제르바이잔(Azerbaijan)
- Azerbaijan Public Health Association
- Centre of Independent Social Researches "Karvan"
• 불가리아(Bulgaria)
- Association Women against Tobacco(Bulgaria)

- Foundation Women against Tobacco - Bulgaria
- 체코공화국(Czech Republic)
  - Czech Coalition against Tobacco
  - Czech Committee of European Medical Association Smoking or Health
  - Working Group or Prevention and Treatment of Tobacco Dependence, Czech Medical Association
- 핀란드(Finland)
  - Action on Smoking and Health(Finland)
  - Cancer Society of Finland
- 프랑스(France)
  - Alliance Contre le Tabac/French Alliance against Tobacco
  - Comité National Contre le Tabac(CNCT)/French Committee for Smoking Prevention
- 조지아(Georgia)
  - Georgian Medical Association
  - Georgian National Counter Tobacco Center
  - Tobacco Control Alliance(Georgia)
- 독일(Germany)
  - Berlin Working Group on Environment and Development(BLUE 21)
  - Federation of German Consumer Organizations/Verbraucherzentrale Bundesverband(vzbv)
  - German Cancer Research Centre

- German Medical Action Group Smoking and Health
- German Medical Association
- German Smoke-free Alliance
- 그리스(Greece)
  - Hellenic Cancer Society
- 헝가리(Hungary)
  - Health 21 Hungarian Foundation
  - Hungarian National Tobacco Control forum
- 아일랜드(Ireland)
  - Action on Smoking and Health(Ireland)
- 이스라엘(Israel)
  - Israel Cancer Association
- 키르기스스탄(Kirgizstan)
  - NGO Public Center for Tobacco Control of Kirgizstan
- 리투아니아(Lithuania)
  - Kaunas Drug Abuse Help Centre for Youth
  - Lithuanian Association of Non-Smokers
- 노르웨이(Norway)
  - Norwegian Cancer Society
  - The Norwegian Heart and Lung Patient Organization (LHL)
  - Tobacco-Free(Norway)
- 포르투갈(Portugal)
  - Conselho de Prevenção do Tabagismo(Portugal)
- 루마니아(Rumania)

- Aer Pur Rumania
- Romtens Foundation Rumania
- 러시아(Russian Federation)
  - Russian Public Health Association
- 세르비아(Serbia)
  - Non-Smokers Educational Center RP
- 슬로바키아(Slovakia)
  - Stop Smoking(Slovakia)
- 스페인(Spain)
  - Asociación Española Contra el Cáncer
  - SpanisH Association against Cancer
  - Unitat de Tabaquisme, Coorporació Sanitaria Clínic
- 스웨덴(Sweden)
  - Health Professionals against Tobacco
  - Swedish Dentistry against Tobacco
- 스위스(Switzerland)
  - OxyRomandie
  - Swiss Association for Smoking Prevention
- 터키(Turkey)
  - Turkish Committee on Tobacco or Health
- 우크라이나(Ukraine)
  - Alcohol and Drug Information Centre(Ukraine)
- 영국(United Kingdom)
  - Action on Smoking and Health(London)
  - Action on Smoking and Health(Scotland)

- Action on Smoking and Health－Wales(ASH Wales)
- British Medical Association
- British Medical Association－Tobacco Control Project
- Cancer Research UK
- London School of Hygiene and Tropical Medicine
- No Smoking Day
- Scottish Tobacco Control Alliance
- 우즈베키스탄(Uzbekistan)
  - Adventist Development & Relief Agency(ADRA) Uzbekistan
- 국제기구(International－EURO)
  - Association of the European Cancer Leagues
  - Citizen Association "Life without Smoke"
  - Commonwealth Medical Association
  - European Heart Network
  - European Medical Association on Smoking and Health
  - European Network for Smoking Prevention
  - European Respiratory Society
  - European Union of Non－Smokers

⑤ WHO 동남아시아 지역(WHO South－East Asia Region)
- 호주(Australia)
  - Action on Smoking and Health(Australia)
  - Cancer Council Australia
  - Cancer Council Victoria

- Cancer Council Western Australia
- National Heart Foundation(Australia)
- New South Wales Cancer Council(Australia)

- 캄보디아(Cambodia)
  - Adventist Development and Relief Agency(Cambodia)
- 중국(China)
  - Hong Kong Council on Smoking and Health
- 일본(Japan)
  - Japan Association against Tobacco
  - Japan Coalition on a Smokefree Environment
  - Japan Medical－Dental Association on Tobacco Control
  - Japanese Society for Tobacco Control
- 몽고(Mongolia)
  - Adventist Development & Relief Agency(ADRA)
    Mongolia
- 뉴질랜드(New Zealand)
  - Action on Smoking and Health(New Zealand)
  - Campaign against Foreign Control of Aotearoa
  - Cancer Society of New Zealand
  - Smokefree Coalition(New Zealand)
  - Te Reo Marama－Maori Smokefree Coalition
- 팔라우(Palau)
  - Coalition for a Tobacco Free Palau
  - Papua New Guinea
  - Action on Smoking and Health(Papua New Guinea)

- 필리핀(Philippines)
  - Conference of Public Health Advocates Inc.(formerly Public Health Initiatives-Philippines)
  - Filipino Consumers' Will
  - Framework Convention on Tobacco Control Alliance, Philippines(FCAP)
  - Philippine Cancer Society
- 대한민국(Republic of Korea)
  - Korean Association on Smoking and Health(KASH)
- 대만(Taïwan)
  - John Tung Foundation
  - Taiwan International Medical Alliance
  - Taiwan Medical Alliance for Control of Tobacco
- 통가(Tonga)
  - Tonga Family Health Association(TFHA)
- 베트남(Viet Nam)
  - Vietnam Standard and Consumer Association
- 국제기구(International-WPRO)
  - Smoke Free Pacific Action Network-S.P.A.N

⑥ 국제(Global)
- Adventist Development and Relief Agency
- FDI World Dental Federation
- INGCAT
- Initiative de Mobilisation PanAfricaine Pour le Contrôle

de Tabac(IMPACT)

- InterAmerican Heart Foundation
- International Agency on Tobacco or Health
- International Alliance of Women
- International Council of Women
- International Federation of Medical Students Association
- International Network of Women against Tobacco
- International Pharmaceutical Federation
- International Union against Tuberculosis and Lung Disease
- International Union for Health Promotion and Education
- Medical Women's International Association
- Observatoire du Tabac en Afrique Francophone(OTAF)
- Pan African Thoracic Society
- UICC Globalink
- UICC International Union against Cancer
- Women's Environment and Development Organization
- World Assembly of Youth
- World Federation of Public Health Associations
- World Heart Federation
- World Vision International

7) 주요 행사

2008년의 대표적인 주요 행사는 다음과 같다.
① 교육자양성과정-금연과정, 영국 도킹(Training the Trainers
-Smoking Cessation-Course, Dorking, United Kingdom)
② UICC 세계암의회, 스위스 제네바(UICC World Cancer Congress, Geneva, Switzerland)
③ SRNT 유럽 제10회 총회, 이탈리아 로마(10th Annual Conference of SRNT Europe, Rome, Italy)

② 정보원

1) 정보원배포정책

FCTC의 정보원은 'Fact Sheet'와 'Country Data' 그리고 'Press'
에서 찾아볼 수 있다. 'Country Data'를 통해 국가별 브라우징
의 흡연 관련 정보를 열람할 수 있다. 대부분의 자료는 영어
이외에 스페인어, 프랑스어 또는 아랍어로도 제공되며, PDF로
원문 무료열람이 가능하다.

2) 보고서(Fact Sheet)

영문보고서의 목록은 다음과 같다.
- *Tobacco Facts*
- *FCTC*

3) 보도 자료(Press)

2003년부터 2008년까지 FCTC의 웹사이트에서 제공하고 있는 보도 자료는 다음과 같다. 단, 2006년과 2004년의 자료는 제공되고 있지 않다.

[2008]

- *11 Feb 2008, Nations to Launch Negotiations on Treaty to Combat Illicit Tobacco Trade, Framework Convention Alliance*

[2007]

- *4 Dec 2007, Nations from the Region of the Americas Collaborate to Save Lives and Reduce Economic Losses by Cracking Down on Illicit Tobacco Trade, Framework Convention Alliance*

[2005]

- *25 May 2005, Corporate Accountability International Urges Nations of World Health Assembly to Prioritize People's Lives over Corporate Profits, A Statement from Corporate Accountability International Executive Director Kathryn Mulvey*

[2003]

- *26 Sep 2003, Signing of Convention Highlights Australia's Global Leadership in Tobacco Control, Cancer Foundation of Western Australia*

4) 그 외(Briefing Documents)

FCTC는 다음과 같은 브리핑 자료를 열람 가능하도록 제공한다.

- *Briefing Paper for INB－1, February 2008: Comments on the Template for a Protocol on Illicit Trade in Tobacco Products*

FDIWDF

FDI World Dental Federation

FDI 세계치과연합

① 기구

1) 소재지

소재국가	프랑스
주　　소	FDI World Dental Federation 13 Chemin du Levant, l'Avant Centre F‑01210 Ferney‑Voltaire, FRANCE
전　　화	+33 4 50 40 50 50
팩　　스	+33 4 50 40 55 55
전자우편	info@fdiworldental.org
홈페이지	http://www.fdiworldental.org/federation/fed_home.html

2) 성격

FDI 세계치과연합(WDF)은 FDI의 국가치과협회의 연합이다.

3) 설립연혁

WDF는 1900년 파리에서 Fédération Dentaire Internationale로

서 설립되었다. 그 후 전 세계의 치과의사들을 대표하는 주요
기구로서 활동해 오고 있으며 매년 세계회의를 개최해 전 세계
의 치과의들이 한자리에 모여 관련 이슈에 대한 토론을 할 수
있도록 하고 있다.

4) 비전 및 임무

WDF의 주요 임무는 FDI와 함께 전 세계의 치과의료사업을
한자리에 모이게 하며, 의료전문성을 대표하고, 정보교환을 촉
진시키는 데에 있다.
① 모든 이들을 위한 최상의 구강 및 일반건강 촉진
② 회원 지원
③ 회원협회의 관심사를 증진시키며 회원들에게 정보 제공
④ 치과의료사업의 도덕성, 예술성, 과학성, 실제성의 촉진 및
   증진

5) 조직

① 협의회(Council)
   협의회는 FDI의 모든 사업을 진행 및 평가하는 권한을 갖
   고 있다. 또한, 총회의 임무 및 사명과 목적을 규정한다.

② 위원회(Committees)
   위원회는 집행위원회(Executive Committee), 재정위원회
   (Finance Committee), 보상위원회(Remuneration Committee),
   커뮤니케이션 및 회원 지원위원회(Communications & Me-

mber Support Committee), 치과실습위원회(Dental Practice Committee), 교육위원회(Education Committee), 과학위원회(Science Committee), 세계치과개발 및 건강 증진위원회(World Dental Development and Health Promotion Committee)로 이루어진다.

③ 부서(Sections)

WDF의 부서는 대중보건팀(Section of Public Health), 치과서비스변호팀(Section of Defence forces Dental Services), 그리고 세계여성치과의사팀(Section of Women Dentists Worldwide)으로 나뉜다.

④ 지역기구(Regional Organization)

다음은 지역기구의 연락처이다.

- 아프리카지역기구(ARO: African Regional Organization)

  African Regional Organization(ARO)

  대 표: Prof Malick Sembène,

  주 소: 5252, Dakar – Fann, SENEGAL

  전 화: +221 822 08 59/+221 824 86 59

  팩 스: +221 822 30 17/+221 822 80 39

  전자우편: msembene@ucad.refer.sn

- 아시아태평양지역기구(APRO: Asia Pacific Regional Organization)

  Asia Pacific Regional Organization(APRO)

대 표: Dr. Mirza M.A.

주 소: Jl Balai Rakyat Ⅱ No. 4, Pondok Bambu Duren
awit, Jakarta Timur 13430, INDonESIA

전 화: +6221－86612784

팩 스: +6221－3853459

전자우편: mirza_abuhamzah@yahoo.co.uk

• 유럽지역기구(ERO: European Regional Organization)

European Regional Organization(ERO)

대 표: Dr. Patrick Hescot

주 소: ADF, 7, rue Mariotte, 75017 Paris, FRANCE

전 화: +(01) 44 90 72 89

팩 스:+(01) 44 90 96 50

전자우편: adf@adf.asso.fr

• 남미지역기구(LARO: Latin American Regional
Organization)

Latin American Regional Organization(LARO)

대 표: Dr. Adolfo Rodrigues Nuñez

주 소: c/o Asociación Odontológica Dominicana Inc, Av
Privada Esq Miguel Angel Monclús No 169,
Santo Domingo, DOMINICAN REPUBLIC

전 화: +1(809) 543 0880

팩 스: +1(809) 534－0104

전자우편: arn@verizon.net.do

- 북미지역기구(NARO: North American Regional Organization)
  North American Regional Organization(NARO)
  대 표: Dr. Joyous Pickstock
  주 소: 110 Pickstock Place, PO Box CB 13420, Nassau, BAHAMAS
  전 화: +1(242) 322 8589
  팩 스: +1(242) 326 3577
  전자우편: drjpick@batelnet.bs

6) 회원

FDI는 135개 국가의 총 191개의 회원협회로 이루어져 있다. WDF의 회원은 FDI와 마찬가지로 정규회원, 비정규회원, 제휴회원, 후원회원, 개인회원으로 구성된다.

7) 세계치과의회(World Dental Parliament)

세계치과의회는 1년에 한 차례 열리는 포럼으로서 전 세계의 전문가 대표들이 함께한다. 190개 이상의 회원협회의 대표들과 백만 명 이상의 치과의사들이 FDI의 총회에 참석하기 위해 모인다.

8) 세계여성치과의사(Women Dentists Worldwide)

1996년 FDI의 유럽지역기구는 '치과의료사업의 여성(Women in Dentistry)이라는 그룹을 형성하였고, 2001년 말레이시아에서 열

린 FDI 세계치과정기의회(FDI Annual World Dental Congress)
에서 이 그룹은 전 세계 네트워크로 발전하였다.

② 정보원

1) 정보원배포정책

FDIWDF의 정보원은 'Annual Report', 'Latest Releases', 그리
고 'Resources'로 이루어진다. 'Resources'는 가이드라인 데이
터베이스(Guidelines), 구강보건정보(Facts and Figures), 출판물
(Publications)로 나뉜다.

2) 총회보고서(Annual Reports)

총회보고서는 PDF로 무료열람이 가능하며, 영어, 프랑스어, 독
일어, 스페인어로 열람이 가능하다. 2008년 현재 2007/2008 보
고서와 2006/2007 보고서가 웹페이지상에서 열람 가능하다.

3) 발간 자료(Publications)

(1) 가이드라인 데이터베이스(Guidelines)
국가 및 국제 가이드라인, 체계적 검토, 메타 분석 등에 대
한 참고문헌 또는 링크를 제공하고 있다. 모든 자료는 인터
넷 웹페이지상에서 원문 무료열람이 가능하다.
[환자 관련(Patient Issues)]

- *Disabled and Special Care Patients*
- *Dry Mouth, Saliva and Oral Health*
- *Emergency Treatment*
- *Endocarditis and Oral Health*
- *Odontophobia, Psychology, Fear*
- *Oral Mucosal Problems*
- *Pain*
- *Quality of Life and Oral Health*
- *Sleeping Disturbances(Sleep Apnea)*
- *Sports*
- *Wear of Teeth*

[대중보건 관련(Public Health Issues)]
- *Abuse, Child Neglect and Family Violence*
- *Access to Oral Health Care*
- *Cancer, Oral and Oropharyngeal*
- *Caries, Public Measures*
- *Diet and Oral Health*
- *Fluorides −Topical and General Use*
- *Fluorides −Waterfluoridation*
- *General Health and Oral Health Relationship*
- *HIV and AIDS*
- *Periodontal Diseases, Public Measures*
- *Prevention of Oral Ill −Health*
- *Tobacco and Oral Health*

[치과예방조치(Precautions in the Dental Office)]

- *Cross − Infection Control*
- *Dermatitis, Allergies & Latex Use*
- *Environmental Issues*
- *Nitrous Oxide*
- *Safety of Employees, Precautions*
- *Toxicology and Biocompatibility of Dental Materials*
- *Unit Waterlines Contamination*

[재료, 기술, 과정(Materials, Techniques & Procedures)]

- *Amalgam Usage*
- *Anaesthetics and Sedation*
- *Antibiotics and Antimicrobials*
- *Fissure Sealants*
- *Pharmacotherapy*
- *Prophylaxis for Patients*
- *Tooth Bleaching and Cosmetics*

[치과수련(Dental Disciplines)]

- *Cariology*
- *Endodontics*
- *Forensic Dentistry*
- *Gerodontics*
- *Implantology*
- *Laser Dentistry*

- *Oral Surgery*
- *Orthodontics*
- *Pediatric Dentistry*
- *Periodontics*
- *Prosthetic Dentistry*
- *Maxillofacial Radiology*
- *Restorative Dentistry*
- *Temporomandibular Dysfunction*

[교육 및 과학 관련(Education & Scientific Issues)]
- *Complementary Dentistry*
- *Education*
- *Epidemiology and Research*
- *Evidence－Based Dentistry*
- *Guideline－Development and Quality Assurance*
- *Standards and Standardization*

[치과의사의 세계(Dentists' World)]
- *Assisting and Diagnostic Devices for the Professionals*
- *Auxillaries and Manpower*
- *Clinical Decision Making*
- *Ethics and Malpractice*
- *Marketing and Advertising*
- *Patient Records and Journal Keeping*
- *Practice Management and Maintenance*

(2) 구강보건정보(Facts and Figures)

　　국가별 구강에 관련된 정보를 PDF로 열람할 수 있다. 국가
　　별 검색은 알파벳 순서로 브라우징이 가능하다.

(3) 출판물(Publications)

　　① 저널

　　　　국제치과저널(International Dental Journal), 유럽치과보
　　　　철학저널(European Journal of Prosthodontics), 치주병
　　　　학국제아카데미저널(Journal of the International Academy
　　　　of Periodontology)의 세 종류가 있으며, 모두 구독신청
　　　　후 구독료를 지불해야 한다.

　　② 치과학개발(Developing Dentistry)

　　　　PDF로 무료열람이 가능하다.

　　　　• issue 1/08

　　　　　　- ***Developing Dentistry Archives***

　　　　• issue 1/06

　　　　　　- ***Practical guide: Infection Control for the Delivery***
　　　　　　of Basic Oral Emergency Care

　　　　• issue 1/05

　　　　　　- ***Practical guide: Basic Oral Emergency Care by***
　　　　　　Auxiliaries for Under - Served Populations

　　　　• issue 2/04

　　　　• issue 1/04

　　　　• issue 2/03

- issue 1/03
- issue 2/02
- issue 1/02
- issue 2/01

③ 서적(Books)

서적은 직접 구매 후 열람이 가능하며, 구매 가능한 목록은 다음과 같다.

- *Disability and Oral Care*(2001)
- *Oral Health Care in Africa —Kenya Leads the Way*(1997)
- *Introduction to Dental Public Health*(1994)
- *Oral Cancer*

4) 보도 자료(Latest Releases)

- 16.06.08 — *FDI Appoints David Alexander as Executive Director*
- 16.06.08 — *La FDI Choisit David Alexander Comme Directeur Exécutif*
- 16.06.08 — *La FDI Nombra a David Alexander Para el Puesto de Director Ejecutivo*
- 16.06.08 — *FDI Ernennt David Alexander Zum Exekutivdirektor*
- 19.05.08 — *Leaders of the World's Health Professions Step up their Support for Professional Self Regulation*
- 19.05.08 — *Les Responsables des Professions de Santé*

Dans le Monde Renforcent Leur Soutien à Une Autorégulation Professionnelle

- 19.05.08 – *Líderes de las Profesiones de La Salud Apoyan La Autorregulación Profesional*
- 19.05.08 – *Weltverbände der Gesundheitsberufe Unterstützen berufliche Selbstregulierung*
- 02.04.08 – *Cancelled – Conference for Oral Health in the Americas*
- 02.04.08 – *La Conférence Pour La Santé Bucco – Dentaire Aux Amériques Est Annulée*
- 02.04.08 – *Cancelada – Conferencia Sobre La Salud Bucal en las Américas*
- 02.04.08 – *Gesamtamerikanische Mundgesundheitskonferenz Findet Nicht Statt*
- 22.02.08 – *FDI Seeks Executive Director*
- 22.02.08 – *La FDI Recherche un Directeur Exécutif*
- 22.02.08 – *La FDI Busca Director Ejecutivo*
- 22.02.08 – *FDI Sucht Exekutivdirektor*
- 07.12.07 – *Postponed: Conference for Oral Health in the Americas*
- 07.12.07 – *Report de La Conférence Pour la Santé Bucco – Dentaire Dans les Amériques*
- 07.12.07 – *Postergada: La Conferencia de Salud Bucodental en las Américas*
- 07.12.07 – *Verschoben: Mundgesundheitskonferenz Für Nord*

−, Mittel Und Südamerika

- 14.11.07 *− People with Diabetes Need to Pay Special Attention to Oral Health*
- 14.11.07 *− Les Personnes Diabétiques Doivent Faire Particulièrement Attention à Leur Santé Bucco − Dentaire*
- 14.11.07 *− Las Personas Con Diabetes Deben Prestar Atención a su Salud Bucodental*
- **14.11.07 *− Menschen Mit Diabetes Müssen Besonders Auf Ihre Mundgesundheit Achten***
- 13.11.07 *− World Health Professions Alliance PublisHes Core Competencies for Health Consultants*
- 13.11.07 *− L'Alliance Mondiale des Professions de Santé Publie des Compétences de Base Pour Consultants de Santé*
- 03.11.07 *− La Alianza Mundial de las Profesiones de Salud Publica las Competencias Principales Para los Consultores de Salud*
- 03.11.07 *− WHPA Veröffentlicht Kernkompetenzen Für Gesundheitsberater*
- 04.10.07 *− FDI Joins Global Campaign to Make the United Nations a Smokefree Place*
- 04.10.07 *− La FDI se Joint à la Campagne Mondiale Visant à Faire des Nations − Unies un Environnement 100% Sans Fumée*
- 04.10.07 *− FDI SchlieBt Sich der Globalen Kampagne Für Rauchfreie Vereinte Nationen an*

- 25.09.07 — *Africa to Take the Lead in Integrating Oral Health into Chronic Disease Programmes*
- 25.09.07 — *L'Afrique est la Première à Intégrer la Santé Bucco — Dentaire Aux Programmes de Maladies Chroniques*
- 25.09.07 — *Afrika übernimmt bei der Integration der Mundgesundheit in Die Programme Zur bekämpfung Chronischer Krankheiten Die Führung*
- 19.09.07 — *Fluoride Toothpaste Helps Prevent Tooth Decay Confirm Leading Experts from Stomatology*
- 19.09.07 — *Les Experts en Odontologie Confirment Que le Dentifrice Fluoré Aide à la Prévention de la Carie Dentaire*
- 19.09.07 — *Destacados Expertos en Estomatología Confirman Que la Pasta Ddentífrica Fluorada Ayuda a Prevenir la Caries Dental*
- 19.09.07 — *Führende Stomatologen Bestätigen den Nutzen Von Fluoridzahnpasta für die Kariesprävention*
- 02.07.07 — *FDI Hosts World Noma Day Planning Meeting at Head Office*
- 02.07.07 — *Réunion au Siège de la FDI Pour Préparer la Journée Mondiale du Noma*
- 02.07.07 — *Reunión de Planificación en la Oficina Central de la FDI Del Día Mundial Sin Noma*
- 02.07.07 — *Treffen Zur Planung des Welt — Nomatags in Der FDI Hauptverwaltung*

- 25.06.07 − *FDI Joins Campaign in Protection against Second − Hand Smoke*

- 25.06.07 − *La FDI Adhère à la Campagne de Protection Contre le Tabagisme Passif*

- 25.06.07 − *La FDI se Adhiere a la Campaña Para Proteger Contra la Exposición al Humo de Tabaco Ajeno*

- 25.06.07 − *FDI Nimmt an der Kampagne Zum Schutz Vor Passivrauchen Teil*

- 31.05.07 − *FDI Urges Dental Professionals to Make their Workplaces Smoke − Free*

- 31.05.07 − *FLa FDI Exhorte Les Professionnels Dentaires à Rendre Non Fumeur Leur Lieu de Travail*

- 31.05.07 − *La FDI Urge a Los Profesionales Dentales a Que Conviertan Sus Lugares de Trabajo en un Espacio Libre de Humo*

- 31.05.07 − *FDI Fordert Von Zahnmedizinern Rauchfreie Arbeitsumgebungen*

- 24.05.07 − *FDI Supports WHO's Action Plan for Oral Health Worldwide*

- 24.05.07 − *La FDI Soutient le Plan D'action de l'OMS Pour Une Santé Bucco − Dentaire Mondiale*

- 24.05.07 − *La FDI Apoya el Plan de Acción de la OMS Para la Salud Bucodental Global*

- 24.05.07 − *FDI Unterstützt WHO − Aktionsplan Für Mundgesundheit Weltweit*

- 23.05.07 — *The FDI and the World Health Organization's Pan American Health Organization Join Forces to Improve Health in the Americas*
- 23.05.07 — *La FDI la Oficina Regional Para las Américas de la Organización Mundial de la Salud(OPS/OMS) se Unen Para Mejorar la Salud en las Américas*
- 02.04.07 — *Second Workshop to Address Oral Health Opens in Rwanda*
- 02.04.07 — *Deuxième Colloque sur la Santé Bucco — Dentaire au Rwanda*
- 02.04.07 — *2do. Taller de Salud Bucodental en Ruanda*
- 02.04.07 — *Zweiter Workshop Für Mundgesundheit in Ruanda*
- 13.02.07 — *WHO Renews Focus on the Neglected State of Global Oral Health*
- 13.02.07 — *L'OMS se Concentre à Nouveau sur L'état Négligé de la Santé Bucco — Dentaire Mondiale*
- 13.02.07 — *La OMS Reactiva su Atención en la Desatendida Área de la Salud Bucodental Global*
- 13.02.07 — *Globale Mundgesundheit ist Für Die WHO Ein Prioritätsthema Mit Nachholbedarf*
- 01.12.06 — *FDI Encourages Safe Dental Practices to Prevent the Spread of HIV/AIDS*
- 01.12.06 — *La FDI Encourage Des Pratiques Dentaires Sûres Pour Prévenir la Prolifération du VIH/SIDA*
- 01.12.06 — *La FDI Promueve Prácticas Dentales Seguras*

Para Impedir la Propagación del VIH/SIDA

- 01.12.06 – *Die FDI Setzt Sich Für Sichere Zahnmedizinische Praktiken Ein, um Die Weitere Verbreitung Von HIV/AIDS zu Verhindern*

FENS

Federation of European Nutrition Societies
유럽영양학협회연합

① 기구

1) 소재지

소재국가	스페인
주 소	Prof. J. Alfredo Martínez Professor of Nutrition Dpt. Physiology and Nutrition University of Navarra Investigation Building C/Irunlarrea, s/n 31008 Pamplona Spain
전 화	｜34 948 425600 ext. 6424
팩 스	+34 948 425649
홈페이지	http://www.fensweb.org/

2) 성격

유럽영양학협회연합(FENS)은 25개의 유럽영양학협회로 구성된 연합체이다.

3) 설립연혁

FENS는 1980년, 총 16개의 유럽 국가를 대표하는 영양학협회
로 설립되었다.

4) 비전 및 임무

건강의 세계적인 촉진을 위한 유럽의 영양개발을 위해 노력한다.
① 영양 관련 지식의 촉진 및 배포
② 4년마다 의회 소집
③ 유럽 전역에 걸친 영양학의 과학적 교환 및 형성과 양성 촉
　진

5) 회원

현재 본 연합의 회원협회 국가들은 다음과 같다.
오스트리아(Austria), 불가리아(Bulgaria), 체코(Czech Republic),
에스토니아(Estonia), 프랑스(France), 그리스(Greece), 아이슬란
드(Iceland), 이탈리아(Italy), 폴란드(Poland), 루마니아(Rumania), 스
페인(Spain), 스위스(Switzerland), 영국(United Kingdom), 벨기
에(belgium), 크로아티아(Croatia), 덴마크(Denmark), 핀란드
(Finland), 독일(Germany), 헝가리(Hungary), 아일랜드(Ireland), 노
르웨이(Norway), 포르투갈(Portugal), 세르비아 몬테네그로(Serbia
& Montenegro), 스웨덴(Sweden), 네덜란드(the Netherlands)

6) 주요 행사

FENS의 주요 행사는 유럽영양학컨퍼런스(European Nutrition Conference)이다. 이 컨퍼런스는 4년에 한 번 개최되며, 가장 최근에 열렸던 컨퍼런스는 2007년 7월 파리에서 열린 제10회 유럽영양학컨퍼런스이다.

② 정보원

1) 정보원배포정책

FENS의 정보원은 'Nutrition Journal'과 'Useful Links'로 나뉜다.

2) 영양학 저널(Nutrition Journal)

다음과 같은 저널의 목록을 제공한다.
- *Annals of Nutrition & Metabolism*(FENS 공식저널)
- *British Journal of Nutrition*
- *Ecology of Food and Nutrition*
- *Journal of Nutrition*
- *Lancet*
- *Nutrition and Dietetics*
- *Public Health Nutrition*
- *Scandinavian Journal of Nutrition, Näringsforskning*
- *The American Journal of Clinical Nutrition*

- *European Journal of Clinical Nutrition*

3) 링크(Useful Links)

- 영양학위원회(Nutrition Council) 및 관련 링크
  - International Union of Nutritional Sciences(IUNS)
  - European Academy of Nutritional Sciences(EANS)
- 다른 영양학기관
  - Nutrition Information and Various Nutrition Home Pages
  - The US National Academies Food and Nutrition Board
  - The Netherlands Nutrition Centre
  - Features of the Early Nutrition Programming Project

FIP

International Pharmaceutical Federation

국제약학연합

1 기구

1) 소재지

주　　소	andries Bickerweg 5 2517 JP the Hague the Netherlands
전　　화	+31 70 3021970
팩　　스	+31 70 3021999
전자우편	fip@fip.org
홈페이지	http://www.fip.org/www2/index.php

2) 설립연혁

국제약학연합(FIP)은 국가약학협회의 세계적 연합체이다. 회원제를 통해서 FIP는 전 세계의 백만이 넘는 약사들과 약학자들을 연결하고 그들에게 서비스를 제공한다. FIP는 1912년 네덜란드 헤이그에 설립되었으며 지금까지 헤이그에 그 본부를 두고 있다. 하나의 조직체로서 FIP는 여러 해에 걸쳐 새로운 활동사업을 벌이며 그 규모를 확대시킨다. FIP는 하나의 마음으

로 그 회원들과 함께하며 회원들에게 보다 나은 서비스를 제공
하기 위하여 긍정적인 변화를 추구한다.

3) 설립목적

FIP는 전 세계 약사 및 약학자들에게 서비스를 제공하고 그들
을 대표할 목적으로 설립되었다.

4) 조직

① FIP 협의회

FIP의 최고의 조직은 FIP 협의회이다. 회원기구라 불리는
모든 국가제약협회와 국가약학협회는 이 협의회에서 비례제
투표권을 행사할 수 있다. FIP의 준회원 협회들은 이 협의회
에 참여할 수는 있으나 투표권이 주어지지는 않는다.

② FIP국(bureau)

FIP의 역사적 배경에 의거하여 FIP의 위원회(board)는 FIP
국(bureau)이라 불린다. 총 9인의 부국장 중 4인은 협의회
에 의해서 선출된다.

③ 집행위원회

집행위원회는 총 3인으로 구성되며, 이 위원회는 FIP의 모
든 활동들을 지휘한다.

④ 제약관행 및 약학위원회(Boards of Pharmaceutical Practice and Pharmaceutical Sciences)

FIP는 전 세계의 개인 약사와 약학자들을 대표하기도 한다. 약사들은 제약관행위원회(BPP: Board of Pharmaceutical Practice)가 대표하며 약학자들은 약학위원회(BPS: Board of Pharmaceutical Sciences)가 대표한다.

5) 회원

FIP가 협회들의 연합형태라고는 하나 약사들 및 약학자들은 개인회원으로서 FIP에 등록할 수 있다.

6) 주요 사업

FIP의 활동은 환자관리의 장기적 효과를 증진시키기 위해 형성된다. 모든 활동들은 WHO의 '모두를 위한 건강'이란 목적에 부합하도록 만들어진다.

7) FIP와 WHO

FIP는 WHO의 공식적 관계(Official Relations)의 지위를 취득한 비정부기구이다. FIP는 또한 세계보건업동맹(WHPA: World Health Professions Alliance)의 창립멤버이기도 하다. 이 연맹은 현재 국제간호사협의회, 세계의학협회, 세계치학연방, 그리고 FIP로 나뉘었다.

FIP는 WHO의 위원회와 회의 등에 활동적으로 참여하고 있으며 이를 통해 의료관리시스템에서의 약사들의 역할을 발전시키고자 한다. FIP의 대표자들은 매년 열리는 WHO의 다양한 회의에 참석하여 중요한 정보들과 관련 정보들을 회원들에게 전파한다. WHO의 대표자들은 또한 FIP 회의에 참가한다. FIP는 지역 약학 포럼을 지원하며, 이 포럼들은 WHO의 지역사무소과 긴밀한 관련을 맺고 있다.

② 정보원

1) 정보배포정책

FIP의 정보원은 'Publications'와 'Health Topics'에서 찾아볼 수 있다. 'Publications'에서 제공하는 자료들은 회원들만이 열람 가능하며, 열람을 원할 시 직접 주문 구매하여야 한다. 'Health Topics'에서는 주제별 보고서를 열람할 수 있다.

2) 정보 자료

① 간행물

FIP의 간행물에는 '국제약학저널(International Pharmacy Journal)', 'FIP 뉴스', 'FIP 뉴스레터', '약학저널(Journal of Pharmaceutical Sciences)'이 있으며 모두 주문구매 후 구독 가능하다.

② 주제별 보고서(Health topics)

주제별 보고서는 PDF로 다운받아 열람이 가능하다. 대표적
인 자료는 다음과 같다.

[인적 자원]

- *FIP Global Pharmacy Workforce and Migration Report*

[금연]

- *Quit Smoking in the Middle East, Mostafa Mohamed, Egypt*
- *Pharmacists against Tobacco Actions in Kuwait, Klara Tisocki, Kuwait*
- *On-line Training in Support of Smoking Cessation, Jenny Bergin, Australia*
- *Malaysian Smoking Cessation Initiatives, Mohammad Haniki Nik Mohamed, Malaysia*
- *What is WHO EMRO Regional Office Doing to Minimise Tobacco Use?, Ibrahim El-Kerdany, Egypt*
- *How can FIP Help Pharmacists in their Fight against Tobacco?, Bente Frøkjær, Denmark*
- *World No Tobacco Day 31 May 2005-FIP Publication: Pharmacists against Tobacco-How to Get Started?*
- *Pharmacy Smoking Cessation Services-Contributing to Public Health. Sue Sharpe, Chief Executive, Pharmaceutical Services Negotiating Committee(PSNC), UK*
- *Smoking Cessation Project in Australia. Patrick Reid,*

Pharmacy Guild of Australia

- *The Pharmacy as an Active Part of the Public Health System Offer on Smoking Cessation in Denmark. Helle Jacobsgaard, Pharmacist, the DanisH Pharmaceutical Association*

- *Rx for Change Tobacco Cessation Programme. Karen Hudmon, Yale University School of Medicine, Department of Epidemiology and Public Health, USA*

- *Pharmacists for Promoting a Future Free of Tobacco in India. Maddirala V. Siva Prasada Reddy, South East Asian Pharmaceutical forum, India*

- *French Campaign against Tobacco. Josette Dubray, French Council of Pharmacists, France*

- *What's Working in Smoking Cessation in the Pharmacy Profession in the USA−Eliminating Tobacco From Healthcare Facilities. Fred S. Mayer, R.Ph., M.P.H., President, Pharmacists Planning Service, Inc.(PPSI) and Pharmacy Council on Tobacco Dependence(PCTD), USA*

- *Smoking Cessation Campaign in Japan. Nobuo Yamamoto, Executive Officer, Japan Pharmaceutical Association and Vice President, Western Pacific Pharmaceutical forum*

- *Pharmacists'smoking Cessation Initiatives in the Western Pacific Region. John Ware, President, Western Pacific Pharmaceutical Forum, Australia*

- *Pharmacy Students' Activities. Simon Bell, Immediate*

Past President, International Pharmaceutical Students'
Federation(IPSF)
- *Pharmacists against Tobacco − How to Get Started?*
- *Pharmacists and Action on Tobacco*

[허위의학]
- *Report of the SEARPharma Forum Study on the Extent*
  of Counterfeit Medicines in India
- *FIP Board of Pharmacy Practice Symposium on "the*
  World Wide Problem of Counterfeit Medicines" During
  the FIP Congress in Cairo, Egypt 2005
- *Counterfeit Drugs − Coming to a Pharmacy Near You*
  (Condensed Version, Prepared for the American Council
  of Science and Health)

GFHR

Global Forum for Health Research

세계보건연구포럼

1 기구

1) 소재지

소재국가	스위스
주 소	Global Forum for Health Research 1−5 route des Morillons PO Box 2100 1211 Geneva 2 Switzerland
전 화	+41 22 791 4260
팩 스	+41 22 791 4394
전자우편	info@globalforumhealth.org
홈페이지	http://www.globalforumhealth.org/Site/000_Home.php

2) 성격

세계보건연구포럼(GFHR)은 스위스 법에 의거하는 독립적인 비영리 재단이다.

3) 설립연혁

GFHR은 1998년 스위스에서 독립적인 국제재단으로 설립되었다.

4) 비전 및 임무

세계보건연구포럼의 비전은 가난한 자들의 건강문제를 다루는 연구 및 혁신의 가능성을 지닌 세계이다.
① 현재 및 미래의 모든 국가의 고위급 정책입안가들의 참여
② 연구와 혁신에 관한 국제관계자들의 결합과 파트너십 중재
③ 건강에 관한 연구 촉진
④ 모든 분야의 연구와 혁신을 위한 자원 증가
⑤ 정책결정에 있어서 증거이용 장려
⑥ 이용 가능한 연구결과 촉진 및 분배

5) 조직

① 재단위원회(Foundation Council)
재단위원회는 가장 높은 수준의 정책결정조직이다. 본 위원회는 기구의 넓은 의미의 안내와 목적 및 우선순위 분야에 대한 정의 그리고 장기적 비전에 대한 책임을 갖고 있다.
본 위원회는 전략기술자문위원회(STRATEC: Strategic and Technical Advisory Committee)의 지원을 받는다.

② 기부단(Donors)
본 기구는 다음과 같은 기구들의 후원을 받는다.

록펠러재단(Rockefeller Foundation), 세계은행(World Bank), 세계보건기구(World Health Organization), 캐나다정부, 아일랜드정부, 멕시코정부, 노르웨이정부, 스위스정부

6) 주요 활동

GFHR은 가난한 자들의 건강 증진을 위한 연구기금 및 정책에 관한 정책입안가들을 위해 포럼을 주최한다.

7) 협력기관

다음은 GFHR의 협력기관이다.

① 국제기구

- 유엔기금/유엔인구활동기금/세계보건기구/세계은행 인간재생산에 관한 연구, 개발, 연구훈련을위한특별프로그램 (UNDP/UNFPA/WHO/World Bank Special Programme of Research, Development and Research Training in Human Reproduction)
- 유니세프/유엔기금/세계은행/세계보건기구 열대질병 연구및훈련을위한특별프로그램(UNICEF/UNDP/World Bank/WHO Special Programme for Research and Training in Tropical Diseases)
- 유네스코(UNESCO: United Nations Educational, Scientific and Cultural Organization)
- 세계보건기구(WHO: World Health Organization)
- 세계보건기구정신건강(WHO Mental Health: Evidence and

Research)
- 세계보건기구 동지중해지역기구(WHO Regional Office for the Eastern Mediterranean)
- 세계은행(World Bank)

② 비정부기구 및 파트너기구
- 개발을위한보건연구협의회(COHRED: Council on Health Research for Development)
- 유럽재단센터(EFC: European Foundation Centre)

③ 연구기관 및 대학
- 이프카라보건연구개발센터및스위스열대연구소(Ifakara Health Research and Development Centre and Swiss Tropical Institute)
- 인도의학연구협의회(Indian Council of Medical Research)
- 존스홉킨스대학(Johns Hopkins University)

④ 정부
- 멕시코보건부(Ministry of Health, Mexico)
- 이집트정부(Government of Egypt)
- 중국보건부(Ministry of Health, People's Republic of China)
- 말리정부(Government of Mali)
- 스페인보건정부(Ministry of Health, Spain)
- 브라질보건부과학기술국(Ministry of Health, Department of

Science and Technology, Brazil)
* 덴마크외교부(Ministry of Foreign Affairs/DANIDA)

⑤ 출판사
* ProBrook Publishing Limited
* RealHealthNews
* The Lancet

② 정보원

1) 정보원배포정책

GFHR의 정보원은 'Publications'와 'Latest News'에서 찾아볼 수 있다. 발간 자료(Publications)는 주제별 또는 제목별 브라우 징 검색이 가능하며, 모든 자료는 PDF로 무료열람이 가능하다. 또한 일부 서적은 온라인상으로 도서구매도 가능하다.

2) 발간 자료(Publications)

* *2007 Review: Catalysing Innovative Solutions for the Health of the Poor*
* *Health Partnerships Review*
* *Equitable Access: Research Challenges for Health in Developing Countries. A Report on Forum 11*
* *Aspectos de la Investigación Sobre la Salud Sexual y*

Reproductiva en Países Con Ingresos Bajos e Intermedios

- *Global Forum Update on Research for Health Volume 4, Equitable Access: Research Challenges for Health in Developing Countries*
- *Book of Abstracts − Forum 11*
- *Young Voices in Research for Health 2007*
- *BIAS FREE Framwork − Chinese Translation*
- *Research Capacity for Mental Health in Low − and Middle −Income Countries: Results of a Mapping Project*
- *Learning from Experience: Health Care Financing in Low −and Middle −Income Countries*
- *Por Quepesquisa em Saúde? Textos Para tomada de Decisão*

3) 보도 자료(Latest News)

- *Initiative for a European Council on Global Health Launched*
- *"Today, We have No Architecture for Global Research for Health"*
- *The Global Forum for Health Research will Hold a Symposium*
- *Global Forum to Host a Global Consultation on Research*
- *Preparatory Work for the Second Session of the WHO*
- *Malaria Product Portfolio*
- *New Global Partnership Architectures for Health Research*

- *Foundation Council News*
- *Forum Friends*
- *Research Agenda for TB Elimination*
- *CHNRI Launched as Independent Foundation*
- *Matriz Combinada/Combined Approach Matrix*
- *Launch of HR4D: Health Researchers and Health Policy –Makers to Alk at Last*
- *Partnership between the Global Forum and COHRED*
- *Road –Traffic Injuries: A Public Health Priority*
- *IC –Health Launched as an Independent Foundation*
- *Monitoring Financial Flows for Health Research 2005: Behind the Lobal Numbers*
- *SVRI Launches New Website*
- *Global Forum Foundation Council: New Members*
- *World Health Day 2006: Human Resources for Health Research*
- *Denmark and Brazil Strengthen Commitments to Global Immunization Programmes*
- *Innternational Women's Day*
- *Sexual Violence Research Initiative(SVRI) Secretariat Relocated to South Africa and Calling for Nominations for Coordinating Group Members*
- *BIAS FREE Framework*
- *Stop TB Partnership Kochon Prize*
- *£5m DFID Fund to Alliance*

- *Road Traffic Injuries Research Network(RTIRN) in Sri Lanka*
- *Call for Proposals*
- *Global Forum Calls for More Support for Public－Private Partnerships*

GHC

Global Health Council
세계건강협의회

① 기구

1) 소재지

주　　소	1111 19th Street, NW − Suite 1120 Washington, DC 20036
전　　화	＋1 202 833 5900
팩　　스	＋1 202 833 0075
전자우편	achristensen@globalhealth.org
홈페이지	http://www.globalhealth.org/

2) 설립연혁

세계건강협의회(GHC)는 전 세계적으로 가장 큰 회원연합체로서 세계 곳곳의 건강을 증진시키기 위해 활동한다. GHC의 회원은 의료전문가 및 NGO를 비롯한 의료 관련 기관들, 기금단체, 기업, 정부기관, 학술기관 등을 포함한다. GHC는 1972년 미국에 본부를 둔 비영리 회원제 기관인 국제건강을 위한 국가협의회(National Council of International Health)로서 출범하였다. 그 후 1998년 현재의 GHC로 기관 명칭을 변경하였다.

3) 설립목적

GHC의 설립목적은 세계건강에 있어서의 평등성을 추구하고 건강을 증진하고자 하는 데에 있다.

4) 조직

GHC는 현재 워싱턴 DC와 버몬트에서 사무소를 운영하고 있다. 워싱턴 DC의 사무소는 연구 분석, 정부관계, 정책분석 및 커뮤니케이션, 대중홍보에 관련된 업무를 담당하며, 버몬트 사무소는 운영, 행정, 콘퍼런스, 재정, 회원관리, 출판 및 웹사이트와 관련된 업무를 보고 있다.

5) 회원

GHC의 회원제는 개인회원제, 기관회원제, 그리고 기업 및 후원회원제로 분류된다. 개인회원이 되기 위해서는 세계건강에 관심이 있는 학생 등 모든 개인이 해당되며, 기관회원이 되기 위해서는 세계건강 및 개발 분야에 종사하고 있는 기관이면 가입이 가능하다. 기업 및 후원회원제는 세계건강정책 및 프로그램 등에 있어서 효과적인 전략을 찾고 있는 기업들이 가입을 하게 된다.

6) 주요 사업

GHC는 크게 다음과 같은 활동을 한다.
아동건강을 위한 캠페인, 홍보, 정책개발, 시상, 콘퍼런스, 세계

에이즈 원탁회의, 장학사업, 말라리아 원탁회의, 출판, 연구 및 분석, 대학 등의 학술기관 홍보

② 정보원

1) 정보배포정책

GHC의 정보원은 'Resources', 'Press' 그리고 'Publications'에서 찾을 수 있다. 'Resources'에서는 GHC 관련 일반정보 및 서적을 열람할 수 있으며, 'Press'에서는 GHC의 보도 자료를, 'Publications'에서는 보고서 등의 출판물을 온라인 열람할 수 있다.

2) 정보 자료

① Resources

다른 기관의 웹사이트 중에서 GHC의 활동과 관련된 서적이 열람이 가능한 웹 링크를 제공한다. 대표적인 서적 목록은 다음과 같다.

- *Women's Empowerment in Ethiopia: New Solutions to Ancient Problems*
- *Adoption of Health Technologies in India*
- *Challenges in Reforming the Health Sector in Africa: Reforming Health Systems under Economic Siege*
- *Rethinking AIDS Prevention*

- *Community Involvement Resources*
- *Global Public Health Communication: Challenges, Per-spectives and Strategies*
- *YouthNet Briefs 10 − 18*
- *Updated Provider Checklists for Reproductive Health Services*
- *Youth Peer Education Toolkit: Standards for Peer Education Programmes*
- *Theatre − Based Techniques for Youth Peer Education*
- *Give Us Your Best and Brightest*
- *Global Public Health Communication*
- *Children's Story is the Latest Weapon in War against Avian Flu*
- *Health Program Planning: An Educational and Ecological Approach*
- *The Leading 500 New Foundations Funding Women and Girls*
- *Rx for Survival*
- *Glossary of HIV/AIDS Related Terms and Phrases*
- *YouthNet Briefs*
- *Dying to be Men*
- *Public Health: Power, Empowerment & Professional Practice*
- *Africa's Prestigious Journal on Reproductive Health*
- *Our Bodies, Ourselves*

- *Where There is No Dentist*
- *Synergy Project PublisHes HIV/AIDS Case Studies*
- *Directory of Associations of People Living with HIV/AIDS*
- *From Population Control to Reproductive Health*
- *Creative Child Advocacy: Global Perspectives*
- *AIDS in Asia*
- *Communicating Health: An Action Guide to Health Education and Health Promotion*
- *Forced Back*

② 보도 자료

최근의 보도 자료는 다음과 같다.

[GHC 보도 자료]

- *Maternal Mortality Rates Nearly Unchanged Since 1990* −Oct. 12, 2007
- *New Poll Finds Wide Support for Child Survival Efforts* −Oct. 10, 2007
- *Global Health Experts Testify on Strengthening PEPFAR before House Committee on Foreign Affairs* − Sept. 25, 2007
- *Senate Approves FY 08 State/foreign Operations Bill: Bolsters Support for Maternal and Child Health Programs* −Sept. 11, 2007
- *UK Prime Minister Gordon Brown Announces New International Health Partnership and Seeks Support*

From Other Donor Nations − Sept. 6, 2007

- *Senate Passes Latest Version of FY 08 Appropriations Bill with Increases for Global Health* − June 29, 2007
- *House Appropriates 2008 Funds for Global Health issues* − June 26, 2007
- *U.S. Rep. Betty McCollum to Receive Congressional Leadership Award for Global Health* − June 13, 2007
- *House Expected to Support Increased Funding for Several Core Global Health Programs* − June 7, 2007
- *White House Calls for Doubling the Investment in Global AIDS Programs* − May 31, 2007
- *Global Health Leaders Celebrate Exemplary Humanitarians and Media Professionals* − May 31, 2007
- *The Global Health Council Announces Launch of Global Health TV* − May 30, 2007
- *Population and Community Development Association to Receive Gates Award for Global Health* − May 29, 2007
- *Urgent Global Attention Needed on Millennium Development Goals 4 & 5* − May 25, 2007
- *Health Experts Gather in Washington for 34th Annual International Conference on Global Health* − May 24, 2007
- *Candlelight Memorial for HIV/AIDS Action Held in over 100 Countries around the World* − May 21, 2007

- *Senate and House Introduce Legislation to Save Millions of Children in Developing Nations* – May 18, 2007
- *Senate Resolution on U.S. Engagement In Global Health Issues Introduced Today* – May 3, 2007
- *Global Health Council Receives Ford Foundation Grant for International HIV/AIDS Advocacy Network* – May 2, 2007
- *Health Experts Meet with Congress to Examine U.S. Progress in Controlling Malaria* – *Apr.* 26, 2007
- *Senate Appropriations Subcommittee Meets on Future of U.S. Health Assistance for Millions of Women and Children in the Developing World* – Apr. 19, 2007
- *The Global Health Council Joins the World Health Organization's Call for Improving Health System Security* – Apr. 6, 2007
- *President's 08 Budget Request Reflects Highs and Lows on Global Health Issues* – Feb. 6, 2007
- *U.S. House Numbers for FY07 Budget Increase Investments in HIV/AIDS and Malaria, Underfund Child and Maternal Health* – Jan. 31, 2007
- *State of the Union Address Highlights Leadership on Aids and Malaria: Other Global Health Programs Remain Underfunded* – Jan. 24, 2007

[GHC를 다룬 보도 자료]

- *India Reports Maximum No. of Childbirth Deaths* - The Times of India - Oct. 16, 2007

- *Global Maternal Maternity Rate Remains Unchanged Since 1990* - The Economic Times of India - Oct. 14, 2007

- *PEPFAR Reauthorization: Issues for Consideration* - Worldpress.org - Oct. 12, 2007

- *The Fight for Global Child Survival* - The Christian Broadcasting Network - Oct. 11, 2007

- *In U.S. Poll, Most Fail a Quiz on Global Causes of Child Deaths* - New York Times - Oct. 11, 2007

- *PEPFAR Programs Should Focus on Sustainable HIV Prevention Model, Experts Say at Reauthorization Hearing* - AllAfrica - Sept. 27, 2007

- *Experts Call for Broadened Approach to AIDS Relief* - CQ Healthbeat News - Sept. 26, 2007

- *U.S. Delays Terror Screening for Aid Groups* - The Washington Post - Aug. 28, 2007

- *Foreign Aid Groups Face Terror Screens* - The Washington Post - Aug. 23, 2007

- *Hilton Humanitarian Prize of $1.5 Million Goes to tostan* - Press Release Newswire - Aug. 13, 2007

- *Reviving the HIV Vaccine Hunt* - United Press International - July 16, 2007

- *White House Treats Malaria as a Global 'Human Crisis'* − *The Washington Times* − July 8, 2007
- *ADRA Showcases Innovative Reporting Mechanism at Global Health Council* − *Reuters* − July 5, 2007
- *Dorothy Granada Receives Best Practices in Global Health Award* − *Episcopal Life Online* − June 28, 2007
- *PEPFAR Mobilizing Around Global AIDS: The Opportunities and Challenges* − *InterAction* − June 27, 2007
- *Profile: Bogaletch Gebre: Ending Female Genital Mutilation in Ethiopia* − *Lancet* − June 23, 2007
- *Participating in the Broader Health Agenda* − *Reuters AlertNet* − June 18, 2007
- *Drug* − *Resistant TB is Best Battled at the Source* − *USA Today* − June 10, 2007
- *TB Case Reveals Loopholes in U.S. Security* − *ABC News* − June 7, 2007
- *U.S. Tuberculosis Case Raises Questions on Global Disease Issues* − *USINFO.State.Gov* − June 7, 2007
- *Andrew Speaker's T.B.: Just the "Tip of the Iceberg?"* − *ABC News* − June 6, 2007
- *'We Made a Mistake'* − *MSNBC News* − June 6, 2007
- *"We Dodged a Bullet on This one"* − ABC News − June 6, 2007
- *Honoring Thailand's Exuberant AIDS Czar* − *Washington Post Foreign Service* − June 1, 2007

- *Drug - Resistant TB - PRI the World - June 1, 2007*
- *Thai Health Program Receives 2007 Gates Award for Global Health - Philanthropy News Digest - May 31, 2007*
- *$1M Gates Award for Mechai's NGO - the Nation - May 31, 2007*
- *Bush Announces Request for $30B, Five - Year Extension of PEPFAR - AllAfrica.com - May 31, 2007*
- *Thai HIV/AIDS Advocate Mechai Receives Gates Award for Global Health - The Henry J. Kaiser Family Foundation - May 30, 2007*
- *Bush Calls for Billions in AIDS Funding - National Public Radio - May 30, 2007*
- *Gates Foundation Honors Thai Population, HIV Program with $1 Million(740,000) Award - International Herald Tribune May 29, 2007*
- *Cabbages and Condoms, a Winning Idea - The New York Times - May 29, 2007*
- *Population and Community Development Association to Receive Gates Award for Global Health - PharmaLive - May 29, 2007*
- *Life - Saving School Health Program Highlighted at Global Health Conference in DC on Wednesday, May 30 at 5pm - EarthTimes.org - May 25, 2007*
- *Middlebury High Student Named First Leahy Scholar*

- *—Rutland Herald —*May 24, 2007
- *South Africa: SA Commemorates Global Aids Memorial Day —AllAfrica.com —*May 20, 2007
- *Remember the Living on AIDS Memorial Day —the Moscow Times.com —*May 18, 2007
- *In Loving Memory, This Week's International AIDS Candlelight Memorial —Monday Publications —*May 16, 2007
- *PEPFAR'S Story so Far —CQ Healthbeat News —*May 7, 2007
- *GlobeMed Hosts Benefit Dinner for Public Health —the Daily Northwestern —*May 7, 2007
- *Congressional Briefing Addresses Obstetric Fistula — Ms. Magazine —*May 4, 2007
- *Forty New Cases of TB Detected Every Hour in the Americas, PAHO Reports —MedicalNewsService.com —*March 28, 2007
- *China's AIDS Heroine —Epoch Times —*March 26, 2007
- *Indonesia Blocking Access to Bird Flu Virus —The Cox News Service —*March 16, 2007
- *25 New Englanders to Watch in Washington —The Boston Globe —*March 8, 2007
- *Court: U.S. Funders Can Demand Anti —Prostitution Pledge —oneWorld.net —*March 7, 2007
- *Plan to Fund Vaccines for Third World —Philadelphia*

Enquirer - Feb. 9, 2007

- *Experts Say Outreach Initiatives Failing to Connect with African Girls at Risk for HIV - CQ Healthbeat News* - Jan. 23, 2007

- *The Coming Pandemic: Myth or Reality - Vermont Public Radio* - Jan. 17, 2007

- *Analysis: AIDS Plan Faces Deadly Deficit - Science Daily* - Jan. 5, 2007

③ 출판물

'연간보고서' 외에 다음과 같은 출판물을 열람할 수 있다.

[정기간행물]

- *HealthLink®*

- *AIDSLink®*

[의료보고시(Technical Report)]

- *Global Health Opportunities*

- *Faith in Action*

- *Commitments*

- *Reducing Malaria's Burden*

- *MTCT*

- *Evidence for Action*

- *Child Health Report*

- *Banking on Reproductive Health*

- *Preventing TB*

- *Making Sense of Research*
- *Safer Childbirth*
- *Promises to Keep*
- *Privacy Guide*
- *Differential Pricing & Financing of Essential Drugs*

[정책보고서]
- *A Critical Shortage of Health Care Workers*
- *The Impact of Tariff and Non-Tariff Barriers on Access to Essential Drugs for the Poorest People*
- *Success Stories: Reaching the Child Survival Millennium Development Goal*
- *Strengthening PEPFAR for Women and Girls*
- *End Restrictions on Travel to the U.S. by People with HIV*
- *Getting Back to Global Child Health*
- *Health Equity for the World's Children Would Save Millions of Lives*
- *Decrease Violence to Decrease Risk of HIV among Women and Girls*
- *Prevention: Our Chance to Reverse the HIV/AIDS Pandemic*
- *Anti-Prostitution Policy Requirement*
- *Overcoming Neglected Tropical Diseases with Cost-Effective, Integrated Programs*
- *Promoting Investments in Research to Strengthen Health Systems: Why and How*

GWA

Gender and Water Alliance

젠더와물동맹기구

① 기구

1) 소재지

주 소	P.O. Box 114, 6950 AC Dieren, the Netherlands
전 화	+31 313 427230
팩 스	+31 313 427230
전자우편	secretariat@gwalliance.org
홈페이지	http://www.genderandwater.org/

2) 설립연혁

젠더와물동맹기구(GWA)는 2000년 3월에 열린 제2차 세계물포
럼(WWF: Second World Water forum)에서 조직되었다.

GWA는 글로벌 네트워크로서 물 자원 관리에 있어서 젠더주류
화에 기여하고 있다. 본 기구는 네덜란드 법률에 근거한 협회
로 등록이 되어 있으며 전 세계적으로 약 104개국의 1,000명
이 넘는 회원을 두고 있다.

GWA의 재정은 네덜란드와 영국정부에 의해 지원받고 있으며, 파트너 기관과 함께 수행하고 있는 프로젝트에서 일부 조달하고 있다.

3) 설립목적

GWA의 설립목적은 통합적물자원관리(IWRM: Integrated Water Resources Management)에 있어서의 젠더주류화를 위한 효과적인 정책 및 실천을 달성하는 데에 있다.

4) 조직

GWA는 독립적인 운영위원회(Steering Committee)에 의해 운영되고 있다. 이 위원회는 3년에 한 번씩 회원들에 의해 선출된다. 운영위원회는 다른 지역을 대표하는 물 영역의 젠더전문가 8인으로 구성된다. 또한 이 위원회는 2년의 임기를 가지는 국제기구의 3인의 대표에 의해 자문을 구하게 된다. GWA 본부는 1인의 국장(Executive Director), 1인의 최고프로그램책임자(Senior Programme Officer), 5인의 프로그램책임자(Programme Officer), 그리고 1인의 행정재정책임자(Administrative Financial Officer)에 의해 운영되며, 네덜란드의 디렌(Dieren)에 위치하고 있다.

5) 관련 기관

GWA의 근본방침 중 하나는 협동을 강화하고 물과 위생 분야의 관련 담당자들과의 시너지를 향상시키는 것이다. 이러한 배경을 바탕으로 결과중심의 파트너십을 위해 GWA는 전 세계 관련 국제기구들과 연관되어 활동한다.

6) 주요 사업

2006∼2010년의 GWA 활동은 다음의 5가지 계획을 중심으로 이루어진다.
① 네트워크 강화
② 젠더주류화 정책에 관한 지식 및 정보 기록 공유
③ 물 자원 관리(IWRM)에 있어서의 젠더주류화 능력 함양
④ 국가 물 관련 정책의 이행과 개발에서의 젠더이슈 결합
⑤ 물 관련 국제콘퍼런스에서의 젠더평등이슈의 프로필 강화

② 정보원

1) 정보배포정책

GWA의 정보원은 '젠더와 물 자원 관리 정보기이드(Gender and IWRM Resource Guide)'와 'Other Resources'에서 찾아볼 수 있다. 젠더와 물 자원 관리 정보가이드는 기본개념을 포함한 참고자료를 제공한다.

2) 정보 자료

① Other Resources

사례연구, GWA 도큐먼트, 보고서, 출판물, 연설문 및 발표
문, 성명서 및 선언서 등의 자료 열람이 가능하다.

[사례연구]

- *Addressing Water and Poverty*
- *All Case Studies from the Guide*
- *Case Studies e-Conference 2002*
- *Community Based Disaster Risk Mitigation- Gujarat*
- *Engendering Environment and Natural Resources Management*
- *Gender Equality Results in the Punjab Community Water Supply and Sanitation Sector Project Pakistan*
- *Gender in Integrated Rural Water Supplies and Sanitation Programme in Zimbabwe*
- *Gender, Water and Poverty in Bangladesh*
- *Incorporating a Gender Perspective in Rural Water and Sanitation Projects*
- *Mainstreaming Gender in Sanitation and Hygiene in Uganda*
- *Mainstreaming Gender in South African Sanitation Programmes: A Blind Spot or Common Practice?*
- *MAMA-86 and the Drinking Water Campaign in the Ukraine*
- *Pro-poor Water Supply and Sanitation-Nepal*
- *Rural Women Securing Household Water in Jordan*

- *Summary of Case Studies in "Gender in Court" at 3rd World Water forum*
- *Tajikistan－Community Situation Indicators*
- *Women, Mobilization and the Revitalization of Water Resources: The Case of North－Eastern Brazil*

[도큐먼트]

- *First General Assembly*
- *General Information Leaflet about GWA*
- *Progress Report 2006*
- *Sidestream or Mainstream Leaflet*
- *Strategic Plan 2006－2007 and Annual Plan 2007*
- *Strategic Plan 2006－2010 and Annual Plan 2006*

[보고서]

- *Accra Conference on Water and Sustainable Development in Africa,* April 2002
- *First Asia Pacific Water Forum*(December 2007) Attended By GWA Chair
- *Report of Gender Seminar "Capturing the Big Picture of Gender in Water"*
- *Report of Seminar on Water and Micro－Finance: Exploring Innovative Partnerships,* October 2007
- *Report of Survey on Use of Manuals and Guidelines for Gender Mainstreaming*

- *Report of the International Training of Trainers for Strategizing Gender Mainstreaming in Water and Sanitation Management*
- *Report of Workshop of Drafting the Minimum Agenda*
- *Report on "Gender in Court" − 3rd WWF*
- *Report on the Workshop of Gender Review of Chapters of the Comprehensive Assessment*
- *Report on Workshop and Staff Training on Gender and Water*, October 2006
- *SACOSAN 2003 Participation Report*
- *Summary of Gender Issues Profiled in Final Comprehensive Assessment* Book
- *Synthesis Report of GWA Activities at the 4th World Water forum*

[출판물]

- *Analysis of Sanitation Policies in S.Africa, Zambia & Zimbabwe*
- *Advocacy Manual for Gender & Water Ambassadors*
- *Brief Overview on the Current Situation on Gender and Water Management in Egypt*
- *Considering Gender Issues in Flood Mitigation*
- *Fact Sheet Gender and Water in Mongolia*
- *For Her − It's the Big Issue: Putting Women at the Centre of Water Supply, Sanitation and Hygiene*

- *Gender Mainstreaming Field Manual for Water Supply & Sanitation Sub Sector*
- *Gender Mainstreaming Guidelines and Checklists for the Water Sector*
- *Gender Mainstreaming in Integrated Water Resource Management. Gender, Efficiency and Sustainability.*
- *Gender Perspectives on Policies in the Water Sector*
- *Gender Responsiveness in ADB Water Policies and Projects*
- *Gender, Water and Sanitation: A Policy Brief*
- *GEWAMED Newsletter, Issue no. 3, December 2006*
- *Impact Measurement and Accountability in Emergencies: the Good Enough Guide*
- *Millenium Development Goals, Gender and Water*
- *Minimum Agenda*
- *Navigating Gender in African Cities*
- *Policy Development Manual*
- *Productive Uses of Domestic Water: A Household - Level Study from Vietnam*
- *Publications of GWA*
- *Sidestream or Mainstream Leaflet*
- *Synthesis Report: "Effective Gender Mainstreaming in Water Management for Sustainable Livelihoods: From Guidelines to Practice"*
- *Tapping into Sustainability*

- *The 22nd Quarterly of UN−Habitat's Programme: Water for Cities*
- *The Gender Approach to Water Management to T Modules*
- *Water, Sanitation and Hygiene Education for Schools*
- *Women's Collective Action and Sustainable Water Management*

[연설문 및 발표문]

- *All India Conference, 2002, Inaugural Session Address*
- *Arab Water Regional Conference*
- *SACOSAN*
- *Speeches by GWA Chair*
- *Stockholm World Water Weeks*
- *The Need to Join in Partnerships for Mainstreaming Gender in Water Management*
- *World Water Forum*

[성명서 및 선언서]

- *African Sanitation and Hygiene Conference 2002, Final Statement*
- *3rd World Water Forum: Ministrial Declaration*

HINARI

HINARI

Health InterNetwork Access to Research Initiative

연구이니셔티브를위한건강네트워크

1 기구

1) 소재지

주 소	World Health Organization EIP/KMS/E - Health, HINARI 20, Avenue Appia, CH - 1211 Geneva 27 Switzerland
전 화	+41 22 791 4150
전자우편	hinari@who.int
홈페이지	http://www.who.int/hinari/en/

2) 설립연혁/설립목적

연구이니셔티브를위한건강네트워크(HINARI)는 생물의학 또는 관련 사회과학에 관한 주요 저널을 개발도상국의 지역, 비영리 기관에 무료 또는 매우 낮은 가격으로 온라인상으로 제공하는 기관이다. HINARI는 2000년 유엔 새천년정상회담(UN Millennium Summit)에서 코피아난 사무총장에 의해 소개되었고, 2001년 7월 설립에 대한 성명이 채택되었다. 그 후 2002년

1월, Blackwell, Elsevier Science, the Harcourt Worldwide STM Group, Wolters Kluwer International Health & Science, Springer Verlag and John Wiley의 6개의 주요 출판사의 약 1,500여 개의 저널과 함께 HINARI가 탄생되었다. 2002년 5월에 22개의 다른 출판사들이 합류하였고, 이로 인해 총 2,000개 이상의 저널이 HINARI에 등록되었다. 그 후 지속적으로 많은 출판사들과 저널이 HINARI에 등록되고 있다.

3) 회원

국가의 지방그룹 또는 비영리기관들은 HINARI의 회원으로 등록이 가능하다. 등록 가능한 국가들의 리스트는 2001년 세계은행(World Bank) 자료의 GNP를 기준으로 제공되고 있다. 미화 1,000달러 미만의 GNP 상태에 있는 국가의 기관들은 온라인상에서 무료로 자료이용이 가능하다. 미화 1,000에서 3,000달러의 GNP 상태에 있는 국가의 기관들은 연간 미화 1,000달러의 회원비를 지불하여야 한다. 등록 가능한 기관들은 국립대학, 연구기관, 전문학교(의학, 간호학, 약학, 대중의료, 치의학), 학술병원, 정부기관, 국가의학도서관 등이다. 이 기관들의 모든 직원 및 학생들은 HINARI의 저널에 접근이 가능하다.

② 정보원

1) 정보배포정책

HINARI의 정보원은 'Journals'에서 찾아볼 수 있다. 주제별 검색, 리스트 색인, 그룹별 검색, 출판언어별 검색, 출판사별 검색이 가능하다. 자료의 열람은 회원로그인 후 가능하다. 2007년 10월 현재 총 4,073개의 저널의 내용을 열람할 수 있다.

HMN

Health Metrics Network

의료메트릭스네트워크

① 기구

1) 소재지

주 소	Health Metrics Network Secretariat WHO, 20 Avenue Appia 1211 Geneva 27, Switzerland
전 화	+41 22 791 5494
팩 스	+41 22 791 5855
홈페이지	http://www.who.int/healthmetrics/about/en/

2) 설립연혁

의료메트릭스네트워크(HMN)는 국가, 지역, 세계의 더 나은 의료정보를 촉진하기 위한 글로벌 파트너십이다. 개발도상국, 다자간기구, 양자간기구, 재단, 그 외 글로벌 의료파트너십, 기술전문가들 등의 파트너들로 구성된다. HMN은 역량 강화 및 전문성 구축과 의사결정 과정에서의 이용가능성, 양질, 분배, 데이터 이용 강화를 위한 의료 및 통계자료를 정리할 수 있는 방법을 모색한다.

3) 설립목적

HMN은 협력적 기금과 주요국가 의료정보시스템 개발을 이용
함으로써 시간에 맞추는 정확한 의료정보의 이용 및 이용가능
성을 증가시키고자 하는 전략적 목표를 가지고 있다. 세부 목
표는 다음과 같다.

① 의료정보시스템의 표준을 기술하는 국가 His(HMN 체제)
  개발을 위한 조화로운 체제 형성

② 기술 및 결정적인 재정적 지원을 제공함으로써 HMN 체제
  에 적합한 국가 His 강화

4) 조직

HMN은 위원회(Board), 기술자문위원회(Technical Advisory
Group) 그리고 본부(Secretariat)로 구성된다.

5) 주요 사업

HMN은 기구의 목표를 달성하기 위해 His 개발을 위한 전략을
정하고 이 전략을 실행하고 있는 국가의 지원을 강화하는 활동
을 한다.

② 정보원

1) 정보배포정책

HMN의 정보원은 'News & Events'에서 찾아볼 수 있다. 뉴스 레터를 비롯하여 매달 갱신되는 자료들을 열람할 수 있다. 또 한, 영상자료 및 보도 자료도 열람 가능하다.

2) 정보 자료

① 뉴스레터
- *HMN Newsletter* vol. 7
- *HMN Newsletter* vol. 6
- *Newsletter* vol. 5
- *Newsletter* vol. 4
- *Newsletter* vol. 3
- *Newsletter* vol. 2
- *Newsletter* vol. 1

② 월간 업데이트
- *HMN Monthly Update*: October 2007
- *HMN Monthly Update*: August 2007
- *HMN Monthly Update*: May 2007
- *HMN Monthly Update*: April 2007
- *HMN Monthly Update*: March 2007
- *HMN Monthly Update*: February 2007

- January 2007: *Grants for 25 Countries in Round Two*
- December 2006: *HMN Board Approves Strategic Plan*

③ 보도 자료

- 21 March 2007 *－European, Central Asian Nations Back HMN Reforms of Health Information Systems*
- 9 March 2007 *－Viet Nam Press Cuttings*
- 9 March 2007 *－6 Asian Nations Reveal Findings of Assessment of HMN－Backed Health Information System Reform*
- 19 February 2007 *－Eritrea Health Update Issue 2, No. 2*
- 23 January 2007 *－HMN Board Approves Grant to Belize*
- 27 October 2006 *－HMN Workshop－Better Health Information Systems*
- 28－29 September *－Health System Metrics Meeting in Glion*
- 28 September 2006 *－HMN and IMMPACT Co－Host Vital Meetings on Maternal Mortality Measurement*

HN TPO

HealthNet TPO

TPO 건강네트

① 기구

1) 소재지

주　　소	tolstraat 127, Amsterdam, Netherlands
전　　화	+31 20 620 00 05
팩　　스	+31 20 42015 03
전자우편	office@healthnettpo.org
홈페이지	http://www.healthnetinternational.org/Healthnet TPO(EN)/

2) 설립연혁

TPO 건강네트(HN TPO)는 전쟁, 재앙, 빈곤에 의해 영향을 받은 지역에서 활동하는 지식기반의 비영리기구이다. 지역주민과 함께 연동하면서 HN TPO는 지속 가능한 건강관리 개발로서의 응급구호를 제공한다.

HN TPO는 국제건강네트(HNI: HealthNet International)와 중복문화적심리사회기구(TPO: Transcultural Psychosocial Organization)가 합병하여 만들어진 기구이다.

HNI는 전염성 질병의 예방, 진단 및 치료와 건강관리시스템을 강화하는 지식 및 경험을 보유하고 있으며, TPO는 전쟁 및 자연재해의 피해자를 위한 심리사회 및 정신건강관리 분야의 전문성을 보유하고 있다.

HNI의 혁신적인 프로그램에 기반을 둔 실제적인 경험과 TPO의 이론적 배경은 혁신적 의료시스템의 개발 및 실행을 촉구한다.

이를 바탕으로 HN TPO는 자기의존과 지속 가능한 건강관리를 촉진시키는 혁신적이며 관습을 벗어난 해결점을 제공한다.

3) 설립목적

HN TPO는 질병에 대처하고자 하는 이니셔티브를 수행할 수 있도록 지역주민을 교육시키고, 정신사회적 관리를 제공하며, 인프라스트럭처를 복구하고, 기관시스템을 강화하는 데 그 목적을 두고 있다.

4) 조직

네덜란드에 본부를 두고 있는 HN TPO는 전쟁, 재해, 빈곤에 의해 영향을 받은 국가에서 활동한다. 위원회(Board)와 총장(General Director)을 비롯한 운영팀(Management Team)이 조직의 주축을 이룬다.

운영팀은 총장에 의해 관리되며, 위원회는 HN TPO의 아이덴티티 및 기구의 목적을 관리한다.

그 외에 운영 및 지원부(Operations & Support Department)가 프로젝트를 담당하고 있으며, 대중의료 및 연구부(Public Health & Research Department)는 콘텐츠 개발 및 관리를 담당한다.

또한, 국장실(Directors Office)은 커뮤니케이션, 기금마련사업, 전반적 경영, 인적 관리 그리고 재정을 담당한다.

5) 주요 사업

HN TPO의 활동은 하나의 질병이나 주제에 집중하는 체제가 아니라 광범위한 프로그램의 수행을 통해서 이루어진다.

이 기구는 전쟁의 희생자를 도울 뿐 아니라 에이즈나 말라리아 치료약을 제공하기도 한다. 또한 장기간 동안 이용 가능한 건강관리시스템을 구축할 수 있도록 지원한다. 의사와 간호사가 교육과 함께 지역사회에 의료정보를 전달하기도 한다. 그 외에 병원 유지를 위한 재정시스템을 촉구하기도 한다.

HN TPO는 지역인구와 긴밀한 협조를 이루고 있다. 지역기구에 지식, 정책결정, 기술교육, 재정적 지원 등을 제공한다. 본 기구는 새로운 의료시스템을 개발하거나 연구하는 등의 혁신적 활동을 위해 노력한다.

6) 파트너십

1996년 HN TPO는 WHO 협력센터(Collaborating Centre of the WHO)로 등록되었으며 암스테르담 소재의 Vrije 대학의 파트너로서 활동을 시작하였다. 또한 HN TPO는 WHO 동지중해 지역사무소의 연구자문위원회 대표로 활동하고 있다.

프로젝트를 수행하고 있는 국가에서는 지역구조기구들과 협동하여 활동한다.

그 외에 Eureko/Achmea 보험사와 파트너십을 맺고 있다. 이 파트너십은 건강관리와 보험시스템 분야에서의 지식을 공유하는 데 그 목적이 있다.

7) 프로젝트

HN TPO 프로젝트의 주요 주제는 다음과 같다.

① 정신건강(Mental Health)

기본적인 의료 프로그램을 바탕으로 한 전쟁 후 지역의 심리사회적 치료와 정신건강관리를 위한 정책 촉진

② 질병 관리(Disease Control)

HIV/AIDS, 말라리아, 결핵과 같은 전염성 질병의 예방, 진단 및 치료

③ 의료재정(Health Financing)

재정 및 보험시스템 구축

④ 의료시스템 개발(Health Systems Development)

병원 및 케어센터 강화 및 구축, 인프라스트럭처 복구, 의료진 교육, 건강정보 제공

8) 국가프로그램

아시아, 중앙아프리카, 동유럽의 18개 국가에서 건강관리시스템을 재구축하기 위한 프로그램을 수행하고 있다. 이들은 전쟁 및 참사에 의해 심각하게 의료시스템의 영향을 받는 국가들이다. HN TPO는 총 30개가 넘는 프로그램을 수행하고 있고, 이

프로그램들은 말라리아에서 정신건강관리까지 이르며, 의료보험시스템 구축도 해당된다. 가장 큰 규모로 이루어지고 있는 프로그램은 아프가니스탄, 캄보디아, 중앙아프리카에서 찾아볼 수 있다.

② 정보원

1) 정보배포정책

HN TPO의 정보원은 'Library online'에서 찾아볼 수 있다. 원하는 자료를 키워드검색, 저자별검색, 도서명검색을 통해서 찾아볼 수 있다. 출판물의 경우 PDF로 열람이 가능하며, 그 외의 자료는 온라인 원문열람이 가능하다.

2) 정보 자료

① 뉴스(News)

최근 연구 자료 및 뉴스레터뿐 아니라 출판물의 링크를 제공한다.

[뉴스레터]

- *CRED CRUNCH: Newsletter of the Center for Research of the Epidemiology of Disasters*

[최근 연구 자료]

- Global Forum for Health Research(2004): *Strengthening Health Systems: The Role and Promise of Policy and Systems Research*

- Bower, P., Rowland, N. & Mellor Clark, J. et al(2006): *Effectiveness and Cost Effectiveness of Counselling in Primary Care(Review)*

- Jamison, D. J., Breman, J. G. & Measham, A. R.(2006): *Disease Control Priorities in Developing Countries(2nd Edition)*

- Eisenman, D., Weine, S., Green, B., de Jong, J.T. V.M., Rayburn, N., & Ventevogel, P. et al(2006): *The isTSS/Rand Guidelines on Mental Health Training of Primary Healthcare Providers for Trauma −Exposed Populations in Conflict −Affected Countries*

[최근 출판물]

- De Jong, J.T.V.M & Komproe, I. H.(2006): *A 15 − Year Open Study on a Cohort of West −African out − Patients with a Chronic Psychosis*

- Kamperman, A. M., Komproe, Ⅰ. H. & de Jong, J.T.V.M.(2007): *Migrant Mental Health: A Model for Indicators of Mental Health and Health Care Consumption*

② 보도 자료(In Press)

보도 자료에 소개된 출판물을 찾아볼 수 있다.

- A.M. Kamperman, I. H. Komproe & J.T.V.M. de Jong: *Social Embeddedness and Its Moderating Effects on Coping and Social Support Mechanisms Related to Well－being in Two Dutch Immigrant Populations with Different Network Properties. Anxiety, Coping & Stress*

③ 진행 중인 연구주제(In Research)

현재 진행 중인 연구주제를 소개한다.

- A Study on Mental Health Care Consumption, the Role of Healing Churches, Help Seeking Behavior and Explanatory Models in D.R. Congo
- A Social Anthropological Analysis of Community Oriented Psychosocial Interventions in Cambodia
- An Epidemiological Survey Comparing Asylum Seekers and Status－Holding Refugees in the Netherlands
- A Randomized Controlled Trial of Class－Room Based Interventions(CBI) among Children Affected by Armed Conflict and the Tsunami Disaster in Burundi, Indonesia, Sudan and Sri Lanka
- Measuring the Psychological Impact on Kosovar and Sri Lankan Communities Affected by Land Mines

④ 주요 출판물(Key Publications)

질병 관리(Disease Control), 의료재정(Health Financing), 의료시스템 개발(Health Systems Development), 정신건강 (Mental Health)의 네 가지 주제별 출판물을 제공한다. 최 근 목록은 다음과 같다.

[질병 관리]

- Brooker, S., Leslie, T. & Kolaczinski, K.(2006): *Emerging Infectious Diseases*

- Jamison, D. J., Breman, J. G. & Measham, A. R.(2006): *Disease Control Priorities in Developing Countries- (2nd Edition)*

- Durrani, N., Leslie, T. & Rowland, M. et al(2005): *Efficacy of Combination Therapy with Artesunate Plus Amodiaquine Compared to Monotherapy with Chloroquine, Amodiaquine or Sulfadoxine – Pyrimethamine for Treatment of Uncomplicated Plasmodium Falciparum in Afghanistan*

- Graham, K., Kayedi, M. H. & Rowland, M. et al.(2005): *Multi – Country Field Trials Comparing Wash – Resistance of PermaNetTM and Conventional Insecticide – Treated Nets against Anopheline and Culicine Mosquitoes*

- Kolaczinski, J., Graham & Rowland, M.et al.(2005): *Malaria Control in Afghanistan: Progress and Challenges*

- Murray, H. W., Berman, J. D. & Davies, C. R. et al(2005): *Advances in LeisHmaniasis*

- Onwujekwe, O., Malik, E. & Mustafa, S. H.(2005): *Do Malaria Preventive Interventions Reach the Poor? Socioeconomic Inequities in Expenditure on and Use of Mosquito Control Tools in Sudan. Oxford University Press in Association with the London School of Hygiene and Tropical Medicine*
- Townson, H., Nathan, M. B. & Zaim, M.(2005): *Exploiting the Potential of Vector Control for Disease Prevention*
- World Health Organization et al(2005): *Malaria Control in Complex Emergencies. An Inter-Agency Field Handbook*

[의료재정]

- De Jong, J.T.V.M & Komproe, I. H.(2006): *A 15-Year Open Study on a Cohort of West-African out-Patients with a Chronic Psychosis*
- Bower, P., Rowland, N. & Mellor Clark, J. et al(2006): *Effectiveness and Cost Effectiveness of Counselling in Primary Care(Review)*
- Carrin, G., Waelkens, M. P. & Criel, B.(2005): *Community-Based Health Insurance in Developing Countries: A Study of Its Contribution to the Performance of Health Financing Systems*
- Gilson, L. & McIntyre, D.(2005): *Removing User Fees*

for Primary Care in Africa: The Need for Careful Action

- Jacobs, B. & Price, N.(2005): *Improving Access for the Poorest to Public Sector Health Services: Insights from Kirivong Operational Health District in Cambodia*
- De Jong, J.T.V.M., Komproe, I. H. & O'Connell, K.A.(2005): *Effectiveness and Cost－Effectiveness of Mental Health Care in Low－Income Developing Countries: Burundi, Gaza, Nepal and Uganda*
- Nabyonaga, J., Desmet, M. & Karamag, H. et al(2005): *Abolition of Cost－Sharing is Pro－Poor: Evidence from Uganda*
- Van de Put, W.A..M.C. & Veer, G. Van Der(2005): *Counseling in Cambodia: Cultural Competence and Contextual Costs*
- Russell, S.(2005): *Illuminating Cases: Understanding the Economic Burden of Illness Through Case Study Household Research*
- Sepehri, A., Chernomas, R. & Akram－Lodhi, H.(2005): *Penalizing Patients and Rewarding Providers: User Charges and Health Care Utilization in Vietnam*
- Sinha, T., Ranson, M. K., Chatterjee, M. & Achary, A.(2005): *Barriers to Accessing Benefits in a Community －Based Insurance Scheme: Lessons Learnt from SEWA Insurance, Gujarat*

142

[의료시스템 개발]

- Kamperman, A. M., Komproe, Ⅰ. H. & de Jong, J.T.V.M.(2007): *Migrant Mental Health: A Model for Indicators of Mental Health and Health Care Consumption*
- De Jong, J.T.V.M & Komproe, I. H.(2006): *A 15 - Year Open Study on a Cohort of West - African out - Patients with a Chronic Psychosis*
- Alonso, A. & Brugha R.(2006): *Rehabilitating the Health System After Conflict in East Timor: A Shift from NGO to Government Leadership*
- Eisenman, D. P., Green, B. L., de Jong, J.T.V.M., Rayburn, N., P. Ventevogel, F Agani, & Weine, S.(2006): *Guidelines on Mental Health Training of Primary Care Providers for Trauma Exposed Populations*
- Tashobya, C. K., Ssengooba, F. and Oliveira - Cruz, V.(Eds) (2006): *Health Systems Reforms in Uganda: Processes and Outputs. London: Health Systems Development Programme*
- Bartlett, L.A.Shairose Mawji, S. & Whitehead, S. et al(2005): *Where Giving Birth is a Forecast of Death: Maternal Mortality in Four Districts of Afghanistan, 1999 - 2002*
- Lancet(2005): *A Crucial Time for Afghanistan's Fledgling Health System*
- de Jong, J.T.V.M., Komproe, I. H. & O'Connell, K.A.

(2005): *Effectiveness and Cost - Effectiveness of Mental Health Care in Low - Income Developing Countries: Burundi, Gaza, Nepal and Uganda*

- De Jong, J.T.V.M. & Van Ommeren, M. H.(2005): *Mental Health Services in a Multicultural Society: Interculturalization and Its Quality Surveillance*

- Kolaczinski, J., Graham & Rowland, M.et al.(2005): *Malaria Control in Afghanistan: Progress and Challenges*

- Wagstaff, A.(2005): *Health Systems in East Asia: What can Developing Countries Learn from Japan and the Asian Tigers?*

- World Health Organization(2005): *The World Health Report: 2005: Make Every Mother and Child Count*

[정신건강]

- Kamperman, A. M., Komproe, Ⅰ.H. & de Jong, J.T.V.M.-(2007): *Migrant Mental Health: A Model for Indicators of Mental Health and Health Care Consumption*

- Tol, W. A, Komproe, I. H., Jordans, M.J.D. & De Jong J.T.V.M., e.a.(2007): *Disability Associated with Psychiatric Symptoms among Torture Survivors in Rural Nepal*

- Jordans, M.J.D., Keen, A. S., Pradhan, H. & tol, W. A.(2007): *Psychosocial Counselling in Nepal: Perspectives of Counsellors and Beneficiaries*

- De Jong, J.T.V.M & Komproe, I. H.(2006): *A 15 − Year Open Study on a Cohort of West − African out − Patients with a Chronic Psychosis*

- De Jong, J.T.V.M.(2006): *Non Governmental Organizations and the Role of the Mental Health Professional*

- De Jong, J.T.V.M.(2006): *The Achilles Heel of the Debate on Culture, Trauma and PTSD*

- Eisenman, D. P., Green, B. L., de Jong, J.T.V.M., Rayburn, N., P. Ventevogel, F Agani, & Weine, S.(2006): *Guidelines on Mental Health Training of Primary Care Providers for Trauma Exposed Populations*

- Kamperman, A. M., Komproe, I. H. & J.T.V.M. de Jong(2006): *Migrant Mental Health. A Model for Indicators of Mental Health and Health Care Consumption. Health Psychology*

- Kamperman, A. M., Komproe, I. H. & de Jong, J.T.-V.M.(2006): *Social Embeddedness and Its Moderating Effects on Coping and Social Support Mechanisms Related to Well − being in Two Dutch Immigrant Populations with Different Network Properties*

- Osterman, J. & de Jong, J.T.V.M.(2006): *Cultural Issues. In:* M. J. Friedman, Keane, T. M., Resick, P. A.(eds.) PTSD: *Science & Practice − A Comprehensive Handbook*

- tol, W. A. & Jordans, M.J.D., Regmi, S. et al(2005):

Cultural Challenges to Psychosocial Counselling in Nepal

- tol, W. A. & Jordans, M.J.D. & Regmi, S. et al(2005): ***Cultural Challenges to Psychosocial Counselling in Nepal***

- De Jong, J.T.V.M.(2005): ***Analysing Critique on PTSD in an Attempt to Bridge Anthropology and Psychiatry***

- De Jong, J.T.V.M.(2005): Deconstructing Critiques on the Internationalization of PTSD

- De Jong, J.T.V.M., Komproe, I. H. & O'Connell, K.A.(2005): ***Effectiveness and Cost‐Effectiveness of Mental Health Care in Low‐Income Developing Countries: Burundi, Gaza, Nepal and Uganda***

- De Jong, J.T.V.M. & Van Ommeren, M. H.(2005): ***Mental Health Services in a Multicultural Society: Interculturalization and Its Quality Surveillance***

- De Jong, J.T.V.M., I. H. Komproe, J. Spinazzola, B. Van Der Kolk, & M. Van Ommeren.(2005): ***DESNOS in Three Post Conflict Settings: Cross‐Cultural Construct Equivalence***

- Jordans, M.J.D. & de Jong, J.T.V.M.(2005): ***Psychosocial Assistance for Children in Areas of Armed Conflict. In: Children in Armed Conflict***

- Laban, C. J., Gernaat, H.B.P.E., Komproe, I. H, Schreuders, G. A. & de Jong, J.T.V.M.(2005): ***Impact*** *of a Long Asylum Procedure on the Prevalence of Psychiatric Disordes in Iraqi Asylum Seekers in the Netherlands*

- Kamperman, A. M.(2005): *Deconstructing Ethnic Differences in Mental Health of Surinamese, Moroccan and TurkisH Migrants in the Netherland*

- Kamperman, A. M., Komproe, I. H. & de Jong, J.T.V.M.-(2005): *Mental Health of Immigrants: Discrepancy between Psychiatric Disorders and Subjective Symptoms and Disabilities*

- Punamäki, L., Komproe, I. H., Quota, S., El Masri, M. & De Jong, J.T.V.M.(2005): *The Role of Peritraumatic Dissociation and Gender in the Association between Trauma and Mental Health in a Palestinian Community Sample*

- Punamäki, L., Komproe, I., Quota, S., El Masri, M. & De Jong, J.T.V.M.(2005): *The Deterioration and Mobilization Effects of Trauma on Social Support: Childhood Maltreatment and Adulthood Military Violence in a Palestinian Community Sample*

- Schwartz, S., tol, W. A., Sharma, B. & de Jong, J.T.V.M.-(2005): *Investigating the Tibetan Healing System: A Psychosocial Needs Assessment of Tibetan Refugees in Nepal*

- Trinidad, R. B., Kamperman, A. M. & de Jong,

J.T.V.M.(2005): ***Explanatory Models in Mental Health Care: Characteristics of Migrant and Dutch Clients Who Persist in Non－Psychological Explanations of Mental Illness***

- Van Duijl, M., Cardeňa, E., & de Jong, J.T.V.M. (2005): ***The Validity of DSM－Ⅳ Dissociative Disorders Categories in South－West Uganda***
- Van de Put, W.A..M.C. & Veer, G. Van der(2005): ***Counseling in Cambodia: Cultural Competence and Contextual Costs***

IAPO

International Alliance of Patients' Organizations

국제환자기구동맹

☐ 기구

1) 소재지

주　　소　703 the Chandlery 50 Westminster Bridge
　　　　　Road London SE1 7QY United Kingdom
전　　화　+44 20 7721 7508
팩　　스　+44 20 7721 7596
전자우편　info@patientsorganizations.org
홈페이지　www.patientsorganizations.org

2) 설립연혁

국제환자기구동맹(IAPO)은 전 세계의 환자기구의 대표들에 의
해 1999년 비영리재단으로 설립되었다. 이 기구의 기원은 1994
년에서 1996년 사이에 열린 건강관리 컨퍼런스에서 찾아볼 수
있다. IAPO는 환자권리를 위한 정보 및 건강관리에 대한 이슈
를 다룬다.

3) 설립목적

① 환자기구의 파트너십 실현 및 역량 강화를 통한 영향력 최
   대화
② 건강관리 정책과 국제·지역·국가 건강 관련 아젠다 및
   정책에 관한 환자권리 국제 홍보
③ 의료 및 건강 전문가들과 정책입안가, 학자들, 연구자, 관련
   산업대표들과의 협력

4) 조직

IAPO의 사업은 이사회(Governing Board)에 의해 관리된다. 이
사회는 정회원과 준회원들 중 선거를 통해 뽑힌 대표들로 구성
된다. 이사회의 대부분은 환자 본인들이거나 환자의 보호자 같
은 환자를 대표할 수 있는 회원들이다. 이사회는 IAPO 직원들
과의 활발한 의사소통을 위하여 1년에 두 차례에 걸친 회의를
갖는다. 이사회의 집행위원회(Executive Committee)는 위원장,
위원장보, 비서관 그리고 재무관으로 구성된다. 집행위원회는
이사회 회의에서 직원을 위한 추가적 지원을 담당한다.

5) 회원

IAPO는 정회원과 준회원 제도를 운영한다. 정회원은 환자들을
위한 기구들을 의미하고 준회원은 환자 중심의 건강관리에 대해
활동하는 기타 건강과 관련된 비영리 기구들을 의미한다.

2 정보원

1) 정보배포정책

IAPO의 정보원은 'News'와 'Publications'에서 찾아볼 수 있다. 'News'에서는 IAPO의 활동 및 개발상황, 회원 환자 기구 및 환자중심의 건강관리 일반에 대한 내용을 열람할 수 있다. IAPO는 수많은 출판물을 제작하고 있으며, 그중 일부는 인터넷상에서 다운로드를 통한 열람이 가능하고, 직접 주문구매도 가능하다.

2) 정보 자료

① News

회원기관의 회원인 경우 정기적으로 이메일을 통한 자료를 받아 볼 수 있다. 또한, IAPO의 뉴스 기록관에 있는 자료들을 키워드 검색을 통해 열람할 수 있다. 대표적인 자료는 다음과 같다.

* *People－Centred Health Care: Reorienting Health Systems in the 21st Century－Tokyo, Japan*
* *3rd Global Patients Congress: Patient－Centred Healthcare Posters Information Prescriptions－London, UK*
* *World Health Editors Network(WHEN) HIV/AIDS Briefing Meeting－London, UK*
* *IAPO Addresses the WHO Intergovernmental Working Group on Public Health, Innovation and Intellectual*

Property

- *IAPO Calls on WHO to Bring Patient Groups to the Centre of Discussions on Public Health, Innovation and Intellectual Property*
- *IAPO Seminar on Intellectual Property and Public Health ‐ Geneva, Switzerland*
- *Capacity Building Support on IAPO's Listserv*
- *Welcome Back Emma*
- *IAPO Responds to WHO IGWG Draft Global Strategy and Plan of Action on Public Health Innovation and Intellectual Property*
- *3rd Global Patients Congress ‐ Budapest, Hungary*
- *IAPO Patients Exchange Listserv ‐ Now Open to All IAPO Members*
- *Health First Europe Launches their Healthcare Directory 2007*
- *WHO Regional Office for EUROPE: Patients for Patients Safety Workshop ‐ Dublin, Ireland*
- *Message from IAPO's Immediate Past Chair: Albert van der Zeijden ‐ Looking Back and Looking forward*
- *IAPO Twinning Service*
- *IAPO Website Updated*
- *Message from the Incoming IAPO Chair: Myrl Weinberg, President, National Health Council, USA*
- *WHO Regional Office for South East Asia: Patients for Patient Safety Workshop!*

- *Patients Safety Trek to Base Camp of Nanga Parbat Mountain*

② Publications

IAPO의 출판물은 개요서, 정책성명 등을 포함한다. 대표적 인 목록은 다음과 같다.

- *IAPO Briefing Paper on Paediatric Medicines and Clinical Research*
- *IAPO Briefing Paper on Biosimilar Medicines*
- *IAPO Declaration on Patient −Centred Healthcare*
- *IAPO Policy Statement on Patient Involvement*
- *What is Patient −Centred Healthcare? A Review of Definitions and Principles*
- *Briefing Paper on Plant −Made Pharmaceuticals*
- *IAPO Policy Statement on Health Literacy*

IASO

International Association for the Study of Obesity

국제비만연구협회

① 기구

1) 소재지

소재국가	영국
주　　소	231 North Gower Street, London NW1 2NR, United Kingdom
전　　화	+44 20 7691 1900
팩　　스	+44 20 7387 6033
전자우편	enquiries@iaso.org
홈페이지	www.iaso.org

2) 성격

국제비만연구협회(IASO)는 56개국을 대표하는 52개의 회원협회로 이루어진 국가비만협회들을 위한 상부기구이다.

3) 설립연혁

비만은 21세기 초반부터 질병의 하나로 인식되어 왔다. 그 이

전, 1961년 영국에서 비만과 관련한 기구의 설립에 대한 논의가 이루어졌었고, 1966년 운영위원회(Steering Committee)에 의해 그 구체적인 사안이 검토되어, 1967년 영국에서 열린 회의에서 '비만협회'(Obesity Association)가 계획되었다. 1968년 비만에 대한 심포지엄(Symposium on Obesity)이 열리면서 비만협회의 두 번째 회의가 이루어졌다.

협회는 그 후 현재의 IASO로 발전하였고, IASO는 현재 56개국을 대표하는 52개의 협회가 활동하고 있다.

4) 비전 및 임무

IASO의 임무는 비만에 대한 과학적 연구 및 대화를 통한 체중 관련 질병의 이해 촉진에 대한 글로벌 건강 증진이다.

5) 조직

본 기구의 주요 조직은 총회(General Council)와 협회회원(Affiliate Members)으로 구성되어 있다.

6) 비만전문가포럼(Obesity Expert forum)

IASO의 비만전문가포럼은 IASO 회원 및 의료 분야를 대표하는 기관들 간의 논의를 위한 전략적 방안을 형성함으로써 비만과 관련된 현대질병에 대한 문제를 다루고자 한다.

이 포럼은 2년에 한 번 열리며, 포럼의 주제는 그 시기에 가장 이슈화되는 논제를 다루게 된다.

7) 주요 행사

① 제5회 비만에 관한 아시아-오세아니아의회(5th Asia Oceania Congress of Obesity)
- 회의기간: 2009년 2월 5일~8일
- 회의장소: 인도 뭄바이(Mumbai, India)
- 회의내용: www.aiaaro.com/aoco-conf.htm

② 제17회 비만에 관한 유럽의회(17th European Congress on Obesity)
- 회의기간: 1009년 5월 6일~9일
- 회의장소: 네덜란드 암스테르담(Amsterdam, the Netherlands)
- 회의내용: www.easoobesity.org/eco2009

8) 협력기관

다음은 IASO의 산하기관이다.
- 국제비만대책기구(IOTF: International Obesity Task force)
  홈페이지: http://www.iotf.org/
- 신체활동대책기구(PATF: Physical Activity Task force)
  홈페이지: http://www.iaso.org/patf.asp
- 교율 및 관리 대책기구(EMTF: Education and Management Task force)
  홈페이지: http://www.iaso.org/emtf.asp
- 비만전문교육 전문가인증(SCOPE: Specialist Certification of Obesity Professional Education)

홈페이지: http://www.iaso.org/popout.asp?linkto =
http://www.scope‑online.org/

- 국제비만상법(OIT: Obesity International Trading Ltd)
  홈페이지: http://www.iaso.org/popout.asp?linkto =
  http://www.oit.org.uk

② 정보원

1) 정보원배포정책

IASO의 정보원은 'Publications'와 'Annual Report'에서 찾아볼 수 있다. '발간 자료(Publications)'에서 IASO의 뉴스레터 및 저널로의 링크를 제공하고 있다. 저널은 회원등록 후 구독가능하다. 연간보고서(Annual Report)는 최근 연간보고서를 PDF 형태로 무료열람이 가능하다.

2) 연간보고서(Annual Report)

- *IASO Annual Review 2004‑2005*
- *IASO Annual Review 2003‑2004*

3) 발간서적(Publications)

다음과 같은 IASO의 저널 및 뉴스레터를 열람할 수 있는 웹페이지로의 링크를 제공하고 있다.

- *International Journal of Pediatric Obesity*
- *International Journal of Obesity*
- *Obesity Reviews*
- *Diabetes, Obesity and Metabolism*
- *IASO Newsletters*
- *Obesity Online(NAASO)*
- *IASO e-Bulletins*
- *Obesity Research & Clinical Practice*

4) 정보원 검색

IASO는 국제비만대책기구(IOTF)의 데이터베이스 시스템을 이
용하여 비만과 관련된 정보를 검색할 수 있도록 하고 있다.
IOTF의 데이터베이스 분류는 다음과 같다.

- 국제 성인비만유행(Global Obesity Prevalence in Adults)
- 국제 아동체중 초과(Global Childhood Overweight)
- 유럽 아동기 및 사춘기 체중 초과(Child & Adolescent Overweight in Europe)
- EU 27개국 성인체중 초과 및 비만(Adult Overweight &
  Obesity in EU 27)
- EU 27개국 및 스위스 아동체중 초과(Child Overweight EU
  27 & Switzerland)
- 아동체중 초과유행 국제추세(Global Trends in Childhood
  Overweight Prevalence)
- 유럽 성인비만유행 추세(Trends in Adult Obesity Prevalence

in Europe)
- 지역보건당국에 의한 영국 비만유행 추세(Trends in Obesity Prevalence in the UK by Local Health Authority)

ICDA

International Confederation of Dietetic Associations
국제식이성협회연합

① 기구

1) 소재지

소재국가	캐나다
주 소	ICDA Secretary C/O Dietitians of Canada 480 University Avenue, Suite 604 toronto, ontario M5G 1V2 Canada
전 화	+1 416 596 0858
팩 스	+1 416 596 0603
전자우편	ICDA@internationaldietetics.org
홈페이지	http://www.internationaldietetics.org/

2) 성격

국제식이성협회연합(ICDA)은 국가식이성협회의 연합체이다.
이 연합은 전 세계의 약 150,000명의 식이성 전문가들이 참여
하고 있다.

3) 설립연혁

ICDA는 1952년 암스테르담에서 열린 국제식이성의회(International Congress of Dietetics)에서 그 기원을 찾아볼 수 있다. 2000년 제13회 국제식이성의회가 열리면서 국가식이성협회의 대표들은 현재의 이름인 ICDA라는 새로운 이름을 수용하였으며, 그 첫 임무를 결정하게 되었다. 2006년 ICDA는 캐나다에서 법인화되었다.

4) 비전 및 임무

ICDA는 국가식이성협회 및 그 회원들을 지원하는 임무를 갖고 있다.
① 통합된 커뮤니케이션 시스템
② 전문성에 대한 강화된 이미지
③ 식이성에 대한 교육 및 실습의 표준 인식 증가

5) 조직

본 협회의 자산, 기록 및 사업은 위원회(Board of Directors)에 의해 관리된다. 위원회는 법령에 의해 그 권한을 발휘할 수 있으며 필요에 따라 정책을 제안 및 수용할 수 있다.

6) 국가식이성협회대표단

국가식이성협회의 대표단은 다음과 같은 임무를 가진다.
① 본부와의 협력을 기본으로 하여 현재의 국가식이성협회의

파일로 된 정보 유지

② ICDA와 국가식이성협회 회원 간의 커뮤니케이션 촉진

③ 국가식이성협회 회원을 위한 홍보

④ 국가식이성협회 회원들에게 ICDA를 대표

⑤ 국제식이성의회 기간 중 대표회의 참가

⑥ ICDA의 인식증가를 위한 활동 및 회원협회에 의한 ICDA 후원 장려

7) 회원

국가식이성협회는 국가협회를 구성하고 있는 회원들로 구성된다. 국가식이성협회 회원들은 다음과 같은 회원활동을 한다.

- 국제식이성의회 주최
- 국제식이성의회에서 국제적 참여 지원
- ICDA를 위한 프로젝트 담당 및 후원
- 전 세계의 식이요법(Dietetics Around the World) 출판
- OCDA 대표
- 회원비 지불 및 국제식이성의회 대표회의 참가를 위한 대표단 지원

② 정보원

1) 정보원배포정책

ICDA의 정보원은 'Newsletter'와 'Education and Work of Dietitians'에서 찾아볼 수 있다. 교육 및 식이요법전문가활동 (Education and Work of Dietitians)에서는 ICDA의 보고서를 열람할 수 있다.

2) 뉴스레터(Newsletter)

뉴스레터는 원하는 정보를 최근 뉴스레터(Current Newsletters), 뉴스레터 검색(Search Newsletters), 뉴스레터 기록관(Archived Newsletters)을 통해 찾아볼 수 있도록 하고 있다. 가장 최근호 (Vol.15 issue 1, 2008)의 뉴스레터 정보는 다음과 같다.

[Announcements]

* *New Member of ICDA – Hungarian Dietetic Association*
* *American Dietetic Association Foundation's 2008 Edna and Robert Langholz International Nutrition Award*

[Congress Updates]

* *International Congress of Dietetics, 8 – 11 September 2008, Yokohama, Japan*

[National Association Reports]

* *Update on DIETS Thematic Network*

- *Dietary Consultation with a Dietitian*
- *Resources for Diabetes Management*

[Awards]

- *First International Nutritionist Dietitian(FIND) Fellowship for Study in the USA*
- *Colgate Palmolive Fellowship to Support Research in Nutrition and Oral Health/Dental Education*
- *Wimpfheimer-Guggenheim Fund for International Exchange in Nutrition, Dietetics and Management 2009 Competitive Essay Award*

[Calendar of Events]

- August 16-20, 2008, *World Congress of Paediatric Gastroenterology, Hepatology and Nutrition*
- September 6-9, 2008, *37th EDTNA-ERCA Conference*
- September 8-11, 2008, *15th International Congress of Dietetics*
- September 25-26, 2008, *2nd DIETS(Dietitians Improving Education & Training Standards) Conference*
- October 25-28, 2008, *ADA Food and Nutrition Conference and Expo*

3) 교육 및 식이요법전문가활동(Education and Work of Dietitians)

- *2002 ICDA Survey Part 1 Glossary of Terms*
- *2002 ICDA Survey Part 1 Work and*
- *2002 ICDA Survey Part 2 Development of Code of Ethics and Professional Standards*
- *2004 Report on Education and Work of Dietitians*
- *Ethics and Standards: The Underpinnings of Quality Professional Practice*

ICN

International Council of Nurses

국제간호사협의회

① 기구

1) 소재지

주　　소	International Council of Nurses 3, Place Jean Marteau 1201 － Geneva, Switzerland
전　　화	＋41 22 908 0100
팩　　스	＋41 22 908 0101
전자우편	icn@icn.ch
홈페이지	http://www.icn.ch/

2) 설립연혁

국제간호사협의회(ICN)는 128개국 이상의 국가를 대표하는 간호사들이 모인 국가간호사협회(NNAs: National Nurses' Associations)의 연합단체이다. 1899년에 설립된 ICN은 의료종사자들을 위한 세계 최초이자 가장 큰 국제기구이다. 간호사를 위해 간호사에 의해 운영되고 있는 ICN은 모두를 위한 간호의 질을 높이고 세계적으로 올바른 건강정책을 확보하며 간호지식의 증진을 위해 활동한다.

3) 설립목적

① 간호, 건강, 사회정책, 세계적인 전문성 및 사회경제 기준에
영향력 발휘
② 간호 및 간호사 경쟁기준을 증진시키기 위해 국가간호사협
회(NNAs) 지원
③ 강력한 국가간호사협회 개발 촉진
④ 국제적으로 간호사 및 간호 대표
⑤ 간호기술 증진 및 ICN 증진에 기여하기 위한 기금 및 신탁
마련 및 관리

4) 사명

ICN의 사명은 세계적으로 간호업을 대표하며 전문직업으로 증
진시키고 건강정책에 영향을 발휘하는 데에 있다.

5) 중심가치

ICN은 다음과 같은 다섯 가지의 중심 가치를 바탕으로 활동한다.
① 가공의 리더십
② 포괄성
③ 유연성
④ 파트너십
⑤ 성과

6) 조직

　① 국가대표협의회(Council of National Representatives)
　　국가대표협의회(CNR)는 ICN의 수뇌부이다.
　② 이사회
　　ICN의 이사회는 CNR의 대리부서로서 활동한다.
　③ 집행위원회
　　회장 및 세 명을 넘지 않는 부회장이 집행위원회를 대표한다.
　④ 위원회
　　위원회는 특정한 목적에 의하여 그때그때 소집된다.
　⑤ 최고경영자
　　최고경영자는 ICN의 회원 국가간호사협회의 회원이자 간호
　　사이어야 한다. 최고경영자는 ICN 이사회에 의해 지명되며
　　위원회의 비서관 역할을 하게 된다.

7) 회원

　회원 자격으로서의 간호사라 함은 간호사 교육 프로그램을 완
　수히고 그가 속한 국가에 의해 인정받고 자격증을 소유한, 간
　호실습을 마친 간호사를 말한다.

8) 주요 사업

　ICN은 특히 전문적인 간호실습에 큰 관심을 갖고 활동한다.
　세부적인 활동영역은 다음과 같다.
　① 간호실습의 국제분류(ICNP®: International Classification of

Nursing Practice)

② 발전된 간호실습

③ 사업

④ HIV/AIDS, 결핵, 말라리아

⑤ 여성건강

⑥ 기초건강관리

⑦ 가족건강

⑧ 식수위생

9) 프로그램

ICN은 전문실습, 규제, 사회경제 복지의 세 가지 주요 프로그램을 운영함으로써 간호와 건강을 증진시키고자 한다.

② 정보원

1) 정보배포정책

ICN의 정보원은 'Book Shop'과 'News Room' 그리고 'Fact Sheets'에서 찾아볼 수 있다. 'Book Shop'에서는 ICN의 보고서 및 서적을 볼 수 있는데, 보고서는 온라인상으로 무료열람이 가능하나 서적은 직접 구매를 통해서 열람이 가능하다. 'Fact Sheets'에서는 간호직업과 관련된 정보를 제공한다.

2) 정보 자료

① Book Shop

대표적인 목록은 다음과 같다.

[보고서]

- *2004 - 2006 ICN Biennial Report*
- *Nurses in Mental Health 2007*

[서적]

- *Positive Practice Environments: Quality Workplaces = Quality Patient Care*
- *The Orientation of Nurses in New Work Settings*
- *Responsible Self - Medication: Nursing Perspectives*

② News Room

보도 자료를 열람할 수 있다. 최근의 목록은 다음과 같다.

- Press Release 13 September 2007. *Nurses in Mental Health: Always Essential, Needed Everywhere, too Often Missing*
- Press Release 24 July 2007. *ICN and WMA Welcome the Release of Bulgarian Nurses*
- Press Release 31 May 2007. *Complex Humanitarian Emergencies the Focus of New Nursing Network*
- Press Release 30 May 2007. *Nurses: Love the Job, But Not the Work Environment*

- Press Release 29 May 2007. *Where Are the Nurses At the World Health Organization?*

- Press Release 29 May 2007. *Global Nursing Caucus Calls for Justice for Bulgarian Nurses, Palestinian Doctor and Libyan Children*

- Press Release 29 May 2007. *Nursing Leaders from Around the World Demand That UN Member States Move Quickly on a Women's Agency*

- Press Release 29 May 2007. *ICN Award for Partners in Development Goes to Merck & Co., Inc.*

- Press Release 29 May 2007. *Dealing with the Unexpected: Nurses Hold Global Conference in Yokohama*

- Press Release 12 May 2007. *ICN Calls for Positive Practice Environments to Ensure Quality Patient Care*

- Press Release 3 May 2007. *A Defining New Publication on Leadership from ICN*

- Press Release 27 April 2007. *Responding to the Scourge of Malaria Among Refugee Populations: The International Council of Nurses, the UN Agency for Refugees and Merck & Co., Inc.*

- Press Release 30 March 2007. *ICN to Launch a Student Nurse Network*

- Press Release 28 March 2007. *Oxfam Director to Speak at ICN's International Nursing Conference*

- Press Release 22 March 2007. *Five Nurses Win the*

Newly Launched ICN/Lilly Award for Work in Tuberculosis and Multi - Drug Resistant TB

- Press Release 5 March 2007. *the Time for a UN Agency for Women is Now Says the International Council of Nurses*
- Press Release 17 January 2007. *ICN Global Nursing Conference to Focus on Dealing with the Unexpected*
- Press Release 11 January 2007. *Activist Nurse, President of MSF - Sweden, Receives ICN's Top International Nursing Award*
- Press Release 9 January 2007. *Nurse Politicians from Around the World Connected through New ICN Network*

③ Fact Sheets

다음과 같은 분류하에 관련 정보를 제공한다.

[고령화]

- Dementia
- Elder Abuse
- Healthy Ageing
- Nutrition and Older People

[아동건강]

- Childhood Nutrition
- The Girl Child
- Maternal and Infant Nutrition

- Prevention of Child Abuse
- Safeguarding the Childhood of Children

[전염병]
- HIV/AIDS in the European Union
- The Human Papillomavirus
- Influenza(the "Flu", or the "Grippe")
- Mobilising Nurses for HIV/AIDS Prevention and Care
- Pneumococcal Pneumonia
- Sexually Transmitted Infections
- Shingles(Herpes Zoster)
- Tuberculosis Exposure in the Health Care Setting: Prevention of Occupational Transmission
- Tuberculosis Fact Sheet
- The WHO "Treat 3 Million by 2005"(3x5) Initiative

[젠더와 건강]
- Equal Opportunity: Gender Issues
- Mainstreaming a Gender Perspective into the Health Services

[면역안전]
- Adverse Events Following Immunization(AEFI)
- First Do No Harm: Auto-Disable Syringes for Immunization Safety

- ICN on Selecting Safer Needle Devices
- Immunisation Safety: An Essential Nursing Function
- Immunisation Safety: Safe Waste Disposal Practices Save Lives
- Preventing Needlestick Injuries

[국제상업]
- International Trade Agreements
- Trade Related Aspects of Intellectual Property Rights(TRIPS)

[정신건강]
- Developing Nursing Resources for Mental Health
- Mental Health: Tackling the Challenges

[이민]
- International Centre on Nurse Migration
- International Nurse Migration & Remittances

[전염되지 않는 질환]
- Lowering Cholesterol through Nurse Case Management
- Obesity
- Osteoporosis: the Silent Thief

[영양]
- Childhood Nutrition

- Food Safety: An Essential Public Health Function of Nurses
- Maternal and Infant Nutrition
- Nutrition and Older People

[직업병]
- ICN on Disinfectants and Sterilants
- ICN on Selecting Safer Needle Devices
- Latex Allergy or Hypersensitivity
- Occupational Stress and the Threat to Worker Health
- Violence: A World – Wide Epidemic

[환자보호]
- ICN on Disinfectants and Sterilants
- ICN on Selecting Safer Needle Devices
- Medication Errors
- Patient Safety
- Patient Safety: Medication Use and the Ageing Population

[연구결과]
- Nursing Sensitive Outcome Indicators

[여성건강]
- The Girl Child
- Maternal and Infant Nutrition

- Women's Health
- Women and Stroke

IDF

International Diabetes Federation

국제당뇨병연맹

① 기구

1) 소재지

주 소	Avenue Emile De Mot 19 B‒1000 Brussels, Belgium
전 화	+32 2 5385511
팩 스	+32 2 5385114
전자우편	info@idf.org
홈페이지	http://www.idf.org/

2) 설립연혁

국제당뇨병연맹(IDF)은 전 세계 160개국의 200개가 넘는 당뇨병협회의 국제연맹으로서, 당뇨병으로 고생하고 있는 사람들의 삶의 질을 향상시키기 위해 활동한다. 50년이 넘게 IDF는 글로벌 당뇨병 옹호활동의 선구자 역할을 해 왔다. IDF의 업무추진팀은 전 세계 당뇨병 커뮤니티의 주요 관련자들을 한자리에 불러 모아 공통의 목적을 위해 노력하며 협동할 수 있도록 한다. 주요 관련자들은 당뇨병 환자 본인과 그 가족들, 당뇨병 의

료 및 관련 분야의 전문가들, 당뇨병 관련 기구들의 대표들, 상
업적 기구들의 관련자들을 포함한다. IDF는 유엔 공보국
(Department of Public Information of the United Nations)과 연
합되어 있으며 WHO와 공식적인 협력관계에 있다. 또한 범미보
건기구(PAHO: Pan American Health Organization)와도 공식적
협력관계를 맺고 있다.

3) 설립목적

IDF는 당뇨병에 대한 세계적인 인식을 높이고 적합한 당뇨병
관리를 촉진하며 다른 종류의 당뇨병 치료법 개발을 위한 활동
을 고취하고자 한다.

4) 조직

IDF의 조직은 크게 다음과 같이 분류할 수 있다.
① 총회(General Council)
② 운영위원회(Executive Board)
③ 경영위원회(Board of Management)
④ 운영사무소(Executive Office)
⑤ 지명위원회 및 특별지명위원회(Nominating Committee and the
Special Nominating Committee)

5) 회원

회원구성은 크게 회원협회(Member Associations), 개인회원

(Individual Members), 명예회원(Honorary Members)으로 나뉜
다. 회원협회는 다시 정회원(Full Members), 임시회원
(Provisional Members), 준회원(Associate Members)으로 나뉘
고, 개인회원은 평생회원(Life Membership)과 3년회원(3 - Year
Membership)으로 나뉜다.

6) IDF 법인파트너(IDF Corporate Partners)

법인파트너란 당뇨병 퇴치를 지원하는 신탁기관, 재단, 기업,
산업그룹을 일컫는다. 법인파트너는 국제 당뇨병팀으로서 가치
있는 역할을 수행하고 있으며, 이들의 활동은 IDF의 사명과 일
치하고 있다. IDF의 법인파트너는 구체적으로 장기파트너(Long
-Term Partner-Lawrence Circle), 법인파트너(Corporate Partner
-Mayes Circle), 기부기관(Contributor)으로 나뉜다. 현재 IDF
에 등록되어 있는 파트너들은 다음과 같다.
Abbott, Amylin, AstraZeneca, Bayer Corporation, Becton
Dickinson, Eli Lilly and Company, GlaxoSmithKline, LifeScan,
Merck KGaA, Medtronic, Merck and Co., Novartis, Novo
Nordisk A/S, Pfizer, Roche Diagnostics, Sanofi - Aventis,
Servier, Takeda

② 정보원

1) 정보배포정책

IDF의 정보원은 'News Room'과 'IDF Bookshop'에서 찾아볼 수 있다. 'News Room'에서는 당뇨병과 관련된 사항들을 열람할 수 있으며, 관련 출판물들은 'Bookshop'을 통해서 구매할 수 있다. 출판물은 영어, 프랑스어, 스페인어로 나뉘어 판매하고 있다.

2) 정보 자료

① News Room
  최근의 대표적인 목록은 다음과 같다.
  [2007년]
  - *First United Nations World Diabetes Day Unites Global Diabetes Community to Fight the Epidemic*
  - *Global Landmarks Mark First United Nations World Diabetes Day*
  - *Diabetes Communities Unite to Celebrate World Diabetes Day November 14*
  - *IDF Launches New Guideline for the Management of Postmeal Glucose*
  - *More Than Eight Decades Since Its Discovery, Insulin is Still Not Reaching Many Who Require It to Live*
  - *New Definition Helps Identify Children at Risk of*

Metabolic Syndrome

- *International Diabetes Federation Launches US$ 10 Million Grant Programme to Improve Diabetes Care*
- *IDF Consensus on Diabetes Prevention*
- *The Stealthy Killers — Sleep Summit to Tackle Diabetes — Snoring Link*
- *Sleep Expert issues Wake up Call to Women Who Snore — Diabetes is a Risk*

[2006년]

- *UN Resolution Caps Momentous Year for Diabetes World/FR/ES*
- *Updated Guidelines for the Definition, Diagnosis and Classification of Diabetes*
- *Diabetes Costs Hinder Economic Growth*
- *IDF and Eli Lilly and Company Partner to Uncover Practical Solutions for Better Diabetes Outcomes*
- *Today's Children to Bear Brunt of Diabetes Epidemic*
- *Diabetes Declaration and Strategy for Africa: A Call to Action*
- *Diabetes Epidemic out of Control*
- *Leadership Change in Global Diabetes Community*
- *November 14 is World Diabetes Day*

② Bookshop

구입 가능한 영문출판물의 목록은 다음과 같다.

- *IDF Consensus Definition of the Metabolic Syndrome in Children*
- *Unite for Diabetes Booklet*
- *Guideline for Management of Postmeal Glucose*
- *International Standards for Diabetes Education*
- *International Consensus on the Diabetic Foot－DVD (2007)*
- *Diabetes Education Modules*
- *19th World Diabetes Congress Abstract Book*
- *The IDF Consensus Worldwide Definition of the Metabolic Syndrome*
- *International Curriculum for Diabetes Health Education*
- *IDF Activity Report 2003－2006*
- *Guide for Guideline*
- *A Guide for Clinical Guideline Development*
- *Global Strategic Plan to Raise Awareness of Diabetes*
- *Global Guideline for Type 2 Diabetes*
- *Diabetes and Obesity: Time to Act*
- *Diabetes and Kidney Disease: Time to Act*
- *Diabetes and Foot Care: Time to Act*
- *Cost－effective Approaches to Diabetes Care and Prevention*
- *19th World Diabetes Congress Abstract CD－Rom*

- *Ten Steps to Better Glucose Control: A Practical Guide*
- *International Consensus on the Diabetic Foot(1999)*

IFICF

International Food Information Council Foundation

국제식량정보협의회재단

① 기구

1) 소재지

소재국가	미국
주　　소	1100 Connecticut Avenue, NW Suite 430, Washington, DC 20036
전　　화	+1 202 296 6540
팩　　스	+1 202 296 6547
전자우편	foodinfo@ific.org
홈페이지	http://www.ific.org/index.cfm

2) 성격

국제식량정보협의회재단(IFICF)은 국제식량정보협의회(IFIC)의 교육기관이다. IFIC는 주로 광범위한 범위의 식량, 음료, 농업에 의해 이루어진다. 워싱턴에 위치한 IFICF 및 IFIC는 주로 미국 내에서 활동한다. 또한 본 기관은 유럽, 아시아, 호주, 캐나다, 일본, 뉴질랜드, 남아프리카공화국의 독립적 식량정보기관의 비공식적 네트워크에 참여하고 있다. IFIC는 원래 미국의 통신기관이었으나, 곧 세계의 식량 및 보건문제를 다루는 기관으로 발전하였다.

3) 비전 및 임무

IFIC의 사명은 건강을 위한 식량안전 및 영양에 대한 과학중심의 정보를 영양전문가, 교육자, 기자, 정부담당자, 그리고 소비자에게 정보를 제공하는 관련자들 간의 정보소통에서 찾아볼 수 있다.

IFIC의 목적은 식량안전, 영양, 건강에 관한 과학적 정보를 수집하고 배포하며, 파트너십을 통한 과학전문가들의 공유를 통한 과학과 의사소통 간의 격차를 줄이는 데에 있다.

4) 협력기관

IFICF 및 IFIC는 넓은 범위의 전문기관 및 학술기관과의 파트너십을 형성하여 대중을 위한 과학중심의 정보를 개발 및 전달해 오고 있다. IFICF 및 IFIC는 다음과 같은 기관들과 파트너 관계에 있다.

- 미국 알레르기, 천식, 면역 아카데미(American Academy of Allergy, Asthma and Immunology)
- 미국 가족의사재단 아카데미(American Academy of Family Physicians Foundation)
- 미국 산과의사 및 계보학자 대학(American College of Obstetricians and Gynecologists)

- 미국 스포츠의학 대학(American College of Sports Medicine)
- 미국 당뇨병협회(the American Dietetic Association)
- 여성건강, 산과, 신생아과 간호사 협회(Association of Women's Health, Obstetric, and Neonatal Nurses)
- 미국소비자연맹(Consumer Federation of America)
- 음식알레르기 및 주사 과민증 네트워크(The Food Allergy and Anaphylaxis Network)
- 식품마케팅연구소(Food Marketing Institute)
- 식량기술연구소(Institute of Food Technologists)
- 소아과 간호 개업 국가협회(National Association of Pediatric Nurse Practitioners)
- 통합흑사병관리교육 국가연맹(National Foundation for Integrated Pest Management Education)
- 영양 및 고령화 국가정책 및 자원 플로리다 국제대학(National Policy and Resource Center on Nutrition and Aging, Florida International University)
- 신체관리 및 스포츠 대통령협의회(President's Council on Physical Fitness and Sports)
- 임시상담소 및 연구재단(Scripps Clinic and Research Foundation)
- 미국 농업부(U.S. Department of Agriculture)
- 미국 환경보호국(U.S. Environmental Protection Agency)
- 미국 식약청(U.S. Food and Drug Administration)
- 일리노이즈 대학 건강프로그램을 위한 기능성식품(University of

Illinois Functional Foods for Health Program)

2 정보원

1) 정보원배포정책

IFICF의 정보원은 'Newsroom', 'Publications', 그리고 'News-letter'로 이루어진다. 대부분의 자료의 온라인 무료열람은 제공되고 있지 않으나, 주요내용의 자세한 설명이 제공되고 있다.

2) 보도 자료(Newsroom)

① 보도 자료(News Releases)
대표적인 목록은 다음과 같다.
- *Food & Health Survey Highlights a Potentially Dangerous New "Diet Disconnect"*
- *Food Insight Looks at the Healthful Benefits of Herbs and Spices*
- *Caffeine and Health: Clarifying the Controversies*
- *"What's for Lunch?" Video Release*
- *Summer Food and Fun*
- *Beverages Containing Caffeine Offer Hydration*
- *Nutrition News and Notes: Low−Calorie Sweeteners*
- *Food Insight Discusses Trans Fat: The Progress and the Road Ahead*

- *February is a Good Time to Consider Matters of the Heart: Nutrition Matters*
- *Food Insight Explores the Attitudes of Food-Conscious Consumers*
- *Food Insight Explains the ABC's of Vitamin D*
- *'This is the Season for Holidays and Food'*
- *Confused about Nutrition on Food Labels? Food Insight Offers Global Perceptions of Nutrition Information*
- *This for my Heart, and This for My Bones……*
- *Food Safety Concerns Do Not Include Biotechnology*
- *Food Safety Tips to Keep Consumers Informed*
- *Bring New Healthful Eating Habits "Back to School"*
- *Americans' Six "Diet Disconnects" Food Insight Reviews New IFIC Foundation Consumer Research*

② 소비사 및 주류의션 연구(Consumer and Opinion Leader Research)

주제별, 소비자그룹별, 연구종류별 브라우징이 가능하며 2008년 6월 현재 제공되고 있는 최근 연구 자료는 다음과 같다.

- *Food & Health Survey: Consumer Attitudes toward Food, Nutrition & Health*(05/15/2008)
- *IFIC Foundation Food Label Consumer Research Project: Summary Report*(04/08/2008)
- *Trends in Obesity-Related Media Coverage*(06/09/2008)

3) 발간 자료(Publications)

발간 자료는 배경설명(Backgrounders), 교육 자료(Educational Booklets & Brochures), IFIC 평가서(IFIC Reviews), 자주하는 질문(Q&As: Questions & Answers), 자료집(Fact Sheets), 그리고 그 밖의 자료(Other Materials)로 나뉘어 제공된다.

① 배경설명(Backgrounders)
다음과 같은 소주제별로 나뉘어 정보가 제공되며 대표적인 목록은 다음과 같다.
[영양학정보(Nutrition Information)]
- *Carbohydrates & Sugars*(11/28/2006)
- *Child & Adolescent Nutrition, Health & Physical Activity-*(11/28/2006)
- *Dietary Fats & Fat Replacers*(11/29/2006)
- *Dietary Guidance*(11/29/2006)
- *Food Ingredients*(11/28/2006)
- *Functional Foods*(11/28/2006)
- *International Food Issues & Resources*(11/29/2006)
- *Overweight, Obesity & Weight Management*(11/28/2006)

[식량안전정보(Food Safety Information)]
- *Agricultural Practices & Food Technologies*(09/04/2007)
- *Food Allergies & Asthma*(03/31/2008)
- *Food Biotechnology*(09/04/2007)

- *Food Safety & Defense*(10/26/2007)
- *Food Safety Information*(11/28/2006)
- *International Food Issues & Resources*(09/04/2007)

[과학적 보고 및 위험 커뮤니케이션정보(Scientific Reporting & Risk Communication Information)]
- *Scientific Reporting & Risk Communication Backgrounder*
- *Scientific Reporting & Risk Communication*

② 교육 자료(Educational Booklets & Brochure)
- *10 Tips to Healthy Eating*(02/01/1998)
- *10 Tips to Healthy Eating and Physical Activity for You-* (02/01/1998)
- *A Consumer's Guide to Pesticides and Food Safety (11/01/1995)*
- *Better Eating for Better Aging*(11/01/1999)
- *Caffeine & Women's Health*(08/01/2002)
- *Everything You Need to Know about Acesulfame Potassium*(07/01/1998)
- *Everything You Need to Know about Aspartame*(06/01/2003)
- *Everything You Need to Know about Asthma & Food* (08/01/1997)
- *Everything You Need to Know about Caffeine*(07/01/1998)
- *Everything You Need to Know about Glutamate and Monosodium Glutamate*(01/01/1997)

- *Everything You Need to Know about Sucralose*(07/21/2004)
- *Everything You Need to Know about the Functions of Fats in Foods*(03/01/1998)
- *Fats: How to Enjoy Your Food and be Healthy, too!* (10/26/2006)
- *Fish & Your Health*(01/31/2006)
- *Food Biotechnology: Enhancing Our Food Supply* (07/29/2004)
- *Food Ingredients & Colors*(03/23/2005)
- *Food Irradiation: A Global Food Safety Tool*(05/31/2002)
- *Gestational Diabetes and Low–Calorie Sweeteners: Answers to Common Questions*(02/15/2005)
- *Healthy Eating During Pregnancy*(01/31/2003)
- *Helping Your Overweight Child*(07/30/2004)
- *Improving Public Understanding: Guidelines for Communicating Emerging Science on Nutrition, Food Safety, and Health*(04/09/2003)
- *Listeriosis and Pregnancy: What is Your Risk?*(09/30/2001)
- *Low–Calorie Sweeteners: Their Role in Healthful Eating-* (10/01/2000)
- *Prevent Childhood Choking: It's up to You*(04/22/2003)
- *Starting Solids: Nutrition Guide for Infants and Children 6 to 18 Months of Age*(01/20/2005)
- *Sweet Taste, without the Calories*(07/12/2007)
- *The Benefits of Balance: Managing Fat in Your Diet*

(02/01/1998)

- *Understanding Food Allergy*(05/11/2006)
- *Weight Loss: Finding a Program That Works for You* (12/01/2000)
- *You're the Role Model! Kidnetic.com Real－Life Guide for Parents: Helping Your Kids Eat Right and be Active*(12/12/2006)
- *Your Personal Path to Health: Steps to a Healthier You!*(06/22/2006)

③ IFIC 평가서(IFIC Reviews)

- *Caffeine and Health: Clarifying the Controversies*(03/31/-2008)
- *Glutamate and Monosodium Glutamate: Examining the Myths*(11/01/2001)
- *How to Understand and Interpret Food and Health－Related Scientific Studies*(05/01/2000)
- *IFIC Review: Understanding Food Allergy*(06/30/2001)
- *Low－Calorie Sweeteners and Health*(10/01/2000)
- *Nutrition and Oral Health: Making the Connection*(09/-01/1998)
- *Pesticides and Food Safety*(01/01/1995)
- *Physical Activity, Nutrition and Bone Health*(04/01/2002)
- *Sodium in Food and Health*(02/23/2005)
- *Sorting out the Facts about Dietary Fats*(12/30/2005)

- *The Science of Sugars*(05/16/2008)
- *Uses and Nutritional Impact of Fat Reduction Ingredients*(04/01/2000)

④ 자주하는 질문(Questions & Answers – Q&As)
- *Dietary Fats Q&A*(09/25/2007)
- *Frequently Asked Questions about Sugars and Carbohydrates*(04/05/2005)
- *Interesterified Fats Q and A*(08/03/2007)
- *Questions and Answers about Acceptable Daily Intake* (08/01/1996)
- *Questions and Answers about Acrylamide*(03/09/2005)
- *Questions and Answers about Animal Antibiotics, Antimicrobial Resistance and Impact on Food Safety* (08/29/2007)
- *Questions and Answers about Avian Influenza "Bird flu"*(05/10/2006)
- *Questions and Answers about Benzene*(04/18/2006)
- *Questions and Answers about Bisphenol – A*(04/24/2008)
- *Questions and Answers about Bovine Spongiform Encephalopathy(BSE)*(03/13/2006)
- *Questions and Answers about Cancer, Diet and Fats* (06/01/1999)
- *Questions and Answers about Diacetyl*(08/29/2007)
- *Questions and Answers about Dietary Reference Intakes-*

(08/31/2002)

- *Questions and Answers about Dioxins*(07/19/2006)
- *Questions and Answers about Fat Replacers*(04/01/2000)
- *Questions and Answers about Food Allergy*(05/11/2006)
- *Questions and Answers about Food Colors and Hyperactivity*(06/02/2008)
- *Questions and Answers about Food Irradiation*(10/31/2003)
- *Questions and Answers about Foods from Cloned Animals-*(12/18/2007)
- *Questions and Answers about Fructose*(04/05/2005)
- *Questions and Answers about Functional Foods*(05/16/2005)
- *Questions and Answers about Glycemic Index*(09/16/2002)
- *Questions and Answers about Low-Calorie Sweeteners, Appetite and Weight Management*(08/06/2004)
- *Questions and Answers about Mercury in the Environment and Food*(05/24/2004)
- *Questions and Answers about Nutrition and Oral Health-*(08/01/1998)
- *Questions and Answers about Pesticides and Children's Health*(08/01/1998)
- *Questions and Answers about Sugars*(04/01/1999)
- *Questions and Answers about the 2005 Dietary Guidelines for Americans*(01/11/2005)
- *Questions and Answers about the Nutritional Content of Processed Baby Food*(08/01/1998)

- *Questions and Answers about Trans Fats*(06/10/2003)

⑤ 자료집(Fact Sheets)
- *Fact Sheet: Caffeine and Health*(08/09/2007)
- *Fact Sheet: Caffeine and Performance*(04/02/2008)
- *Fact Sheet: Caffeine and Women's Health*(01/14/2008)
- *Fact Sheet: Dioxins, Diet, and Health*(07/19/2006)
- *Fact Sheet: FDA's Approval Process for Food Animal Antibiotics*(04/24/2008)
- *Facts about Low－Calorie Sweeteners*(05/04/2006)
- *Functional Foods Fact Sheet: Antioxidants*(03/23/2006)
- *Functional Foods Fact Sheet: Omega－3 Fatty Acids* (06/17/2008)
- *Functional Foods Fact Sheet: Plant Stanols and Sterols* (07/31/2007)
- *Functional Foods Fact Sheet: Probiotics and Prebiotics* (06/21/2006)
- *Functional Foods Fact Sheet: Soy*(10/27/2005)
- *Sugar Alcohols Fact Sheet*(12/08/2006)
- *Whole Grains Fact Sheet*(01/25/2007)

⑥ 그 밖의 자료(Other Materials)
- *"Sizzlin' Summer Food Safety Tips"*(04/07/2008)
- *2007 Food & Health Survey CPE Answers*(09/28/2007)
- *2007 Food & Health Survey CPE Questions*(09/28/2007)

- *2007 IFIC Foundation Food and Health Survey: Consumer Attitudes toward Food, Nutrition & Health CPE-*(09/28/2007)
- *2007 IFIC Foundation Food and Health Survey: Consumer Attitudes toward Food, Nutrition & Health CPE-*(09/28/2007)
- *A Consumer's Guide to Food Safety Risks*(01/29/2007)
- *A New Nutrition Conversation with Consumers about Fats in Food*(07/31/2007)
- *A New Nutrition Conversation with Consumers about Fats in Food CPE Answers*(07/31/2007)
- *ACTIVATE/Kidnetic.com Case Study*(12/29/2004)
- *Addressing the Obesity Problem: A Consumer Point of View Case Study*(12/29/2004)
- *Agricultural Biotechnology: Myths & Facts*(11/25/2003)
- *All about Caffeine ADA CPE Program*(07/02/2004)
- *All about Carbohydrates and Health CPE Index*(06/-05/2007)
- *Animal Diseases in the News: What You Need to Know-*(06/30/2005)
- *Bone Health Resources*(03/07/2005)
- *Caffeine Resources*(04/14/2008)
- *Communicating Food and Nutrition Science CPE Program*(11/06/2007)
- *Dietary Fats Case Study*(09/21/2004)

- *Dietary Guidelines Alliance Case Study*(01/01/2002)
- *Dietary Reference Intakes: An Update*(08/01/2002)
- *Fat Replacers: New Choices for Managing Dietary Fat Tool Kit*(11/01/2000)
- *Fats & Fat Replacers Myths and Facts*(07/27/2001)
- *Food & Agricultural Biotechnology: Health Impacts in Developing Nations*(11/20/2007)
- *Food Allergy Poster for Food Service Workers*(11/15/2005)
- *Food Biotechnology 101: A Primer on the Science & the Public Debate CPE Program*(10/13/2006)
- *Food Biotechnology K − 12 Online Education Resources*(04/14/2004)
- *Food Biotechnology: A Communications Guide to Improving Understanding, 2003 Edition*(12/05/2003)
- *Food Science Meets Nutrition CPE Answers*(09/28/2007)
- *Food Science Meets Nutrition CPE Questions*(09/28/2007)
- *Food Science Meets Nutrition: Synergy for the Public Good*(09/28/2007)
- *Food Science Meets Nutrition: Synergy for the Public Good*(09/28/2007)
- *Guidelines for Communicating the Emerging Science of Dietary Components for Health*(03/22/2005)
- *Heart Health Resources*(01/23/2008)
- *Helping Consumers Get the "Big Picture": Practical Approaches to Promoting a Healthful, Balanced Eating*

Pattern(11/02/2007)

- *Holidays and Food Resources*(11/05/2007)
- *It's All about You(for Health Professionals) (05/01/1999)*
- *It's All about You Owner's Manual for Your Body(for Consumers)*(05/01/1999)
- *Key International Organizations*(03/14/2002)
- *Myths & Facts about Low −Calorie Sweeteners*(09/21/2006)
- *New Nutrition Conversation with Consumers CPE Program* (08/19/2004)
- *Resources on Animal Cloning*(12/11/2007)
- *Resources on Celiac Disease*(04/15/2008)
- *Resources on Diet and Cancer*(10/29/2007)
- *Resources on Dietary and Food Guidance*(04/01/2005)
- *Resources on Dietary Fats*(10/26/2006)
- *Resources on Food Allergy*(05/11/2006)
- *Resources on Food Safety*(08/29/2007)
- *Resources on Low −Calorie Sweeteners*(09/13/2006)
- *School Foodservice and Food Allergies: What We Need to Know*(10/29/2004)
- *Sugar Alcohols CPE Program*(05/08/2007)
- *Summer Food and Fun Resources*(04/07/2008)
- *The Lowdown on Low −Calorie Sweeteners and their Role in Healthful Eating*(02/28/2003)
- *The Lowdown on Low −Calorie Sweeteners CPE Program* (06/02/2008)

- *The New Food Label: A Food Label Education Program for High School Students*(07/01/1994)
- *Tools for Effective Communications*(06/21/2004)
- *Turkey Talk about Food Safety*(11/05/2007)
- *Understanding Food Allergy: A Primer for Dietitians* (10/18/2007)
- *What Should Consumers Do Regarding Salmonella in Tomatoes?*(06/11/2008)
- *What the Experts Say about Food Biotechnology*(05/26/2004)
- *Women's Health Resources*(11/30/2005)

4) 뉴스레터

가장 최근호에 실린 주요 내용은 다음과 같다.

- *Gold Medal Nutrition: Fueling for Fitness and Optimal Performance*
- *How to Tell If Your Food Has Gone Bad: IFIC, Expert Chris Bruhn, and Monkeysee.com Provide Food Safety Messages on the Web*
- *Opportunities in Food Safety and Nutrition: Where There's Food, There's a Profession*
- *Breakfast: More Than Meets the Eyes(NewsBite)*
- *2008 Food & Health Survey Now Available!(NewsBite)*
- *Hot off the Presses: IFIC Foundation PublisHes Updated IFIC Review － The Science of Sugars(NewsBite)*

IFMSA

International Federation of Medical Students' Associations

국제의대생협회연합

① 기구

1) 소재지

소재국가	프랑스
주　　소	IFMSA General Secretariat IFMSA, c/o WMA BP 63, 01212 Ferney－Voltaire CEDEX France
팩　　스	＋33 450 405937
전자우편	gs@ifmsa.org
홈페이지	http://www.ifmsa.org/

2) 성격

국제의대생협회연합(IFMSA)은 의학교육의 발전에 기여하고자 하는 세계에서 가장 큰 학생기구 중 하나이다.

3) 설립연혁

1948년 잉글랜드에서는 제2차 세계대전 직후 설립된 국제학생연맹(I.U.S.: International Union of Students)에 의한 이니셔티브로서 국제학생임상콘퍼런스(S.I.C.C.: Student International Clinical Conference)가 열렸다.

1950년 12월 파리에서는 가능한 연맹의 설립에 대한 국제의회가 열리게 되었고, 덴마크가 세계보건기구로부터의 경제적 지원을 받을 수 있는 가능성을 검토하는 역할을 맡게 되었다.

1951년 5월 코펜하겐에서 본 연맹에 대한 간략한 계획이 세워졌으며, 현재의 IFMSA라는 이름이 확정되었다. 그 후 임시조직이 형성되어 연맹의 설립에 대한 추가 조사가 이루어졌다.

1952년 7월 런던에서 제1회 총회가 열렸으며 10개 국가에서 30명의 참가자가 참여하였다.

4) 조직

IFMSA의 최상위 의사결정 조직은 총회(GA: General Assembly)이다. 총회는 매해 한 번씩 열리며, 각 회원기관들은 일정 인원을 대표로 보내게 되어 있다. 매해 총회는 경영위원회(EB: Executive Board)를 조직하게 된다.

5) 회원

총 98개의 국가회원과 함께 국제학생 및 청년기구들로 이루어져 있다. IFMSA의 50% 이상은 의과대학 학생으로 이루어진다.

6) 주요 시범 사업

IFMSA는 국제학생임상콘퍼런스(SICC: Student International

Clinical Conferences)를 비롯하여 IFMSA 여름학교 사업을 진행하고 있다. 여름학교는 특히 개발도상국의 학생들을 스칸디나비아, 영국, 덴마크 등의 국가로 초대하고 있다.

그 외에 의대학생교환 프로그램을 통해서 개발도상국의 학생들에게 선진국에서의 경험을 제공한다.

7) 국제활동

IFMSA는 세계보건기구(WHO), 유엔에이즈(UNAIDS), 유엔인구활동기금(UNFPA), 유엔난민고등판무관(UNHCR), 유네스코(UNESCO), 글로벌보건협의회(Global Health Council), 세계의학협회(World Medical Association), 유럽의과생협회(EMSA: European Medical Students' Association), 유럽청년포럼(European Youth forum) 등과 활발한 교류를 하고 있다.

2 정보원

1) 정보원배포정책

IFMSA의 정보원은 'Publications'과 'News'에서 찾아볼 수 있다. 발간 자료(Publications)는 의대생국제매거진(Medical Students International Magazine), 프로젝트게시판(Projects Bulletin) 그리고 뉴스레터인 *e-Vagus*로 나뉜다. 모든 자료는 온라인상으로 무료열람이 가능하다.

2) 발간 자료(Publications)

① 의대생국제매거진(MSI: Medical Students International Magazine)

- *MSI-17 Migration and Health*
- *MSI-16 Access to Essential Medicine*
- *MSI-15 Rural Health*
- *MSI-14 Health as a Human Right*
- *MSI-13 To Eradicate Extreme Poverty and Hunger*
- *MSI-12 Millenium Development Goals*
- *MSI-11 Anti Tobacco Strategies*
- *MSI-10 Violence*
- *MSI-09 Ageing and Health*
- *MSI-08 Exchanges*
- *MSI-07 The Child*
- *MSI-06 Adolescents and Reproductive Health*
- *MSI-05 Focus on Refugees and Peace*
- *MSI-04 The Future of Medical Education*
- *MSI-03 Public Health*

② 프로젝트게시판(Projects Bulletin)

- *Projects Bulletin-2007-03*
- *Projects Bulletin-2006-08*
- *Projects Bulletin-2007-08*

③ 뉴스레터(e‑Vagus)

최근의 대표적인 자료는 다음과 같다.

- *e‑Vagus 2008‑03 vol.56*
- *e‑Vagus 2008‑01 vol.56*
- *e‑Vagus 2006‑11 vol.55 n.1*
- *e‑Vagus 2006‑09 vol54 n.8*
- *e‑Vagus 2006‑07 vol.54 n.7*
- *e‑Vagus 2006‑06 vo.l54 n.6*
- *e‑Vagus 2006‑02 vol.54 n.5*
- *e‑Vagus 2006‑01 vol.54 n.4*
- *e‑Vagus 2005‑12 vol.54 n.3*
- *e‑Vagus 2005‑11 vol.54 n.2*
- *e‑Vagus 2005‑10 vol.54 n.1*
- *e‑Vagus 2005‑07 vol.53 n.4*
- *e‑Vagus 2005‑04 vol.53 n.3*
- *e‑Vagus 2005‑01 vol.53 no.2*
- *e‑Vagus 2004‑12 vol.53 no.2*
- *e‑Vagus 2004‑11 vol.53 no.1*
- *e‑Vagus 2004‑07 vol.52 no.3*
- *e‑Vagus 2004‑03 vol.52 no.3*
- *e‑Vagus 2004‑02 vol.52 no.2*
- *e‑Vagus 2004‑01 vol.52 no.2*

3) 보도 자료(News)

보도 자료의 예는 다음과 같다.

- Tuesday 26. August 2008, *UICC World Cancer Congress*
- Sunday 06. July 2008, *2008 Gadjah Mada University International Summer Course on Disaster Medicine*
- Thursday 29. May 2008, *19th European Students' Conference*
- Thursday 08. May 2008, *The Second International Conference of Medical Students and Junior Doctors on Family Medicine*
- Wednesday 07. May 2008, *International Congress of Medical Sciences for Students & Young Doctors in Sofia, Bulgaria*
- Wednesday 30. April 2008, *EUROPEAN MEDICAL STUDENTS' COUNCIL 5*
- Wednesday 09. April 2008, *EuRegMe*
- Sunday 02. March 2008, *IFMSA PeaceTest Project Page Has Moved*

IFPMA

International Federation of Pharmaceutical Manufacturers & Associations

국제약업단체연합회

① 기구

1) 소재지

주　　소	15 Ch. Louis‐Dunant, PO Box 195 1211 Geneva 20, Switzerland
전　　화	+41 22 338 32 00
팩　　스	+41 22 338 32 99
전자우편	admin@ifpma.org
홈페이지	http://www.ifpma.org

2) 설립연혁

국제약업단체연합회(IFPMA)는 1968년 8월 1일, 유럽경제공동체(EEC) 여러 나라의 제약업자 회합을 계기로 창립되었다. 비정부·비영리 기구로서 1971년 세계보건기구(WHO)의 승인을 얻었다.

3) 설립목적

IFPMA는 세계인류의 건강과 복지에 대한 공헌과 약업의 도의성을 수립하기 위한 공적·사적 조직의 연대를 목적으로 한다.
① 전 세계 환자들의 이익을 위한 혁신적 약업 글로벌 정책환경 장려
② 의약산업으로의 전문성 기여와 대중건강에 기여하고 있는 국제기구, 국가기관, 정부 및 비정부기구와의 협력적 관계 및 파트너십 촉진
③ 정기적인 연락과 경험 공유 보장

4) 조직

IFPMA의 조직은 총회와 이사회 그리고 사무국으로 구성되어 있다. 총회는 2년마다 개최되며 회의 진행을 위해 의장 1명과 부의장 2명을 선출한다. 총회에서는 새로운 회원에 대한 가입 여부를 결정하고, IFPMA규약을 변경한다. 2002년 현재 60개국이 가입해 있으며, 본부는 스위스의 취리히에 있다.

5) 회원

IFPMA의 회원은 크게 회원협회와 회원사로 나뉜다. 회원협회는 전 세계 약 60개국의 국가 및 지역 의약산업협회들로 구성된다. 2004년 11월부로 일반 의약기업들도 IFPMA의 회원사로 활동할 수 있게 되었다.

6) 주요 사업

의약품의 가격관리를 통해 유통질서를 확립하고, 의약품 연구 개발을 위한 각종 기술협력 및 출판, 심포지엄 등을 주관한다.

7) 관련 단체

IFPMA에서 제공하는 관련 단체는 다음과 같다.
① 의약회사
- Abbott Laboratories
- Akzo - Nobel
- Almirall - Prodesfarma
- AstraZeneca Plc
- Aventis Pasteur
- Agouron
- Bayer
- Boehringer Ingelheim GmbH
- Bristol - Myers Squibb Company
- Chiron
- Chugai Pharmaceutical
- Eisai
- Eli Lilly
- Esteve
- GlaxoSmithKline(GSK)
- Johnson & Johnson
- Menarini SA

- Merck & Co., Inc.
- Merck KGaA
- Novartis International AG
- Organon NV
- Pfizer Inc.
- Roche/F. Hoffman – La Roche Ltd.
- Sanofi – Synthelabo
- Serono International SA
- Schering AG
- Schering Plough
- Sigma Tau
- Takeda
- Wyeth

② 국제기구
- 세계건강이니셔티브(Global Health Initiative) – 세계경제 포럼(World Economic forum)의 이니셔티브
- G8 – 정보센터
- 국제화합콘퍼런스(ICH: International Conference on Harmonisation)
- 국제간호사협의회(ICN: International Council of Nurses)
- 국제환자기구동맹(IAPO: International Alliance of Patients' Organizations)
- OECD(Organization for Economic Co – operation and Development)

- 약학보안연구소(PSI: the Pharmaceutical Security Institute)
- 세계보건기구 미대륙 지부를 위한 건강기구 미대륙 지역 사무소(PAHO: Pan American Health Organization Regional Office for the Americas of the World Health Organization)
- 의료적합기술프로그램(RHO: Program for Appropriate Technology in Health) - PATH 프로그램
- 아틀란틱기업간대화(TABD: Trans Atlantic Business Dialogue)
- 유엔에이즈계획(UNAIDS Joint United Nations Program on HIV/AIDS)
- UNDP(United Nations Development Program)
- UNFPA(United Nations Population Fund)
- UNICEF(United Nations Children's Fund)
- 지속적인 개발을 위한 세계기업협의회(WBCSD: World Business Council for Sustainable Development)
- WHO(World Health Organization)
- 연대병에 관한 연구 및 교육을 위한 유니세프, 유엔개발 프로그램, 세계은행, 세계보건기구 합동 특별 프로그램 (TDR: UNDP/World Bank/WHO Special Programme for Research and Training in Tropical Diseases)
- WIPO(World Intellectual Property Organization)
- World Bank
- World Economic Forum
- WTO(World Trade Organization)

③ 건강협회(Health Associations)

- 에이즈에관한국제의사협회(IAPAC: International Association of Physicians in AIDS Care)
- 국제간호사협의회(ICN: International Council of Nurses)
- 국제정신의학연맹(World Federation for Mental Health)
- 국제심장연맹(World Heart Federation)

2 정보원

1) 정보배포정책

IFPMA의 정보원은 'News & Publications'에서 찾아볼 수 있다. IFPMA의 보도 자료, 미디어상의 관련 자료, 선언문, 출판물 등을 온라인상으로 열람할 수 있다.

2) 정보 자료

① 보도 자료

2007년 한 해 동안의 IFPMA 보도 자료는 다음과 같다.

- 30 November 2007. *R&D Pharmaceutical Industry Intensifies Efforts to Address HIV/AIDS Threat, Including Resistance & Pediatric Needs*
- 10 November 2007. *WHO Inter Governmental Working Group — Addressing Unmet Developing World Health Needs: Sustainable, Practical Solutions*

- 2 November 2007. *Updated IFPMA Survey Shows Growing Pharmaceutical Industry Contribution to Improving Developing World Health*
- 2 November 2007. *Latest IFPMA Developing World Disease R&D Status Report Shows Continued Expansion of Industry Research Effort*
- 28 September 2007. *The IFPMA Welcomes Nicholas Piramal India Limited*
- 10 September 2007. *Kuala Lumpur to Host 2008 IFPMA Asian Regulatory Conference*
- 6 August 2007. *Chennai Court Ruling: India's Innovative Potential Continues to be Stifled by Its Poor Patent Law*
- 13 June 2007. *IFPMA Welcomes WHO's Call for an International Stockpile of Pre-pandemic Influenza Vaccines for Developing Countries*
- 8 June 2007. *Industry Welcomes G8's Commitment to Fight HIV/AIDS*
- 31 May 2007. *G8 Development Summit: R&D Pharmaceutical Industry Committed to Improving Health in Africa*
- 16 May 2007. *Swedish FASS Website Demonstrates New Technology to Allow National Websites to Provide Clinical Trial Searches, in their Own Language, Using the IFPMA Clinical Trials Portal*

- 16 May 2007. *IFPMA's New Partnerships Book Documents the R&D - Based Pharmaceutical Industry's Longstanding and Growing Commitment to Improve Health in Developing Countries*

- 14 May 2007. *IFPMA Influenza Vaccine Supply International Task Force Welcomes Sinovac and PowderMed as its Latest Members*

- 4 May 2007. *IFPMA Statement on Compulsory Licensing of Medicines*

- 25 April 2007. *IFPMA Supports WHO Meeting to Examine Options for Increasing Developing Countries' Access to Potential Pandemic vaccines*

- 18 April 2007. *IFPMA Welcomes WHO Global Partners Meeting on Neglected Tropical Diseases and Urges Cooperation and Integration to Increase Program Coverage*

- 22 March 2007. *Challenges Posed by Tuberculosis Underline Importance of Pharmaceutical Industry R&D Projects in this Therapeutic Area*

- 13 March 2007. *Manufacturers of Human and Animal Vaccines Say they Each Have their Own Distinct Roles to Play in Combating Pandemic Influenza*

- 15 February 2007. *IFPMA Strengthens Ethical Promotion of Medicines with New Marketing Code Internet Resource: www.ifpma.org/ethicalpromotion*

- 9 February 2007. *IFPMA Welcomes Governments' Launch of AMC Pilot Project to Encourage Development of New Pneumococcal Vaccines for the Poorest Countries*
- 8 February 2007. *IFPMA Welcomes New Executive Director of the Global Fund to Fight AIDS, Tuberculosis and Malaria*
- 29 January 2007. *IFPMA Urges Thai Government to Discuss Access to Innovative Medicines with Originator Companies*
- 22 January 2007. *IFPMA Helps to Advance Influenza Pandemic Preparedness*
- 3 January 2007. *New IFPMA Code of Pharmaceutical Marketing Practices*

② 미디어 자료

IFPMA가 제공하는 관련 미디어 자료의 예는 다음과 같다.

- 21 December 2007. *Talks with Pharma -Giants Collapse, CL Seems a Certainty -the Bangkok Post*
- 21 December 2007. *Chronic Diseases in Developing Countries -The Lancet*
- 21 December 2007. *International Cooperation to Combat Chronic Diseases -The Lancet*
- 21 December 2007. *China Fails to Define NCE or Protect Data, Industry Warned -Pharma Times*

- 21 December 2007. *Access to Medicines, Human Rights and Trade Rules: Comparative and International Perspectives － Conference*
- 21 December 2007. *Evidence for New Malaria Vaccines Efficacy － Thaindian News*
- 21 December 2007. *MRSA Test on New Patients Reduces Infections by 40% － The Times*
- 21 December 2007. *Link between Cellular Defense Processes Found, Showing How Cancer Cells Survive － Science Daily*
- 21 December 2007. *Link between Cellular Defense Processes Found, Showing How Cancer Cells Survive － Science Daily*
- 21 December 2007. *UBC Pledges Developing World Access to New Technologies － IP Health*

③ 출판물

모든 출판물은 PDF로 다운받아 열람할 수 있다. 최근 1년 간 출간된 자료의 목록은 다음과 같다.

- *Alianzas Para la Construcción de Sociedades Más Sanas en el Mundo en Desarollo*
- *Des Partenariats Pour Bâtir des Sociétés en Meilleure Santé Dans les Pays en Développement*
- *Value of Innovation*
- *Challenges of Pharmaceutical Innovation*

- *Policy Pillars of Pharmaceutical Innovation*
- *Public - Private Partnerships*
- *Data Exclusivity: Encouraging Development of New Medicines(July 2007)*
- *HIV/AIDS: Partnerships to Improve Access and R&D*
- *Malaria: Partnerships to Improve Access and R&D*
- *Tuberculosis: Partnerships to Improve Access and R&D*
- *IFPMA Tropical Diseases: Partnerships to Improve Access and R&D*
- *Partnerships to Build Healthier Societies in the Developing World*
- *Des Partenariats Pour Bâtir des Sociétés en Meilleure Santé Dans les Pays en Voie de Développement*
- *Alianzas Para la Creación de Una Sociedad Más Sana en Países en Vías de Desarrollo*
- *Partnerships to Build Healthier Societies in the Developing World*
- *Innovación Adaptativa, Propiedad Intelectual e Interés Público: Cómo la Extensión de Patentes Conduce a Más Medicamentos Mejores y Más Seguros*

INRUD

International Network for the Rational Use of Drugs

합리적약물복용을위한국제네트워크

① 기구

1) 소재지

소재국가	미국
주　　소	INRUD Coordinator, Dr. John Chalker 4301 N. Fairfax Dr. Suite 400 Arlington, VA 22203, USA
전　　화	+1 703 534 6575
팩　　스	+1 703 524 7898
전자우편	inrud@msh.org
홈페이지	http://www.inrud.org/

2) 성격

합리적약물복용을위한국제네트워크(INRUD)는 안전하고 효과적이며 비용 효율적 약물복용을 위한 공통의 비전을 공유하는 네트워크 그룹이다. INRUD는 참여회원들, 기술적 협력, 양질의 교육, 가치 있는 방법론적 방법 형성, 약물복용 향상으로의 접근과 관련하여 경험 공유의 중요성을 강조한다.

3) 설립연혁

INRUD는 1989년 특히 자원이 부족한 국가에서의 약물처방, 배포, 사용방법을 향상시키기 위한 효과적인 전략의 설립, 평가, 분포를 위해 설립되었다.

이 네트워크는 현재 약 20여 개 국가에서 24개의 그룹과 WHO, 하버드 의대, 스웨덴 Karolinska 연구소 등으로 이루어져 있다. INRUD 본부는 현재 스웨덴 국제협력단(SIDA: Swedish International Development Cooperation Agency)에 의해 재정적 지원을 받고 있다. 역사적으로 INRUD는 미국 국제개발처 (USAID: US Agency for International Development)와 덴마크 국제개발처(DanisH International Development Agency)를 포함한 다른 기관들의 지원을 받아 오고 있다.

4) 비전 및 임무

INRUD은 약물복용을 향상시키고 올바른 사용법을 전파하기 위한 최선책을 강구하기 위해 활동한다.

5) 조직

INRUD의 이사회는 총 13인의 회원으로 구성된다.

6) 회원

2008년 7월 현재 총 24개의 회원그룹이 있으며, 그룹 구성은 다음과 같다.

방글라데시(Bangladesh), 나이지리아(Nigeria), 캄보디아(Cambo-dia), 페루(Peru), 중국(China), 필리핀(Philippines), 에티오피아(Ethiopia), 스웨덴 Karolinska 연구소(Sweden – Karolinska Institute), 가나(Ghana), 탄자니아(Tanzania), 인도 – 델리(India – Delhi), 태국(Thailand), 인도 – 타밀 나두(India – Tamil Nadu), 우간다(Uganda), 인도네시아(Indonesia), 미국 – 보스턴그룹(USA – Boston Group), 케냐(Kenya), 미국 – 건강관리과학(USA – Management Sciences for Health), 키르기스스탄(Kirgizstan), 베트남(Vietnam), 몰도바(Moldova), 세계보건기구/의학정책 및 표준(WHO/Medicines Policy and Standards), 네팔(Nepal), 짐바브웨(Zimbabwe)

7) 주요전략

- 합리적 약물복용 촉진을 위한 학제적 접근
- 공공기관 및 사적 기관, 대학, NGO 등의 지역전문가의 권고를 바탕으로 한 연구, 기획, 실행 노력 강조
- 기술적 정보, 성공사례, 배워야 할 사항 공유
- 약물복용의 행동적 측면에 관한 이해를 위한 조사연구
- 실용적 연구법 개발

8) 약물복용 향상을 위한 국제컨퍼런스(ICIUM: International Conferences on IMproving Use of Medicines)

국가 및 국제 정책입안가, 프로그램 관리자, 연구원, 임상연구원, 그 외의 관련자들이 함께 모여 약물복용 향상에 관한 글로

벌 연구 아젠다를 형성하기 위해 1997년과 2004년 두 차례에
걸친 국제 컨퍼런스가 개최되었다.

9) 주요 시범 사업

① 연구사업

INRUD는 회원국가들 내에서의 약물복용 개선을 위한 행동
변화에 관한 연구프로젝트를 지원한다.

② 교육사업

교육사업은 약물복용을 개선시키는 또 하나의 중요한 분야
이다. 지역그룹 및 국가보건부, 국제보건기구 등과 함께
INRUD는 매해 2주간의 교육 프로그램을 아시아 및 아프리
카 지역에서 제공하고 있다.

② 정보원

1) 정보원배포정책

INRUD의 정보원은 'News'와 'INRUD Bibliography'로 이루어
진다. 'News'의 정보는 PDF를 이용한 무료열람이 가능하다.

2) INRUD News

INRUD 뉴스는 매해 1회 또는 2회에 걸쳐 웹사이트상에서 출
간된다. 이 뉴스를 통해 회원 국가들의 활동소식과 발간 자료
에 대한 소개, 약물복용과 관련된 중요한 소식 등을 열람할 수
있다. 대표적인 목록은 다음과 같다.

- *INRUD News* Volume 18, Number 2, July 2008
- *INRUD News* Volume 18, Number 1, January 2008
- *INRUD News* Volume 17, Number 1, May 2007
- *INRUD News* Volume 16, Number 1, December 2006
- *RPM Plus Update for December 2006*
- *INRUD News* Volume 15, Number 1, December 2005
- *RPM Plus Update for December 2005*
- *INRUD News* Volume 14, Number 1, November 2004
- *INRUD News* Volume 13, Number 1, December 2003
- *INRUD News* Volume 12, Number 2, April 2003
- *INRUD News* Volume 12, Number 1, October 2002
- *INRUD News* Volume 11, Number 2, April 2002
- *INRUD News* Volume 11, Number 1, October 2001
- *INRUD News* Volume 10, Number 2, March 2001
- *INRUD News* Volume 10, Number 1, June 2000
- *INRUD News* Volume 9, Number 2, December 1999
- *INRUD News* Volume 9, Number 1, May 1999
- *INRUD News* Volume 8, Number 2, November 1998
- *RPM Update for November 1998*
- *INRUD News* Volume 8, Number 1, February 1998

- ***RPM Update for February 1998***
- ***INRUD News*** Volume 7, Number 1, March 1997
- ***RPM Update for March 1997***
- ***INRUD News*** Volume 6, Number 2, September 1996
- ***RPM Update for September 1996***
- ***INRUD News*** Volume 6, Number 1, February 1996
- ***RPM Update for February 1996***
- ***INRUD News*** Volume 5, Number 2, September 1995
- ***INRUD News*** Volume 5, Number 1, February 1995
- ***RPM update for February 1995***
- ***INRUD News*** Volume 4, Number 2, July 1994
- ***INRUD News*** Volume 4, Number 1, October 1993
- ***INRUD News*** Volume 3, Number 2, January 1993
- ***INRUD News*** Volume 3, Number 1, August 1992
- ***INRUD News*** Volume 2, Number 2, December 1991
- ***INRUD News*** Volume 2, Number 1, June 1991
- ***INRUD News*** Volume 1, Number 2, October 1990
- ***INRUD News*** Volume 1, Number 1

3) INRUD 참고문헌(INRUD Bibliography)

INRUD 약물복용 참고문헌은 약물복용과 관련하여 발간된 논문, 서적, 도큐먼트뿐 아니라 미발간 자료의 참고문헌 리스트를 제공하고 있다. 이메일 요청을 통해 CD로 된 자료를 받아볼 수 있다.

4) 정보원 검색

다음과 같은 데이터베이스로의 링크를 제공한다.

① 데이터 정보원(Data Sources)

- Demographic and Health Surveys
- Demographic Databases
- General Practice Research Database(UK MHRA)
- IMS Health
- U.S. Census Bureau
- WHO Global Health Atlas
- World Bank Data Statistics
- World Bank Living Standards Measurement Study Household Surveys
- World Bank Poverty Monitoring Database

② 약물정보자원(Drug Information Resources)

- Australia National Prescribing Service
- British National formulary
- Medscape Drug Reference
- McGraw − Hill's AccessMedicine
- NLM Drug Information Portal
- Royal Pharmaceutical Society of Great Britain(RPSGB) Pharmacy Information Resources
- Scientific American Professional Library from WebMD
- UK Medicines

- U.S. Food and Drug Administration
- WHO Essential Medicines Library
- WHO Model Formulary

③ 도서관 및 검색엔진(Libraries and Search Engines)
- AED Satellife
- Association for Health Information and Libraries in Africa (AHILA)
- Bio‒Mail
- BioMed Central
- BioMedNet
- Contents Direct
- Link Out: Journal List
- Medline
- Medline Plus
- Medscape
- Med Web‒Electronic Newsletters and Journals
- Merck Manuals Online Medical Library
- Meta Press
- Pub‒Med Central
- Scirus(Science Information Search Engine)
- Springer
- WHO Essential Medicines Library
- WHO Library Site

④ 연구조사 방법 및 도구(Research Methods and Tools)
- Apian SurveyPro Survey Software and Online Survey Hosting
- Cancer Control PLANET
- Clean List online
- International Development Research Centre(IDRC) – Health Systems Research(Vol.1)
- International Development Research Centre(IDRC) – Health Systems Research(Vol. 2)
- Measurement Experts(MEI)
- Measuring Continuity of Ambulatory Care
- Qualitative Method Resources
- Questionnaires and Surveys – A Free Tutorial
- WHO Collaborating Centre for Drug Statistics Methodology(Including ATC/DDD)
- WHO International Classification of Diseases(ICD)

⑤ 저널(Journals)
- *Academic Medicine*
- *Africa Journals Online*
- *American Journal of Epidemiology*
- *American Journal of Public Health*
- *Australian Prescriber*
- *British Journal of Clinical Pharmacology(BJCP)*
- *British Medical Journal(BMJ)*

- *BMJ－Archive of Issues by Date*
- *Clinical Pharmacology and Therapeutics*
- *East African Medical Journal*
- *Free Medical Journals*
- *Health Affairs*
- *Health Policy and Planning*
- *Health Policy*
- *International Journal for Quality in Health Care*
- *International Journal of Health Services*
- *International Journal of Clinical Pharmacology & Therapeutics*
- *International Journal of Epidemiology*
- *International Journal of Health Planning and Management*
- *Journal of the American Medical Association(AMA)*
- *Journal of Internal Medicine*
- *Journal of Clinical Epidemiology*
- *Lancet*
- *Managed Care Digest*
- *Medical Care Editorial Manager*
- *Milbank Quarterly*
- *New England Journal of Medicine*
- *PharmacoEconomics*
- *Social Science and Medicine*
- *Transactions of the Royal Society of Tropical Medicine*

& Hygiene
- *Tropical Medicine & International Health*
- *WHO Health InterNetwork Access to Research Initiative(HINARI)*
- *WHO Publications － World Health forum WHO Bulletin*

⑥ 국제개발기구, NGO, 학술기관(International Development Organizations, NGOs, and Academic Centers)
- Action on Antibiotic Resistance(ReAct)
- Boston University Center for International Health
- Foundation for Innovative New Diagnostics(FIND)
- Harvard University(DACP)
- HLSP － Mott MacDonald
- John Snow, Inc. and JSI Research and Training Institute
- Management Sciences for Health(MSH)
- Médecins Sans Frontières(MSF) International
- Medicines for Malaria Venture(MMV)
- Program for Appropriate Technology in Health(PATH)

⑦ 약품가격정보(Drug Price Information)
- HAI － Measuring Medicine Prices
- Frontline － The Other Drug War(PBS)
- MSH International Drug Price Indicator Guide

⑧ 약물규제 및 표준(Drug Regulation and Standards)
- British Pharmacopoeia(BP)
- Clinical Research Guide - NHLBI, NIH, DHHS
- European Directorate for the Quality of Medicines and Health Care(EP)
- European Medicines Evaluation Agency(EMEA)
- International Pharmacopoeia(IP)
- UK Medicines and Healthcare Products Regulatory Agency
- U.S. Food and Drug Administration
- U.S. Pharmacopeia(USP)

⑨ 능력 함양 및 교육 자료(Capacity Building and Training Resources)
- Promoting Rational Drug Use CD - ROM - Front Page
- Promoting Rational Drug Use in the Community - Materials
- Promoting Rational Drug Use Course Materials

INWAT

International Network of Woman against Tobacco

국제흡연반대여성네트워크

① 기구

1) 소재지

소재국가	캐나다
주　소	International Network of Women against Tobacco c/o British Columbia Centre of Excellence for Women's Health E311－4500 Oak St, Box 48, Vancouver, BC, Canada V6H 3N1
전　화	＋1 604 875 2633
팩　스	＋1 604 875 3716
전자우편	info@inwat.org
홈페이지	http://www.inwat.org/

2) 성격

국제흡연반대여성네트워크(INWAT)는 100개국의 1,600여 명이 넘는 회원을 둔 여성흡연철폐운동을 하고 있는 국제 네트워크 이다.

3) 설립연혁

INWAT는 1990년 흡연반대운동 여성리더들에 의해 설립되었다.

4) 비전 및 임무

여성 및 어린 소녀들의 흡연에 관한 복잡한 문제를 알리고자
한다.

5) 조직

INWAT는 위원회 및 위원장(Board of Directors) 그리고 지역
대표들(Regional Representatives)로 운영되며, 이들은 모두 매
해 열리는 흡연과 건강국제컨퍼런스(World Conference on
Tobacco of Health) 이전에 회원모임을 통해 선출된다.

6) 회원

INWAT의 회원가입은 무료이다. 웹페이지상의 지원서를 작성
후 온라인상으로 비로 지원이 가능하다.
INWAT의 회원은 1년에 두 차례 발간되는 전자 뉴스레터를
구독할 수 있게 된다. 또한 토의그룹의 참가명단에 오르게 되
며 여성흡연과 관련하여 토론에 적극 참여할 수 있다.

7) 후원기관

INWAT는 다음과 같은 후원기관에 의해 후원을 받는다.

- 스웨덴 대중보건 국가연구소(National Institute of Public Health, Sweden)
- 캐나다 브리티시 콜롬비아 여성보건센터(British Columbia Centre of Excellence for Women's Health, Canada)
- 네덜란드 스티보로(STIVORO, the Netherlands)
- 미국 미대륙심장재단(InterAmerican Heart Foundation, USA)
- 미국 아동흡연반대운동(Campaign for Tobacco-Free Kids, USA)

8) 주요 시범 사업

① 흡연저지에 관해 일하고 있는 개인 및 기관 간의 연결 도모
② 국제여성과 흡연에 관한 문제 관련 정보의 수집 및 배포
③ 흡연광고 및 촉진에 반하는 전략공유
④ 여성중심의 흡연저지 및 방지에 대한 개발 지원
⑤ 흡연저지 콘퍼런스의 조직 및 기획 지원
⑥ 여성과 흡연에 관한 출판개발 협력
⑦ 여성리더십 개발

② 정보원

1) 정보원배포정책

INWAT의 정보원은 'e-Magazine', 'Tobacco News', 'Country Profiles', 'Reports & Resources' 그리고 'Link'에서 찾아볼 수

있다. 대부분의 자료는 온라인상으로 무료열람이 가능하다.

2) 전자매거진(e - Magazine)

전반적으로 영어로 정보 제공이 되고 있으며, 유럽지역의 경우 프랑스어, 스페인어, 독일어로 된 정보도 출간되고 있다. 최근의 대표적인 목록은 다음과 같다.

- *Sep 07 - Feb 08*
- *Mar - Aug 2007*
- *Sep 06 - Feb 07*
- *Mar - Aug 2006*
- *Sep 05 - Feb 06*
- *Mar - Aug 2005*
- *Fall 2004*
- *Spring 2004*
- *Late Fall 2003*
- *Spring 2003*
- *Late Fall 2002*
- *Summer 2002*
- *Winter 2002*
- *Fall 2001*
- *Spring 2001*
- *Spring 2000*
- *Winter 2000*
- *Summer 1999*
- *Winter 1999*

3) 흡연뉴스(Tobacco News)

Join Together(http://www.jointogether.org/news/)로의 사이트 이
동을 통하여 흡연과 관련된 뉴스를 접할 수 있도록 하고 있다.
대표적인 예는 다음과 같다.

① 주요뉴스(Headlines)

- *New York Bans Smoking in Dorms* 07/10/2008
- *FTC Wants Agency Name Off Cigarette Ads* 07/10/2008
- *Wisconsin is State Most Affected by Alcohol, Analysis Shows* 07/09/2008
- *Slate: Multiple Drugs Cause Most Overdoses* 07/09/2008
- *Rising Alcohol Abuse Seen Among Returning Veterans* 07/09/2008

② 연구소식(Research News)

- *Depression Tied to Quitting Drinking* 07/10/2008
- *85 Percent of Online Pharmacies Don't Require Prescription, CASA Study Finds* 07/10/2008
- *Infant Breathing Hurt by Prenatal Exposure to Tobacco Smoke* 07/10/2008
- *Knowledge of Smoking – Bladder Cancer Link Lacking* 07/09/2008
- *Smokers of Strong Marijuana May be at Greater Risk of Psychosis: Report* 07/07/2008

③ 자금마련뉴스(Funding News)

- *NGO Connection Unveiled by Microsoft* 07/10/2008
- *Kresge Announces New Health Funding Program* 07/10/2008
- *Baseball, Newspaper Charities Focus on Veterans' Mental Health, Job Needs* 07/10/2008
- *Less Federal Money Going to Kids' Programs, Study Says* 07/10/2008
- *Measures and Determinants of Smokeless Tobacco Use, Prevention, and Cessation* 07/10/2008

④ 그 외(Your Turn)

- *Association of Recovery Schools Annual Conference: It Takes a Village to Raise a Child* 07/08/2008
- *Marin to Host Town Hall Meeting on Catastrophic Costs of Alcohol in CA* 07/07/2008
- *Califano Urges NCAA to Ban All Beer and Alcohol Ads at Broadcast Events* 07/02/2008
- *2008 California Youth Conference and Teen Leadership Training Institute* 06/27/2008
- *8th Annual Conference for New England Drug Court Judges, Professionals* 06/27/2008

4) 국가 자료(Country Profiles)

벨기에(belgium), 핀란드(Finland), 독일(Germany), 네덜란드

(Netherlands), 스웨덴(Sweden)의 흡연통제와 관련된 국가 자료를 PDF로 제공하고 있다.

5) 보고서(Reports & Resources)

- *Turning a New Leaf: Women, Tobacco, and the Future*
- *Second Hand Smoke and Women in Europe*
- *Reducing Harm: A Better Practices Review of Tobacco Policy and Vulnerable Populations*
- *Expecting to Quit: A Best Practices Review of Smoking Cessation Interventions for Pregnant and Postpartum Girls and Women*
- *Women, Tobacco and Cancer: An Agenda for the 21st Century*
- *IrisH Women and Tobacco: Knowledge Attitudes and Beliefs*
- *Tobacco Control Policy Strategies, Successes and Setbacks*
- *The Health Consequences of Smoking: A Report of the Surgeon General*
- *Smoking and Reproductive Life*
- *The Princess Slays the Dragon – Ending the Tyranny of the Tobacco Industry*
- *Fact Sheet on Gender, Health and Tobacco*
- *Searching for the Solution: Women, Smoking and Inequalities in Europe*

- *The Tobacco Atlas: Pages 26 - 27 on Women*
- *Smoke - Free Children - the First 10 Years*
- *Filtered Policy: Smoking & Women in Canada*
- *Femmes and Tabacco*
- *Women and Smoking: A Report of the Surgeon General*
- *Women and the Tobacco Epidemic Challenges for the 21st Century*
- *Part of the Solution? Tobacco Control Policies and Women*
- *European Women & Smoking Fact Sheets*
- *Presentations from the INWAT - Europe Expert Seminar on Women and Second - Hand Smoke*
- *Women and Tobacco Presentation Preview - Automatic Presentation*
- *Presentations from the International UNIon Conference on Lung Health*
- *Presentations from 12th World Conference on Tobacco or Health*
- *Marketing to Women*
- *Supported by a Grant to Tobacco Control by the Robert Wood Johnson Foundation*
- *Slide Series*

6) 링크(Links)

[국제]

- GLOBALink International Tobacco Control Community
- International Union against Cancer
- Tobacco Free Initiative – World Health Organization

[호주]

- Quit Victoria

[불가리아]

- Association Women against Tobacco – Bulgaria

[캐나다]

- Canadian Council for Tobacco Control
- Canadian Lung Association
- Health Canada's Tobacco Program
- ICEbeRGS Interdisciplinary Capacity Enhancement: Bridging Excellence in Respiratory Disease and Gender Studies
- National Clearinghouse on Tobacco and Health
- Physicians for a Smoke – Free Canada

[인도네시아]

- Indonesian Women against Tobacco

[스페인]

- www.nicotinaweb.info

[태국]

- Action on Smoking or Health(ASH) Thailand

[영국]

- Action on Smoking or Health(ASH) UK
- Action on Smoking or Health(ASH) Scotland
- NHS Health Scotland

[미국]

- American Cancer Society
- American Heart Association
- American Lung Association
- Americans for Nonsmokers' Rights
- Campaign for Tobacco-Free Kids
- Centers for Disease Control
- Corporate Accountability International
- Morbidity and Mortality Weekly Report CDC
- Tobacco News and Information
- Tobacco Talk Radio
- Women's Tobacco Prevention Network

IPA

International Pediatric Association

국제소아협회

① 기구

1) 소재지

소재국가	스위스
주　　소	International Pediatric Association 1－3, rue de Chantepoulet, P.O. Box 1726 CH－1211 Geneva 1－ Switzerland
전　　화	＋41 22 906 91 52
팩　　스	＋41 22 732 28 52
전자우편	adminoffice@ipa－world.org
홈페이지	http://www.ipa－world.org/

2) 설립연혁

국제소아협회(IPA)는 1910년 유럽 소아과의사 모임의 1912년 제1회 국제소아과의회 준비과정에서 그 시초를 찾아볼 수 있다. 그 후 IPA는 139개국의 144개의 국가소아과사회(National Pediatric Societies), 10개의 지역소아과사회(Regional Pediatric Societies), 국제소아과협회(International Pediatric Chairs

Association) 및 세계소아과전문의협회연합(World Federation of Associations of Pediatric Surgeons)을 포함한 11개의 국제 소아과전문사회(International Pediatric Specialty Societies)의 회원과 함께 비정부기관으로 발전해 왔다.

현재 IPA는 자원봉사 직원들로 이루어진 기구이며 스위스에 본부를 두고 있다.

3) 비전 및 임무

IPA의 임무는 소아과의사들이 모든 아동들의 신체적, 정신적, 사회적 건강을 촉진시키는 리더가 되며, 또한 전 세계 모든 국가의 신생아, 아동, 사춘기 청소년들의 양질의 건강을 실현시키는 데서 찾아볼 수 있다.

4) 회원

IPA는 회원사회(Member Society), 국가소아과사회(National Pediatric Societies), 지역 및 언어사회(Regional & Linguistic Societies), 그리고 하위전문분야사회(Subspecialty Societies)로 이루어져 있다.

5) 주요 행사

- 제13회 아시아-태평양 소아과 의회(13th Asian Pacific Congress of Pediatrics)
  - 회의기간: 2009년 10월 14일~18일

- 회의장소: 중국 상하이(Shanghai, China)
- 회의내용: http://www.chinamed.com.cn/appa2009/

6) 국제활동

IPA는 세계보건기구(WHO) 및 백신 및 면역 글로벌 연맹 (Global Alliance for Vaccines and Immunization)과 함께 활동을 하고 있다.

② 정보원

1) 정보원배포정책

IPA의 정보원은 'News'와 'Resource'에서 찾아볼 수 있다. 'Resource'에서는 IPA의 출판물 및 타 기관의 소아 관련 보고서로의 링크를 제공하고 있으며, 대부분의 자료는 인터넷상에서 무료열람이 가능하다.

2) News(보도 자료)

보도 자료 및 IPA의 뉴스레터를 열람할 수 있다. 최근 자료의 대표적인 예는 다음과 같다.
① 일반
* *Workshop on Children's Health and the Environment*
* *Dr. Ruth A. Etzel, IPA Technical Advisor in Children's*

Environmental Health, Named 2007 Children's Environmental Health Champion by the United States Environmental Protection Agency's Office of Children's Health Protection

- *John Lewy Tribute*
- *Marrakech Newborn Screening Conference*
- *WHO Vaccines and Immunizations Geneva, November 20 - 22, 2006*
- *Report to IPA: High Level Symposium on Child Survival(MDG 4)*
- *UNAPSA Declaration - December 2005*
- *Innocenti Declaration - November 2005*
- *Nairobi Environment Conference - October 2005*

② 지역별

- *Session of the Regional Committee for the Western Pacific Region, World Health Organization(WHO) - Chok - Wan CHAN, IPA*
- *IPA Statement on Equity and Quality Healthcare for Children of the World*
- *Agenda Item 7: Report of the Regional Director*
- *APPA Report on the Rotavirus and Polio Symposia in Pattaya - July 2006*

③ 국가별

- *Japan: Visit to the Japanese Pediatric Society Tokyo, November* 17 – 20, 2006

④ 뉴스레터

- Volume 1 – Number 1, February 1, 2006

3) 발간 자료(Publications)

2008년 7월 현재 발간 자료 웹페이지는 개편 중에 있다.

4) 관련 보고서(Link)

- UNICEF State of the World's Children Report 2007
  홈페이지: http://www.unicef.org/publications/index_36587.html
- Lancet series on Newborn, Child, and Maternal Survival
  홈페이지:

http://www.thelancet.com/collections/neonatal_survival/2006

IRC

International Water and Sanitation Center

국제물위생센터

① 기구

1) 소재지

주   소   Westvest 7, 2611 AX Delft, the Netherlands

전   화   +31 15 219 2939

팩   스   +31 15 219 0955

홈페이지   http://www.irc.nl/

2) 설립연혁

1968년 설립 이래 국제물위생센터(IRC)는 지식의 공유, 촉진, 이용을 촉구함으로써 개발도상국 빈곤층이 물과 위생서비스를 제공받고 이용하고 유지할 수 있는 정부, 전문가, 관련 기관들의 더 나은 지원을 위하여 활동해 오고 있다.

'IRC'라는 약어는 1968년 창립 당시 기관의 명칭이었고 1980년대 중반까지 사용되었던 '물 제공 커뮤니티를 위한 국제 관련 센터(International Reference Centre for Community Water Supply)'에서 유래되어 기관 명칭이 현재의 '국제물위생센터

(IRC International Water and Sanitation Centre)'로 바뀐 후에
도 계속 사용해 오고 있다.

IRC의 파트너들과의 정보와 지식 공유를 위한 활동은 1970년
대 초반에 시작되었다. 5년 동안 이루어진 파트너들과의 합동
학습은 수년간의 이 분야에서의 주제 변화 및 파트너십 개발,
일정 기간 동안의 연구가 다른 기간에 미친 영향 등을 알 수
있게 해 주었다.

3) 설립목적

IRC는 지식의 창조, 공유, 이용을 촉진함으로써 분야 종사자
및 기구들이 개발도상국의 빈곤층에게 지속적인 물과 위생서비
스를 제공할 수 있도록 하는 데에 목적이 있다.

4) 조직

IRC는 2006년 10월 19일자로 자치적 기관으로 거듭났다. 굿거
버넌스라는 최근 개념과 비영리기관으로서의 성격을 추구하기
위해 관리위원회(Supervisory Board)가 설립되었고 기관 내 가
장 높은 운영조직이 되었다.

5) 주요 사업

다음과 같은 세 가지 영역을 중심으로 사업이 이루어지고 있다.

① 지식공유(Knowledge Sharing)

본 기관은 다양한 언어와 형태의 이용 가능한 양질의 정보를
제공한다. 모든 사회적, 교육적, 과학적인 정보를 포함하는
물과 위생을 향상시킬 수 있는 지식과 경험을 가진 국제적으
로 인정받은 전문가를 중심으로 팀을 구성하여 활동한다.

② 저비용 출판 및 보급(Low‐Cost Publishing and Dissemi-
nation)

개발도상국의 정보네트워크를 개발하며, 출판 및 보급을 통
해 타 기관 및 네트워크들이 저비용으로 정보를 이용할 수
있도록 한다.

③ 개발도상국의 정보센터 촉진(Facilitating Resource Centers
in Developing Countries)

본 기관은 지역 정보센터들이 업무개발 및 직원능력 향상을
동해 그들 국가에서 효과적인 지식센터가 될 수 있도록 지원
한다.

6) 파트너십

IRC는 아프리카, 아시아, 라틴아메리카의 파트너 기구들과 강
한 연대를 맺고 있으며, 국제네트워크와의 긴밀한 협조관계를
맺고 있다. IRC와 그 파트너들은 다양한 국제네트워크와의 협력
관계를 바탕으로 서로를 지원한다. IRC는 또한 네덜란드의 관련
기관들 및 유럽과 북미대륙 국가들과의 협동활동을 통해 협조관

계를 유지한다. 그 외에 방글라데시, 부르키나파소, 콜롬비아, 인도, 케냐, 모잠비크, 네팔, 필리핀, 남아프리카, 스리랑카, 짐바브웨에 위치한 기관들과 파트너 관계를 맺고 활동한다.

7) 프로젝트

IRC는 다양한 파트너들과 함께 수많은 프로젝트를 운영하고 있다. 대표적인 프로젝트는 다음과 같다.

① RCD 18개국 프로그램(RCD 18 Countries Programme)
  이 프로그램은 국가단계에서의 물과 관련한 정보공유를 촉진한다.

② JPO 프로그램(JPO Programme)
  주니어 전문가(JPO: Junior Professional Officer) 프로그램은 물과 위생 분야의 젊은 전문가를 위한 네덜란드와 상대국가 간의 교환프로그램이다.

③ EMPOWERS
  유럽의학 물 자원 참여 시나리오(EMPOWERS: Euro-Med Participatory Water Resources Scenarios)는 영국 케어(Care International UK)에 의해 2003년에 시행된 이집트, 요르단, 웨스트 뱅크/가자 국가의 연구사업 및 개발 프로젝트이다.

④ SWITCH

유럽연합(EU)에 의해 재정지원을 받아 통합적 도시 물 관리(Integrated Urban Water Management)의 패러다임 변화를 목적으로 하는 2006년부터 2011년까지로 계획된 5년간의 프로그램이다.

⑤ RiPPLE

RiPPLE은 에티오피아와 나일 지역을 중심으로 한 5년간의 연구조사 프로그램이다. 2006년 7월 1일부터 시작하여 2011년 6월 30일까지 연구사업이 이루어질 예정이다.

⑥ UN‒Habitat‒SCP‒BUS

유엔인간정주(UN Habitat) 지속 가능한 도시프로그램(Sustainable Cities Programme)은 위생 및 물 서비스와 같은 기본 도시 서비스(BUS: Basic Urban Services)를 구성요소로 한다. IRC는 2003년부터 2008년까지 BUS의 지휘를 맡았다.

8) 지역프로그램

IRC의 지역프로그램의 목적은 새천년목표(MDG: Millennium Development Goal)의 WASH 분야를 성취하기 위해 기여하고자 하는 것이다. WASH는 물(Water)과 위생(Sanitation and Hygiene)을 뜻한다. 지역프로그램은 동아프리카, 라틴아메리카, 남아시아, 남부아프리카, 서아프리카로 나뉘어 이루어진다.

9) 주제영역

IRC와 파트너들은 다음과 같은 주제영역을 나누어 연구사업, 출판사업, 정보공유 워크숍 등에 적용한다.

지역 거버넌스(Local Governance), 투명성과 책임성(Transparency and Accountability), 척도의 확장성(Scaling up), 정보 및 커뮤니케이션(Information and Communication), 학교위생(School Sanitation and Hygiene), 물과 생계(Water and Livelihoods), 재정 및 비용복원(Financing and Cost Recovery), 위생촉진(Hygiene Promotion), 환경위생(Environmental Sanitation), 젠더 및 공평성(Gender and Equity), 참여경영(Participatory Management), 지식경영(Knowledge Management), 능력 개발(Capacity Development), 학습연합(Learning Alliances)

② 정보원

1) 정보배포정책

IRC의 정보원은 'Products'에서 찾아볼 수 있다. IRC는 물 분야의 개발에 관한 뉴스와 이벤트에 대한 내용을 제공한다. 또한 정보에 대한 대중의 이용을 촉진한다.

2) 정보 자료

① 뉴스(Source News)

영어, 프랑스어, 스페인어로 물과 위생에 대한 정보를 제공
한다. 대표적인 예는 다음과 같다.

- *International Year of Sanitation: Official Launch by United Nations*
- *Climate Change: Decrease in Freshwater for Coastal Regions More Than Expected*
- *Mozambique: Committees for Water Not Sustainable*
- *Africa, Mali: Small Scale Water Providers Crucial in Meeting the MDGs*
- *Ethiopia: United Kingdom Provides GBP 75 Million for Water and Sanitation Project*
- *Nigeria: Overview of Sanitation Activities*
- *Yemen: Qat Cultivation Threatening Water Resources, Specialists Warn*
- *Jordan: Water Contamination Incidents Highlight Water Shortage Problem*
- *Asia: Cautious Optimism about Water Future in ADB −Commissioned Report*
- *East Asia: Leaders Vow to Increase Investments in Sanitation and Hygiene*
- *Nepal: India funds Water Treatment Plants in Moist Camps*

- *India, Punjab: Water Pollutants may Cause Genetic Mutations, According to Study*
- *Brazil: Sewerage Worst Public Service in Country*
- *Bolivia: Ministry Announces "Water, belonging to All and for All" Declaration*
- *Latin America: LatinoSan 2007 Cali Declaration Unites Region toward Sanitation Targets*

② 출판물(Publications)

IRC는 수년간 물과 위생을 주제로 한 100개 이상의 서적, 팸플릿, 연구논문을 출판해 왔다. 새로운 연구주제들이 정기적으로 추가되고 있다. IRC의 모든 출판물은 날짜별, 주제별 검색이 가능하며 주제별 연구개요 서비스도 제공되고 있다. 최근 출판물 및 연구논문의 목록은 다음과 같다.

- *HIV/AIDS: A Pilot Assessment of Water, Sanitation, Hygiene and Home-Based Care Services in South Africa*
- *Ecosan: Urine Fertiliser Yields Bigger Cabbages in Finland*
- *Peri-Urban Water Conflicts: Supporting Dialogue and Negotiation*
- *Economic and Health Effects of Increasing Coverage to Meet MDG Target 10*
- *The Water Carriers*
- *Water, Sanitation and Hygiene: Quantifying the Health*

Impact at National and Local Levels
* *The African Development Bank and the Water and Sanitation Sector*

③ IRCDOC 데이터베이스

IRCDOC는 16,000개 이상의 참고자료를 도큐먼트 형식으로 제공한다. 기록들은 IRC의 정보전문가에 의한 수작업을 통해 목록화된다. 정보는 키워드검색을 통해 찾을 수 있다.

④ 도서관 서비스(Library Services)

개발도상국의 물 공급 및 위생 관련 정보와 문서서비스를 제공한다. IRCDOC 데이터베이스는 IRC 도서관 서비스를 이용하는 하나의 방법으로 활용되고 있다. 온라인상으로 제공되지 않는 자료들은 이메일로 요청하여 저작권에 위배되지 않는 한에서 사본을 이용할 수 있다. 온라인상으로 열람 가능한 최근의 업데이트된 자료는 다음과 같다.

* *Rethinking Governance in Water Services*
* *Water Monitoring: Mapping Existing Global Systems and Initiatives*
* *Assessing Partnership Effectiveness*
* *The Sanitation Scandal*
* *The African Development Bank and the Water and Sanitation Sector*
* *Water, Sanitation and Hygiene: Quantifying the Health Impact at National and Local Levels*

- *Economic and Health Effects of Increasing Coverage [...] to Meet MDG Target 10*
- *Peri−Urban Water Conflicts: Supporting Dialogue and Negotiation*
- *Hygiene Promotion: A Practical Manual for Relief and Development(2nd ed.)*
- *Partnering to Combat Corruption in Infrastructure Services: A toolkit*
- *Microfinance for Water, Sanitation and Hygiene*
- *Legionella and the Prevention of Legionellosis*
- *Human rights Obligations Related to Equitable Access to Safe Drinking Water and Sanitation*
- *Making Anti−Corruption Approaches Work for the Poor*
- *Infrastructure for All*
- *Roofwater Harvesting: A Handbook for Practitioners*
- *Multi−Stakeholder Platforms for Integrated Water Management*
- *Towards Effective Programming for WASH in Schools*
- *Enhancing Livelihoods through Sanitation*
- *Accountability Arrangements to Combat Corruption*
- *Water: Support from the Inter−American Development Bank Group 1990−2005*
- *HIV/AIDS Checklist for Water and Sanitation Projects*
- *Financial Structuring of Infrastructure Projects in Public −Private Partnerships*

- *Willingness − to − Pay and Design of Water Supply and Sanitation Projects: A Case Study*
- *Mobilizing Market Finance for Water Utilities in Africa*
- *Arsenic in Drinking Water*
- *Sustainability of groundwater Resources and Its Indicators*
- *Hydrology 2020: An Integrating Science to Meet World Water Challenges*
- *How IWRM will Contribute to Achieving the MDGs*
- *Cost Estimates, Budgets, Aid and the Water Sector: What's Going on?*
- *The Challenge of Reducing Non − Revenue Water(NRW) in Developing Countries*
- *Partnerships in the Water and Sanitation Sector*
- *Greywater Management in Low and Middle − Income Countries*
- *Kenya National Water Development Report*
- *Multi − Stage Filtration*
- *Resource Fuide: Mainstreaming Gender in Water Management*
- *Fluoride in Drinking Water*
- *Navigating Gender in African Cities: A Synthesis Report of Rapid Gender and Pro − Poor Assessments in the 17 Cities of the WAC Ⅱ Programme*
- *Capacity Building for Ecological Sanitation: Concepts*

for Eologically Sustainable Sanitation in Formal and Continuing Education

- *SSHE Notes and News, October 2006*

IRC RCM

International Red Cross and Red Crescent Movement
국제적십자사

1 기구

1) 소재지

홈페이지   http://www.redcross.int/EN/default.asp

2) 설립연혁/설립목적

국제적십자사(IRC REM)는 1859년에 있었던 전투와 관련하여 앙리 뒤낭(Henry Dunant)을 주축으로 한 4인의 비전으로부터 시작되었다. 국제적십자사는 그 후 두 차례의 세계대전을 비롯하여 오늘날까지 진 세계적으로 가장 근 규모의 인도주의적 구조활동을 벌이고 있는 네트워크이다. 국제적십자사는 178개 국가의 국가사무소뿐 아니라 제네바에 본부를 둔 국제적십자위원회(ICRC: International Committee of the Red Cross)와 국제적십자사회연합(International Federation: International Federation of Red Cross and Red Crescent Societies)이 모인 단체이다.

3) 조직

국제적십자사는 5개의 위원회로 구성되어 있다. 창립 이래로
현재까지 초대 대표인 앙리 뒤낭을 비롯하여 총 13인의 대표가
국제적십자사를 이끌어 왔다. 상임위원회는 국제컨퍼런스에서
열리는 선거에 의해 열리게 된다.

4) 주요 사업

국제적십자사는 주로 구호활동, 보건, 안전, 혈액 및 골수 기증
등의 활동을 한다.

② 정보원

1) 정보배포정책

국제적십자사의 정보원은 'Archives'에서 찾아볼 수 있다. 국제
적십자위원회(ICRC: International Committee of the Red Cross)와
국제적십자사회연합(International Federation: International
Federation of Red Cross and Red Crescent Societies)의 기록관
으로 연결이 되어 자료를 열람할 수 있도록 되어 있다.

2) 정보 자료

① 국제적십자위원회(ICRC) 기록관
국제적십자사와 관련된 출판물 외에도 인권법 등의 관련 출

판물을 볼 수 있다. 일부 출판물은 archives.gva@icrc.org로
직접 구매요청을 해야 한다.

[국제적십자운동]

- *Red Cross Red Crescent Magazine: Israel－Palestine a Tragedy without End?*
- *Cooperation with National Societies*
- *Retroscope: Lasting Images from the Red Cross and Red Crescent Movement*
- *The Fundamental Principles of the Red Cross and Red Crescent*
- *Code of Conduct for the International Red Cross and Red Crescent Movement and Non－Governmental Organizations(NGOs) in Disaster Relief*
- *Three Emblems, One Movement, Serving Humanity*
- *Red Cross, Red Crescent, Red Crystal*
- *Manual for the Use of Technical Means of Identification by Hospital Ships, Coastal Rescue Craft, Other Protected Craft and Medical Aircraft*
- *Visibility of the Distinctive Emblem on Medical Establis-Hments, Units and Transports*
- *Protective Signs*
- *Resolutions of the 28th International Conference of the Red Cross and Red Crescent*

[국제인도법]

- *How does Law Protect in War? Cases, Documents and Teaching Materials on Contemporary Practice in International Humanitarian Law*
- *Action by the International Committee of the Red Cross in the Event of Violations of International Humanitarian Law or of Other Fundamental Rules Protecting Persons in Situations of Violence*
- *Business and International Humanitarian Law: An Introduction to the Rights and Obligations of Business Enterprises Under International Humanitarian Law*
- *The International Review of the Red Cross: French Selection 2005*
- *The Basics of International Humanitarian Law*
- *Library and Research Service: International Committee of the Red Cross*
- *Report of the Expert Meeting on Multinational Peace Operations: Applicability of International Humanitarian Law and International Human Rights Law to UN Mandated forces*
- *International Humanitarian Law: Answers to Your Questions*
- *Elements of War Crimes Under the Rome Statute of the International Criminal Court – Sources and Commentary*

- *Constraints on the Waging of War: An Introduction to International Humanitarian Law*
- *The People on War Report: ICRC Worldwide Consultation on the Rules of War*
- *Greenberg Research, Inc*
- *Compendium of Case Studies of International Humanitarian Law*
- *International Humanitarian Law: An Introduction*
- *Dictionary of the International Law of Armed Conflict*
- *Index of International Humanitarian Law*
- *DistinguisH: Combatant or Civilian? It's a Vital Distinction*
- *DistinguisH: Combatant or Civilian?*
- *Distinction: Protecting Civilians in Armed Conflict*
- *Rules of International Humanitarian Law and Other Rules Relating to the Conduct of Hostilities*
- *The Protocols Additional to the Geneva Conventions of 12 August 1949*
- *The Geneva Conventions of 12 August 1949*
- *Basic Rules of the Geneva Conventions and their Additional Protocols*
- *Commentary on the Additional Protocols of 8 June 1977 to the Geneva Conventions of 12 August 1949*
- *Summary of the Geneva Conventions of 12 August 1949 and their Additional Protocols*

- *Commentary on the Geneva Conventions of 12 August 1949. Volume II.*
- *Commentary on the Geneva Conventions of 12 August 1949. Volume III.*
- *Commentary on the Geneva Conventions of 12 August 1949. Volume IV.*
- *Commentary on the Geneva Conventions of 12 August 1949. Volume I*
- *Customary International Humanitarian Law*
- *Study on Customary International Humanitarian Law: A Contribution to the Understanding and Respect for the Rule of Law in Armed Conflict*
- *Exploring Humanitarian Law(EHL) −Guidelines for Experimentation and Evaluation*
- *Exploring Humanitarian Law(EHL) −Guidelines for Inserting EHL into the Curriculum*
- *Exploring Humanitarian Law(EHL) −Pack*
- *International Humanitarian Law at the National Level: Impact and Role of National Committees*
- *Protection of Cultural Property in the Event of Armed Conflict*
- *Punishing Violations of International Humanitarian Law a the National Level: A Guide for Common Law States*
- *National Measures to Repress Violations of Internati-*

onal Humanitarian Law(Civil Law Systems): Report on the Meeting of Experts, Geneva, 23－25 September 1997

- *Respect for International Humanitarian Law*
- *Committees or Other National Bodies for International Humanitarian Law: Report of the Meeting of Experts,* Geneva, 23－25 October 1996
- *Leaflet Showing How the ICRC's Advisory Service Functions. The Purpose of the Service is to Assist Civilian and Military Authorities in Implementing International Humanitarian Law*
- *Procedural Principles and Safeguards for Internment/Administrative Detention in Armed Conflict and Other Situations of Violence*
- *Arms Transfer Decisions: Applying International Humanitarian Law Criteria*
- *A Guide to the Legal Review of New Weapons, Means and Methods of Warfare: Measures to Implement Article 36 of Additional Protocol I of 1977*
- *Expert Meeting Report: "Humanitarian, Military, Technical and Legal Challenges of Cluster Munitions"*
- *Convention on Prohibitions or Restrictions on the Use of Certain Conventional Weapons Which May be Deemed to be Excessively Injurious or to have Indiscriminate Effects*

Policing Concepts: Highlights from the Book "to Serve and to Protect"

- *To Serve and Protect: Guide for Police Conduct and behaviour*
- *To Serve and to Protect*
- *Behaviour in Combat: Code of Conduct for Combatants. First Aid*
- *Handbook on the Law of War for Armed Forces*
- *Essentials of the Law of War*
- *Behaviour in Combat: Rules for Behaviour in Combat*
- *Weapon Contamination Manual: Reducing the Impact of Explosive Remnants of War and Landmines Through Field Activities*
- *Mine Action: Preventive Activities in the Field*
- *Arms Transfer Decisions: Applying International Humanitarian Law Criteria*
- *Targeting the Weapons: Reducing the Human Cost of Unregulated Arms Availability*

[보호(Protection)]

- *The ICRC and Civil－Military Relations in Armed Conflict*
- *Strengthening Protection in War: A Search for Professional Standards*
- *Hard Choices: Moral Dilemmas in Humanitarian Inte-*

Human Remains - A Guide to best Practice in Armed Conflicts and Other Situations of Armed Violence

- *The Missing and their Families: Documents of Reference*
- *Operational Best Practices Regarding the Management of Human Remains and Information on the Dead by Non - Specialists*
- *Armed Conflict and Family Links*
- *The Missing: End the Silence Poster*
- *The Missing - Brochure*
- *Waiting for News*
- *Restoring Family Links: A Guide for National Red Cross and Red Crescent Societies*
- *Primary Health Services: Primary Level*
- *Mobile Health Units: Methodological Approach*
- *Management of Dead Bodies After Disasters: A Field Manual for First Responders*
- *Antenatal Guidelines for Primary Health Care in Crisis Conditions*

[원조]

- *Management of Dead Bodies After Disasters: A Field Manual for First Responders*
- *Water, Sanitation, Hygiene and Habitat in Prisons*
- *Hospitals for War - Wounded: A Practical Guide for Setting up and Running a Surgical Hospital in an*

Area of Armed Conflict

- *Manuel de Nutrition Pour L'intervention Humanitaire*
- *Care in the Field for Victims of Weapons of War. A Report from the Workshop Organized by the ICRC on "Pre −Hospital Care for War and Mine Wounded"*
- *Humanitarian Action and Armed Conflict: Coping with Stress*
- *H.E.L.P. Public Health Course in the Management of Humanitarian Aid*
- *Forum: War and Water*
- *Primary Health Services: Primary Level*
- *Mobile Health Units: Methodological Approach*
- *First Aid in Armed Conflicts and Other Situations of Violence*
- *Antenatal Guidelines for Primary Health Care in Crisis Conditions*
- *War and Public Health: Handbook on War and Public Health*
- *Surgery for Victims of War*
- *War Wounds With fractures: A Guide to Surgical Management*
- *War Wounds: Basic Surgical Management: The Principles and Practice of the Surgical Management of Wounds Produced by Missiles or Explosions*
- *Amputation for War Wounds*

- *The Red Cross Wound Classification*
- *Polypropylene Technology*
- *Prosthetics and Orthotics Manufacturing Guidelines*
- *Caring for Landmine Victims*
- *Support for Life: Physical Rehabilitation Programme*
- *Mine Action: Preventive Activities in the Field*

② 국제적십자사회연합(International Federation) 기록관
다음과 같은 정기간행물을 열람할 수 있다.

- *World Disasters Report 2006*
- *Red Cross Red Crescent Magazine*
- *The Federation of the Future*
- *Annual Report 2006*
- *Programmes and Appeal 2006/2007*
- *International Red Cross and Red Crescent Movement: Guidelines for Cash Transfert Programming*
- *Tsunami 26.12.2004*
- *Strategy 2010 Mid－Term Review*
- *Practical Guide on Road Safety*
- *The Bridge*
- *Beyond Conflict*

isH

International Society of Hypertension

국제고혈압연합

① 기구

1) 소재지

소재국가	영국
주　소	isH Secretariat Hampton Medical Conferences Ltd. 113－119 High Street Hampton Hill Middlesex TW12 1NJ, U.K.
전　화	＋44 20 8979 8300
팩　스	＋44 20 8979 6700
전자우편	secretariat@isH－world.com
홈페이지	http://www.isH－world.com/default.aspx?Home

2) 성격

국제고혈압연합(isH)은 과학적 연구 및 지식의 증진에 기여하기 위해 활동하는 기구이다.

3) 설립연혁

isH는 1966년에 설립되었으며, 2007년 12월 잉글랜드와 웨일
스에서 자선단체로 등록되었다.

4) 비전 및 임무

본 협회는 전 세계의 심장혈관 관련 질병과 고혈압으로 인한
발작 그리고 심장질환의 예방과 관리에 관한 모든 방면의 연구
장려 및 촉진을 위해 존재한다.

5) 회원

isH는 전 세계 60개 이상의 국가에서 700명 이상의 회원을 두
고 있다. 회원들은 의사, 학자, 연구원 등을 포함한다.
회원혜택은 매달 발간되는 isH의 공식적인 *the Journal of Hypertension*을 구독할 수 있으며, 유럽고혈압협회(ESH: European
Society of Hypertension)의 회의에 할인가격으로 참석할 수 있다.
또한 정기적으로 발간되는 협회전자뉴스레터인 *Hypertension News*
를 열람할 수 있다.

6) 주요 행사

isH의 대표적인 주요 행사는 다음과 같다.
- 브라질고혈압협회 연간총회(Annual Meeting of the Brazilian
  Society of Hypertension), 2008년 8월 7일~9일, 브라질

리우데자네이루

- 제2회 크롬친화세포종 국제심포지엄(2nd International Symposium on Pheochromocytoma), 2008년 9월 17일~20일, 영국 케임브리지 킹스칼리지
- 제16회 임신 중 고혈압 연구를 위한 국제협회 연간세계의회(ISSHP: 16th Annual World Congress for the International Society for the Study of Hypertension in Pregnancy), 2008년 9월 20일~24일, 미국 워싱턴
- 제7회 베네수엘라 고혈압의회(VII Venezuelan Congress on Hypertension), 2008년 9월 24일~27일, 베네수엘라 카라카스

7) 주요 활동

본 협회의 주요 활동은 약 8,000여 명이 참가하는 2년 주기 과학총회(Biennial Scientific Meetings) 및 세계보건기구를 따르는 개발 및 출판활동, 타 기관 방문프로그램 등이 있다. 또한 isH는 세계적인 과학적 네트워크를 강화하고 있다.

② 정보원

1) 정보원배포정책

isH의 정보원은 'Journal', 'Public Information', 그리고 'Latest News'에서 찾아볼 수 있다. 'Journal'은 1년에 총 12차례 발간되며 열람은 http://www.jhypertension.com/를 통해 문의하여야

한다.

2) 대중정보(Public Information)

관련 기관의 웹사이트로의 링크를 제공하고 있다.

- American College of Cardiology USA
- Council for the High Blood Pressure Research of the AHA USA
- American Society of Hypertension USA
- Argentine Society of Hypertension Argentina
- Asian Pacific Society of Hypertension
- Belgian Hypertension Committee Belgium
- Belorussian Hypertension League Belarus
- Brazilian Society of Hypertension Brazil
- British Hypertension Society UK
- Canadian Hypertension Society Canada
- Chinese Hypertension League China
- Council for High Blood Pressure of the IrisH Heart Foundation Ireland
- Croatian Society of Hypertension Croatia
- DanisH Hypertension Society Denmark
- Egyptian Hypertension Society Egypt
- Estonian Society of Hypertension Estonia
- European Council for Cardiovascular Research
- European Society of Cardiology

- European Society of Hypertension
- French Society of Hypertension France
- German Hypertension Society Germany
- High Blood Pressure Research Council of Australia
- Hellenic Society of Hypertension Greece
- Hellenic Society for the Study of Hypertension Greece
- International Society for the Study of Hypertension in Pregnancy
- International Society of Hypertension in Blacks
- Israeli Society of Hypertension israel
- Italian Society of Hypertension Italy
- Japanese Society of Hypertension Japan
- Journal of Hypertension
- Korean Society of Hypertension Korea
- Latin American Society of Hypertension
- Polish Society of Hypertension Poland
- Portuguese Society of Hypertension Portugal
- Slovak Society of Hypertension Slovakia
- Slovenian Hypertension Society Slovenia
- Southern African Hypertension Society South Africa
- Spanish Society of Hypertension Spain
- Swedish Society of Hypertension Sweden
- Swiss Society of Hypertension Switzerland
- Taiwan Society of Cardiology Taiwan
- Turkish Society of Hypertension and Atherosclerosis Turkey

- Turkish Society of Hypertension and Renal Diseases Turkey
- Uruguayan Society of Hypertension Uruguay
- Venezuelan Society of Hypertension Venezuela
- World Heart Federation
- World Health Organization
- World Hypertension League

3) 보도 자료(Latest News)

웹사이트의 첫 페이지를 통해 가장 최근의 관련 보도 자료를 제공한다. 2008년 7월 현재 제공되고 있는 헤드라인은 다음과 같다.

- *isH Research Fellows*
- *Hypertension 2008 − 8,500 Participants*
- *Foundation for High Blood Pressure Research − 2009 isH Visiting Postdoctoral Award*
- *Scientific Meeting Vancouver 2010*

ISID

International Society for Infectious Diseases

국제전염성질병협회

1 기구

1) 소재지

소재국가	미국
주　　소	International Society for Infectious Diseases 1330 beacon Street, Suite 228 Brookline, MA 02446
전　　화	+1 617 277 0551
팩　　스	+1 617 278 9113
전자우편	info@isID.org
홈페이지	http://www.isID.org/

2) 성격

국제전염성질병협회(ISID)는 전염성 질병 환자들의 관리를 증진시키고, 전염성 질병에 관한 의사 및 연구자들을 교육시키며 전 세계 전염성 질병의 통제를 위해 활동한다.

3) 설립연혁

ISID는 1986년 국제전염성질병의회(ICID: International Congress on Infectious Diseases)와 전염성 질병 및 기생충 질병에 관한 국제연맹(IFIPD: International Federation on Infectious and Parasitic Diseases)의 합병에 의해 설립되었다.

ICID는 1983년 전염성 질병에 관한 연구 및 임상정보의 교환을 위한 과학적 협회로 설립되었다. ICID의 임시 경영위원회에 의해 IFIPD에 대한 초기논의가 이루어졌고, 이를 토대로 1986년 합병이 이루어졌다.

ISID는 155여 개국의 개인회원들로 구성되어 있으며, 전염성 질병 관리의 발전, 이 분야에서의 임상연구원과 과학자들의 전문성 개발 그리고 전 세계 전염성 질병의 관리를 위해 활동해오고 있다.

4) 비전 및 임무

① 연구를 통한 전염성 질병의 지식기반 증가 및 이 분야에 있어서의 개인의 전문성 개발 강화
② 전염성 질병과 미생물학의 기술적 전문성의 확장 및 전파
③ 전염성 질병의 효율적 비용관리와 통제를 위한 파트너십 창조 및 촉진

5) 조직

① 협의회(Council)

ISID는 회원들이 선출한 협의회에 의해 운영된다. 협의회의 대표들은 지리학상의 지역에 의해 구분된다.

협의회는 ISID의 활동을 관리하는 데에 있어서 위원회 및 활동그룹의 참여를 통해 경영위원회를 지원한다.

② 경영위원회(Executive Committee)

경영위원회는 ISID의 모든 활동을 감독하는 역할을 하고 있다. 이 위원회는 ISID의 위원들로 이루어져 있으며 경영위원장(Executive Director)을 지명한다.

③ 지명위원회(Nominations Committee)

지명위원회는 경영위원회의 공석을 채우기 위해 적당한 개인회원들을 추천하는 역할을 한다.

6) 회원

ISID의 회원은 155개국에서 모인 20,000명 이상의 개인들로 이루어져 있다. 이 회원들은 전염성 질병에 대한 관심을 공유하며 국경을 넘은 과학적 교환의 중요성에 대한 인식을 공유하고 있다. 이 회원들은 크게 정규회원과 통신회원으로 나뉜다.

① 정규회원(Regular Membership)

전염성 질병에 관심이 있는 모든 개인은 ISID의 회원이 될수 있다. ISID의 회원은 연간제로 이루어지고 있으며, $150

의 연간 회원비를 지불해야 한다. 단, 저소득국가나 학생의
경우 $50의 회원비를 지불하면 된다.

② 통신회원(Corresponding Membership)

통신회원은 회원비 없이 회원가입이 가능하다. 단, 정규회원과
비교하여 ICID 할인과 저널구독의 혜택은 주어지지 않는다.

7) 프로그램

ISID의 프로그램은 건강관리전문가들의 교육 및 훈련을 통한
정보 및 적합한 기술의 전파를 중심으로 이루어지고 있다. 이
프로그램들은 콘퍼런스, 워크숍, 훈련과정, 연구원 과정을 포함
한다. 새로운 질병, 에이즈, 적합한 항생제 사용 등에 관한 내
용들이 ISID 프로그램 과정에서 다루어진다.

① 국제 에이즈 임상과정 양성프로그램(International HIV/AIDS
   Clinical Training Program)

   이 프로그램은 1년간 진행되는 과정으로서 전염성 질병 임
   상연구원 및 다른 건강관리자들을 위한 교육과정이다. 1998
   넌부터 ISID는 47개국에서 약 100명의 임상연구원을 양성
   해 왔다. 프로그램의 과정은 에이즈에 감염된 성인과 아동에
   관한 공식강의, 사례논의, 실제임상과정으로 이루어진다. 에
   이즈감염, 상이한 진단결과, 환자관리, 해로운 프로토콜, 에
   이즈감염환자 치료 등에 관한 다양한 발표에 중점을 둔다.
   이 과정은 또한 실제적인 연구실 임상연구도 다룬다.

② 소규모 장학프로그램(Small Grants Program)

소규모 장학프로그램은 개발도상국의 젊은 조사자들의 준비 조사 프로젝트를 위한 기금사업이다. 이 프로그램의 목적은 전염성 질병 연구 분야의 젊은이들의 전문성 개발을 장려하고 지원하는 데에 있다.

③ 과학적 교환 협력 프로그램(Scientific Exchange Fellowship Program)

ISID의 이 프로그램은 1992년 전염성 질병을 연구하는 연구원들이 그들의 직업에 있어서 좀 더 공식성을 높이며 서로 다른 국가에서 온 연구원들의 협동을 고취하고자 설립되었다. 이 프로그램은 의학도들에게만 제한된 것은 아니며, 개발도상국의 젊은 과학자들을 지원하기 위한 것이다.

④ SSI/ISID 전염성 질병연구 협력프로그램(SSI/ISID Infectious Diseases Research Fellowship Program)

ISID와 스위스 전염성 질병 협회(SSI: Swiss Society for Infectious Diseases)는 SSI/ISID 전염성 질병연구 협력프로그램을 공동으로 지원하고 있다. 본 협력프로그램의 목적은 전염성 질병을 다루고 있는 개발도상국의 내과의들과 과학자들을 지원하는 데에 있다.

2 정보원

1) 정보원배포정책

ISID의 정보원은 'Publications'에서 찾아볼 수 있다. 이 웹페이지를 통해 ISID에서 제공하는 뉴스레터와 ISID가 주최하는 콘퍼런스의 정보 및 콘퍼런스 자료를 PDF로 열람할 수 있다.

2) 발간 자료(Publications)

① ISID News

ISID News는 1년에 네 차례 정기적으로 발간되는 뉴스레터이다. 이 뉴스레터는 모든 회원들에게 제공되고 있다. 온라인상으로 열람 가능한 대표적인 목록은 다음과 같다.

- May 2008, Special Pre‐Congress Issue
- January 2008
- September 2007
- June 2007
- February 2007
- October 2006
- May 2006, Special Pre‐Congress Issue
- February 2006
- November 2005
- June 2005
- February 2005
- October 2004

- July 2004
- January 2004, Special Pre-Congress Issue
- November 2003
- April 2003
- June 2002
- January 2002, Special Pre-Congress Issue
- September 2001
- March 2001

② *IJID: International Journal of Infectious Diseases*

IJID는 ISID의 공식적인 출판물로서 전염병학, 임상적 평가, 진단, 치료, 전염의 통제에 관한 정보를 전 세계를 통해 전염성 질병 연구원들과 임상가들에게 전하고 있다. 이 저널은 세계의 각기 다른 곳의 전염성 질병에 대한 독자들의 의학 및 문화적 요소에 대한 이해를 높이고자 한다.

본 저널은 정규회원들의 구독을 위해 한 달에 두 차례 발간되며, 회원이 아닌 경우 연간 $140의 구독비가 필요하다.

IUATLD

International Union against Tuberculous and Lung Disease

국제결핵및폐질병퇴치연맹

1 기구

1) 소재지

소재국가	프랑스
주　　소	International Union against Tuberculosis and Lung Disease(the Union) 68 boulevard Saint Michel 75006 Paris - FRANCE
전　　화	+33 1 44 32 03 .60
팩　　스	+33 43 29 90 87
전자우편	union@iuatld.org
홈페이지	http://www.iuatld.org/index_en.phtml

2) 성격

국제결핵및폐질병퇴치연맹(IUATLD)은 결핵을 다루는 유일한 자발적 국제기구이다.

3) 설립연혁

IUATLD는 1867년 파리에서 열린 전염성 질병에 관한 제1회 의학전문가국제콘퍼런스(International Conference of Medicine Specialists)에서 제안되었다. 1920년에 열린 콘퍼런스에서 총 31개 국가가 참여한 가운데 현재의 형태를 갖춘 국제결핵퇴치연맹(IUAT: International Union against Tuberculosis)이 출범하였다. 그 당시의 연맹은 국가협회 연맹의 형태로 이루어졌다.

본 연맹은 세계대전 이후 1946년에 경영위원회에 의해 재출범하였다. 세계대전 이후 첫 번째 콘퍼런스가 1950년 코펜하겐에서 열렸으며, 총 43개국이 참여하였다.

1953년 지역연맹이 설립되었으며, 1958년 최초로 국제 협력적인 임상실험이 시도되었으며, 17개국의 총 17,391명의 환자들이 참여하였다.

1961년 연맹총장(Executive Director)에 의해 산업국으로부터 새로이 독립한 국가들로의 기술, 자원, 정보 이전을 고취하기 위한 개발도상국의 연맹국가협회를 통한 공동지원프로그램(Mutual Assistance Program)이 제안되었다. 1965년부터 21개국의 75,000명 정도 아동의 결핵피부 국제공동연구가 시작되었다.

1973년 IUAT는 폐질병의 포함을 제안받게 되며, 그 결과 1986년 연맹의 이름을 현재의 IUATLD로 변경하게 되었다.

1991년 국제결핵프로그램(National Tuberculosis Programme) 모델에 대한 구상이 시작되었으며, 이와 관련된 전략은 세계보건기구의 공식정책으로 발전되었다. 1993년부터 1996년까지 교육 및 기술지원 활동이 주로 아프리카 지역에서 이루어졌다.

1998년 본 연맹은 세계보건기구의 다른 국제파트너들과 함께 결핵퇴치 운동에 참여하게 되었다. 2002년까지 지역활동이 중동국가에서 2개, 아프리카국가에서 23개, 유럽에서 14개, 남미에서 8개, 북미에서 2개가 이루어졌다.

4) 비전 및 임무

본 연맹은 결핵퇴치 보건프로그램의 개발, 실행, 평가에 관하여 각국의 우선순위 기준을 기본으로 한 국가자율성 촉진에 중점을 둔다.

① 에이즈 및 커뮤니티의 보건문제를 야기하는 결핵 및 폐질병의 모든 분야에 관한 지식 입수 및 배포

② 의사들, 의사결정자, 의견리더들, 일반 대중에게 결핵 및 폐질환의 위험성 및 이들과 관련된 커뮤니티 보건문제에 대한 심각성 전달

③ 전 세계 회원들의 활동 증진, 지원 및 협력

④ 세계보건기구 및 보건과 개발 분야의 다른 유엔기구, 정부 및 비정부기관들과의 긴밀한 협력체계 형성 및 유지

5) 조직

① 총회(General Assembly)

총회는 다른 위원회들로부터 경영, 재정, 법률 보고서를 받아 연맹의 예산측정 및 감사일정 등을 결정한다.

② 위원회(Board of Directors)

연맹은 위원회에 의해서 경영된다.

6) 회원

① 선출회원(Constituent Members)

선출회원은 보건기구 및 폐질병에 관한 서비스 단체로서 연맹의 목적을 함께 나누는 기관들이다. 각 나라마다 한 명의 회원을 선출할 수 있으며, 이 회원들은 총회에 참석하여 토론 및 투표를 하게 된다.

② 기관회원(Organizational Members)

기관회원은 선출회원이 아닌 기관 및 재단들로 이루어진다. 이 회원들 역시 총회에 참석하여 토론 및 투표를 하게 된다.

③ 명예회원(Honorary Members)

명예회원은 협회에 기여한 바가 있는 개인들로 구성된다. 명예회원은 연맹에 의해 지명된다. 명예회원은 총회에 참석하여 토론 및 투표를 하게 되고, 회원비는 면제된다.

④ 개인회원(Individual Members)

개인회원은 연맹의 목적에 동의하는 개인들로서 회원제도에 가입한 자들이다.

7) 주요 행사

- 제1회 국제연맹동남아시아지역콘퍼런스(1st International Union Conference of the South East Asia Region), 2008년 9월 8일~9월 10일
- 제39회 폐건강연맹세계콘퍼런스(39th Union World Conference on Lung Health), 2008년 10월 16일~20일
- 제17회 아프리카지역연맹콘퍼런스(17th Conference of the Union Africa Region), 2009년 3월 4일~3월 6일
- 제5회 유럽지역연맹콘퍼런스(5th Union Europe Region Conference), 2009년 5월 27일~5월 30일
- 제2회 아시아태평양지역연맹콘퍼런스(2nd Union Asia Pacific Region Conference), 2009년 9월 9일~9월 12일

8) 주요 활동

IUATLD의 주요 활동은 교육과 기술시원 빛 연구활농으로 이루어진다.

9) 파트너 기관

다음은 본 연맹의 파트너 기관 및 기관 웹사이트이다.
- 세계보건기구 - 결핵(World Health Organization(WHO) - Tuberculosis)
  홈페이지: http://www.who.int/health_topics/tuberculosis/en
- 결핵퇴치이니셔티브(Stop TB Initiative)

홈페이지: http://www.stoptb.org/

- 에이즈, 결핵, 말라리아 퇴치를 위한 글로벌기금(The Global Fund to fight AIDS, Tuberculosis and Malaria)

  홈페이지: http://www.theglobalfund.org/

- 질병 관리 및 예방센터(Centers for Disease Control and Prevention)

  홈페이지: http://www.cdc.gov/

② 정보원

1) 정보원배포정책

IUATLD의 정보원은 'International Journal of Tuberculosis & Lung Disease', 'Publications', 'Press Room' 그리고 'Lung Health Image Library'로 이루어진다. 폐건강이미지도서관(Lung Health Image Library)의 웹페이지도 운영하고 있다.

2) *IJTLD: International Journal of Tuberculosis & Lung Disease*

IJTLD는 구독신청 또는 회원가입을 통해 열람이 가능하다. 본 저널은 매월 발간되어 1년에 12권의 저널이 인쇄형태와 전자형태로 회원들 및 구독신청자들에게 배달되고 있다.

3) 발간 자료(Publications)

발간 자료는 기술적 안내(Technical Guides), 파워포인트 발표
자료(Powerpoint Presentation), 간편보고서(Fact Sheets), 그
외 교육 자료(Others Educational Resources)로 구분된다. 대부
분의 자료는 PDF로 무료열람이 가능하다.

① 기술적 안내(Technical Guides)

- *Management of Tuberculosis: A Guide for Low Income
  Countries,* 2000, 5th ed
- *Prise en Charge de la Tuberculose: Guide Pour les
  Pays à Faibles Revenus,* 2000, 5ème éd
- *Manejo de la Tuberculosis: Guia Para los Paises Con
  Escasos Recursos Economicos,* 2000, 5ta ed
- *Technical Guide: Sputum Examination for Tuberculosis
  by Direct Microscopy in Low Income Countries,* 2000,
  5th ed
- *Management of Asthma: A Guide to the Essentials of
  Good Clinical Practice,* 2005, 2nd ed
- *Tobacco Control and Prevention: A Guide for Low
  Income Countries,* 1998
- *Tuberculosis Programs Review, Planning, Technical Sup-
  port: A Manual of Methods and Procedures,* 1998
- *Epidemiologic Basis of Tuberculosis Control,* 1999
- *Bases Epidémiologiques de la Lutte Antituberculeuse,*
  1999

- *Bases Epidemiologicas del Control de la Tuberculosis,* 1999
- *Research Methods for the Promotion of Lung Health, a Guide to Protocol Development for Low Income Countries,* 2001
- *Interventions for Tuberculosis Control and Elimination,* 2002
- *Guide d'Achat des Médicaments Antituberculeux,* 2001
- *Guide for the Procurement of Anti-Tuberculosis Drugs,* 2001
- *Prevención y Control del Tabaquismo,* 1998
- *Tuberculose-Manuel Pour les Étudiants en Médecine,* 1999
- *Guia Para Médicos Especialistas,* 2003
- *Diagnostic Atlas of Intrathoracic Tuberculosis in Children,* 2003
- *Tuberculosis A Manual for Medical Students,* 1999
- *Méthodes de Recherche Pour la Promotion de la Santé Respiratoire, Guide Pour l'élaboration de Protocoles de Recherche Dans les Pays à Faibles Revenus,* 2001
- *A Tuberculosis Guide for Specialist Physicians,* 2003 - Part 1
- *A Tuberculosis Guide for Specialist Physicians,* 2003 - Part 2
- *A Tuberculosis Guide for Specialist Physicians,* 2003 -

Part 3

- *Controlled Clinical Trials in Tuberculosis. A Guide for Multicentre Trials in High Burden Countries,* 2004
- *Atlas Diagnostic de la Tuberculose Intrathoracique Chez L'enfant,* 2003
- *Management of the Child with Cough or Difficult Breathing, a Guide for Low Income Countries,* 2005, 2nd ed
- *Manual de Enfermedades Respiratorias, 2005,* 2nd ed
- *AFB Microscopy Training,* 2005 – Chapters Ⅰ – Ⅱ
- *AFB Microscopy Training,* 2005 – Chapters Ⅲ – Ⅳ
- *AFB Microscopy Training,* 2005 – References
- *Guía Para el Manejo del Asma – Medidas Estandarizadas Esenciales,* 2005, 2a ed
- *Guide Pour la Prise en Charge de L'asthme: Mesures Standardisées Essentielles,* 2005, 2ème ed
- *Normas Internacionales Para la Asistencia Antituberculosa,* 2006
- *International Standards for Tuberculosis Care,* 2006
- *Standards Internationaux Pour le Traitement de la Tuberculose,* 2006
- *Métodos de Investigación Para la Promoción de la Salud Respiratoria, Recomendaciones Para la Elaboración de Protocolos en Países de Bajos Ingresos,* 2001
- *Best Practice of the Care for Patients with Tuberculosis: A Guide for Low Income Countries,* 2007

- *Priorities for Tuberculosis Bacteriology Services in Low −Income Countries,* 2007, 2nd ed−High Resolution *PDF- (5.36 MB)*

- *Priorities for Tuberculosis Bacteriology Services in Low −Income Countries,* 2007, 2nd ed−Low Resolution *PDF(1.34 MB)*

- *Guía de Enfermería: Para la Implementación y Expansión de la Estrategia DOTS/TAES,* 2004

- *Intervenciones Para el Control y la Eliminación de la Tuberculosis,* 2002

- *Prise en Charge de L'enfant Qui tousse ou Qui a des Difficultés Respiratoires: Guide Pour les Pays à Faible Revenu,* 2005, 2ème ed

- *Bonnes Pratiques de Soins Pour les Patients Atteints de Tuberculose: Guide Pour les Pays à Faibles Revenus,* 2007

- *Management of the Child with Cough or Difficult Breathing: A Guide for Low Income Countries,* 1997

- *The Public Health Service National Tuberculosis Reference Laboratory and the National Laboratory Network,* 1998

- *Management of Asthma in Adults: A Guide for Low − Income Countries,* 1996

② 파워포인트 발표 자료(Powerpoint Presentation)

파워포인트 발표 자료는 http://www.tbrieder.org를 통해 직접 구입해야 한다.

③ 간편보고서(Fact Sheets)

- *10 Tuberculosis Facts*
- *10 Facts about Multidrug-Resistant Tuberculosis*
- *10 Facts about Tuberculosis and AIDS*
- *10 Facts about the Cost of Tuberculosis*
- *10 Facts about DOTS*
- *10 Facts about the Economic Benefits of DOTS*
- *10 Tuberculosis Facts about Women*
- *10 Facts about Tuberculosis and Mobile Populations*
- *10 Facts on Pneumonia in Children*
- *10 Facts on Tobacco*
- *A Worldwide Problem: Tobacco*
- *A Worldwide Problem: Asthma*
- *Current Challenges in Tobacco Control*
- *Global Tobacco Control Must Become a Top Public Health Priority*
- *The PATIENTS' CHARTER for Tuberculosis Care(Part of the International Standards for Tuberculosis Care)*

④ 그 외 교육 자료(Other Educational Resources)

- *AFB Smear Staining Poster*

4) 보도 자료(Press Room)

[38th Union World Conference on Lung Health 2007]
- *Analysis of Press Coverage*
- *A Selection of Articles in French*
- *Listen to the Podcasts and Powerpoint Presentations Click here*
- *Watch the Kaiser Foundation Coverage of the Conference*
- *Read the Reports from the HDN Key Correspondents Click Here*
- *Press Pack(Media Advisories and Press Releases)*
- *Final Press Release: Where do We Go from Here?*
- *Union Scientific Awards*

[Presse Pack]
- *Press Review November 2006(in French and EnglisH)*
- *Press Pack November 2006(in EnglisH and French)*
- *Press Pack November 2005*
- *Press Pack October 2004*
- *Press Pack October 2003*

[Press Releases]
- *The Work of the Union in 2005*
- *World TB Day 2005*

- *The Union Invests US$ 3 Million to Apply the DOTS Strategy to HIV*
- *Making a Difference in Child Survival in Malawi, September 2003*
- *Global Launch of World Tuberculosis Day 24th March 2003*
- *Union Announces the Release of Its Updated Website in Three Languages: EnglisH, SpanisH and French*
- *33rd Union World Conference on Lung Health, Montreal 6 - 10 October 2002*
- *Community - Based TB Care in Uganda Receives Funding from the International Union against Tuberculosis and Lung Disease*

IUFoST

International Union of Food Science & Technology
국제식량과학기술연합

① 기구

1) 소재지

소재국가	캐나다
주　　소	IUFoST Secretariat PO Box 61021 No. 19, 511 Maple Grove Drive Oakville, ontario Canada L6J 6X0
전　　화	＋1 905 815 1926
팩　　스	＋1 905 815 1574
전자우편	secretariat@iufost.org
홈페이지	http://www.iufost.org/

2) 성격

국제식량과학기술연합(IUFoST)은 국가회원제 기구로서 식량과학기술에 대한 국제적인 목소리를 내고자 하는 단체이다. 본 기구는 세계의 식량과학자들과 기술자들을 연결하고 있는 국가식량과학기구들로 이루어진 자발적인 비영리 연합체이다.

3) 설립연혁

전 세계의 영양이 필요한 인구를 위한 식량과학자 및 기술자들의 국제기구 설립에 대한 실현가능성에 대한 논의는 1962년 런던 에서 열린 제1회 국제식량과학기술의회(First International Congress of Food Science and Technology)에서 비공식적으로 이루어졌다. 이 의회 이후 국제식량과학기술위원회(International Committee of Food Science and Technology)가 형성되었다.

4) 비전 및 임무

IUFoST는 세계 식량공급 보장을 위한 식량과학기술의 역할 강화와 장거리교육, 워크숍, 통합적식량시스템(Integrated Food Systems) 등의 프로그램을 통한 세계 기아 퇴치에 그 목적이 있다.

5) 조직

① 위원회(Board)

위원회는 이사회(Governing Council)의 목적을 달성하기 위한 전략을 이행하는 역할을 한다.

② 과학협의회(Scientific Council)

과학협의회는 이사회와 위원회로부터 독립적으로 활동하며, 과학기준 및 모든 IUFoST 활동의 통합성을 유지하는 기능을 한다.

③ 이사회(Governing Council)

이사회는 위원회 구성원, 학회장(Academy President) 그리고 6개국을 대표하는 일반 회원으로 구성된다. 사무총장(Secretary‒General)은 본 연합의 재정이사가 역임한다.

④ 총회(General Assembly)

총회는 IUFoST의 정책 및 활동을 개발 및 관리한다. 총회는 정기적인 회의를 주최한다.

⑤ 국제아카데미(International Academy)

식량과학기술국제학회(IAFoST: International Academy of Food Science and Technology)는 본 학회의 연구원으로 활동하고 있는 뛰어난 식량과학자 및 기술자들로 이루어진 단체이다. 본 학회의 연구원들은 특정 기구를 대표할 수 없으며 독립적인 개인으로 활동해야 한다.

⑥ 감사자문위원회(Audit Advisory Committee)

감사자문위원회는 적합한 회계관리 절차수립에 관한 자문역할을 한다.

⑦ 규정자문위원회(Constitution Advisory Committee)

규정자문위원회는 IUFoST 규정 및 세칙의 개정에 관한 업무를 담당한다.

⑧ 지명자문위원회(Nominations Advisory Committee)

지명자문위원회는 임원 등의 역할에 충분한 능력을 가진 자를 추천하는 책임을 갖고 있다.

⑨ 국제식량공학협회(isFE: International Society of Food Engineering)

isPE는 IUFoST의 특별이익단체로서 개인회원을 기반으로 한 연구, 교육과정 및 국제표준화 등에 관한 협동 및 네트워킹을 강화하기 위한 글로벌 협회이다.

⑩ isOPOW

isOPOW는 IUFoST의 상임위원회이다. isOPOW는 음식에 포함되어 있는 수분 및 생물학적 시스템 등에 대한 이해를 증진시키기 위한 활동을 한다.

⑪ 주요교육과정연합(Corc Curricula Working Group)

주요교육과정연합은 식량과학기술 전공의 대학과정의 주요 과목을 개발한다.

⑫ 원거리교육프로젝트팀(Distance Education Task force)

IUFoST는 전 세계의 기아를 완화하는 데 기여하고 있다. 이와 관련하여 부가가치적 식량처리과정을 위한 잘 훈련된 기술자들을 통해 세미나 또는 워크숍과 같은 이 산업의 전문가들을 위한 교육활동을 제공한다.

6) 주요 활동

IUFoST는 교육프로그램, 워크숍, 지역 심포지엄과 식량과학기술 국제아카데미를 통해 글로벌 식량과학기술의 증진을 촉진시킨다.

또한 2년마다 열리는 세계의회, IAFoST, 과학저널, 온라인 저널, 정기적인 과학정보 게시판을 통한 과학적 지식과 아이디어의 세계적 교환을 장려하고 있다.

7) 지역단체, 특별이익단체, 상임위원회(Regional Groups, Special Interest Groups, Standing Committees)

① ALACCTA(Latin American and Caribbean Food Science and Technology Associations)
남아메리카 및 캐리비안 지역의 활동은 ALACCTA로 대표된다. ALACCTA는 남아메리카 및 캐리비안 식량과학기술 협회들이 함께할 수 있는 지역 세미나 및 국제 전문가 과정 등을 매해 개최하고 있다. 현재 총 13개국의 협회들이 ALACCTA에 등록되어 있다.

② EFFoST(European Federation of Food Science and Technology)
EFFoST는 식량과학기술 유럽연합으로 IUFoST의 지역단체의 하나로서 1982년에 비영리협회로 설립되었다.

③ FIFSTA(ASEAN Food Science and Technology)
ASEAN 식량과학기술의 활동은 FIFSTA를 통해 이루어지

고 있다. 최근 베트남의 참여로 인해 현재 총 7개 국가가
공동의 노력을 투자하고 있다.

④ WAAFoST(Western African Association of Food Science
and Technology)
WAAFoST는 서아프리카 식량과학기술협회를 뜻하며, 지역
및 비정부, 비영리 전문기관으로 활동하고 있다.

② 정보원

1) 정보원배포정책

IUFoST의 정보원은 'Latest News', 'Scientific Reports & Resources', 그리고 'Publications & Reviews'로 나뉘어 제공되고
있다. 과학보고서 및 자료(Scientific Reports & Resources)는
과학정보 게시판과 기술보고서, 정보 및 자문 한마디 그리고
데이터베이스로 이루어진다. 출판물은 온라인 열람 서비스는
제공되고 있지 않으나, 최근 발간된 서적에 대한 자세한 설명
이 제공된다.

2) 보도 자료(Latest News)

보도 자료의 최근 대표적인 목록은 다음과 같다. 모든 보도 자
료는 PDF로 다운로드가 가능하다.

- *World Congress Young Scientists Address*
- *IUFoST Global Food Industry Awards*
- *IUFoST Food Science and Technology Handbook*
- *IUFoST Annoucnes New Fellows of the International Academy of Food Science and Technology*
- *Professor M.S. Swaminathan to Deliver DistinguisHed Lecture at the 14th World Congress*

3) 과학보고서 및 자료(Scientific Reports & Resources)

① 과학정보게시판(SIB: Scientific Information Bulletins)
과학위원회(Scientific Council)는 과학정보게시판을 운영하여 유익한 정보를 제공하고 있다.

- BEST PRACTICES IN RISK and CRISIS COMMUNICATION: Advice for Food Scientists and Technologists, October 2007
- BIOTECHNOLOGY and FOOD, February 2005
- BOVINE SPONGIFORM ENCEPHALOPATHY(BSE), February 2004
- EQUIVALENCE IN FOOD SAFETY MANAGEMENT, December 2007
- FOOD DEFENSE, September 2007
- NANOTECHNOLOGY and FOOD, December 2007
- ObeSITY, Revised October 2007
- SAFETY, RisK and the PRECAUTIonARY PRINCIPLE,

August 2007

- TRANS FATTY ACIDS, May 2006

② 정보 및 자문 한마디(Information & Advisory Statements)
  영국의 식량과학기술연구소(IFST: Institute of Food Science
  & Technology)에서 제공하는 정보를 수록하고 있다.
  IUFoST의 웹페이지뿐 아니라 직접 IFST의 홈페이지
  (http://www.ifst.org/)에서도 같은 내용을 열람할 수 있다.
  [정보한마디(Information Statements)]

- AIDS and the Food Handler(February 2003)
- Avian Influenza and Food(March 2007)
- Bovine Spongiform Encephalopathy(BSE) and Variant
  Creutzfeldt − Jakob Disease(vCJD)(November 2004)
- BST(January 2004)
- Campylobacteriosis(October 2007)
- Cyclospora(March 2003)
- Dietary Fibre(April 2007)
- Food Allergy(October 2005)
- Food Irradiation(January 2006)
- Genetic Modification of Food(July 2004)
- 3 − MCPD(February 2003)
- Mycotoxins(February 2006)
- Nanotechnology(February 2006)
- Olestra(January 2004)
- Organic Food(February 2005)

- Phytosterol Esters(Plant Sterol and Stanol Esters) (January 2005)
- Salt(February 2007)
- Trans Fatty Acids(February 2007)
- Verocytotoxin‒Producing E Coli Food Poisoning and Its Prevention(November 2004)

[자문한마디(Advisory Statements)]
- Contamination of Water Supplies(January 2004)
- NEW "Don't Spread Germs: Avoiding Cross‒Contamination in the Home": Contribution to UK 2008 Food Safety Week
- Don't Spread Germs‒Avoiding Cross‒Contamination in the Home(March 2004)
- Food Safety in Our Hands(March 2003)
- Keeping Food Safe: "4C's‒and a K"(May 2007)
- Stop‒Think‒Wash(March 2005)

③ 기술보고서(Technical Reports)
각종 콘퍼런스에서 발표된 자료를 PDF 및 PPT로 열람 가능하다.
[2005년 3월 MIFT‒IUFoST 콘퍼런스]
- ***Kuala Lumpur Programme***
- ***Food Processing: Heat‒formed Compounds Including Acrylamide and Food Safety, Dr. David Lineback,***

President −Elect, IUFoST, USA

- *Safety of Genetically Modified Food Crops, Dr. Ruud Valyasevi*

- *Perspectives to Improve the Global Nutrition Situation: National Development, International Trade and Role of Food Trade in Solving Nutrition Problems, Prof. John Lupien, Adjunct Professor of Food Science, University of Massachusetts, USA*

- *Gaining a Competitive Advantage in Sensory Information, Dr. Herbert Stone, President, IFT and President, Tragon Corporation, USA*

- *EU Food Labelling Regulations, Prof. J. Ralph Blanchfield, Mbe, Chair, IFST External Affairs, UK*

- *Recent Developments in Regulation of Food Safety and Primary Products in Australia and New Zealand, Prof. Ken Buckle, Professor of Food Science and Technology, the University of New South Wales, Australia*

- *Codex and WTO updates on Biotechnology, Functional Foods, Food Quality and Safety, Prof. John Lupien, Adjunct Professor of Food Science, University of Massachusetts, USA*

- *Major Causes of Food Borne Diseases in Europe, Prof. Dr. Ing. Dr. h.c. Walter Spiess, Past President, IUFoST, c/o University of Karlsruhe, Germany*

- *HACCP Application in Ready −to −Serve Meals with*

Fresh Components, Prof. Dr. Ing. Dr. h.c. Walter Spiess, Past President, IUFoSt, c/o University of Karlsruhe, Germany

- *BSE/vCJD ‑ The European ongoing Story, Prof. Ralph Blanchfield*

[2005년 3월 IUFoST 상하이 심포지엄]
- *Shanghai Programme*
- *Benefits of Food Science Information to the Innovation Process, Dr Jeremy Selman, General Manager, International Food Information Service, UK*
- *Business Innovation for Chinese Food Industry: Hong Kong Case Study, Mr Leo Yuen, Hong Kong Food Science and Technology Association, Hong Kong*
- *New Trends in Food Protection, Preserving Food against Spoilage and Pathogens with Natural Solutions, Mr Stephane Constant, Vice President, Food Safety and Protection, Danisco Specialties*
- *Emerging Processing Technologies for New Product Development, Dr Jason Wan, Senior Research Scientist, Food Science Australia, Australia*
- *Development of New Test Methods for the Chinese Food Industry, Prof Shi Xianming, School of Food Science, Shanghai Jiaotong University, China*
- *Keynote Presentation: International Trends in Functional*

Food Development, Dr Mary Schmidl, Adjunct Professor, University of Minnesota, USA

- *Safety Considerations and Evaluations on Functional Foods, Prof Wang Yin, Vice Director, Institute of Functional Food Research, Zhejiang Academy of Medical Sciences, China*

- *Functional Food from Traditional Experience to Modern Production, Prof Cherl − Ho Lee, Korea University, Korea*

- *Advantages and Disadvantages of Food Products with Special Health Benefit, Prof Dr. Hans Steinhart, Director, Institute of Biochemistry and Food Chemistry, University of Hamburg, Germany*

- *Functional Properties of Probiotics and Prebiotics, a Chinese Research Perspective, Dr. Liu Zhenmin, R & D Manager, Junyao Dairy Group, China*

- *Functional Food Ingredients from Tea and Other Plant Sources, Assoc Prof Tu Youying, Department of Tea Science, Zhejiang University, China*

[2004년 5월 FiCEE/IUFoST 베를린 콘퍼런스]
- *Final berlin Programme*
- *The Following Reports from the Berlin Conference are Available Online in MS Power Point*
- *European Food Safety Authority: Progress to Date and*

Future Prospects, Dr. Geoffrey Podger, Executive Director, EFSA, Belgium

- *Impact of EU Food Related Legislation on SME in the New EU Member States, Prof. Arpad Somogyi, Prec − Accession Adviser, EU Twinning Project Food Safety Office, Ministry of Agriculture and Rural Development, Hungary*

- *EU Legislation on Food Additives, Dr. Michael Knowles, Director, Science and Regulatory Affairs, Europe, Eurasia and Middle East SBU, Coca − Cola, Belgium*

- *EU Hygiene Legislation with Regard to Food Ingredients and food Additives, Prof. Andras Sebok, General Manager, Campden & Chorleywood, Hungary*

- *Requirements of Major Retailers with Respect to Auditing Standards/the Role of Third Party Auditing Under Market Developments, Ms. Carole Payne, EFSis Ltd., UK*

- *Microbiological Risk Assessment, Dr. Edda Bartelt, Federal Institute of Risk Assessment, Germany*

- *Risk Assessment of Biological Active Substances in Herbs and Spices, Prof. Dr. Herbert Buckenhüskes, Germany*

- *Advantages and Disadvantages of Food Products with Special Health Benefits, Prof. Dr. Dr. Hans Steinhart, Director, Institute of Biochemistry and Food Chemistry,*

University of Hamburg, Germany

④ 데이터베이스(Database)

식량 관련 사이트로의 링크를 제공하고 있다.

- International HACCP Alliance Food Safety − Related Database

  홈페이지: sciencedata.tamu.edu/search.html

- Food Animal Residue Avoidance Databank(FARAD)

  홈페이지: www.farad.org/faradpro

- Food and Agriculture Organization(FAO)

  홈페이지: www.fao.org

- FAO Databases − FAOSTAT

  홈페이지: apps.fao.org

- AQUASTAT

  홈페이지: www.fao.org/ag/agl/aglw/aquastat/main

- FAOSTAT − Agriculture

  홈페이지: apps.fao.org/page/collections?subset＝agriculture

- FAOSTAT − Nutrition

  홈페이지: apps.fao.org/page/collections?subset＝nutrition

- FAOSTAT − FisHeries

  홈페이지: apps.afo.org/page/collections?subset＝fisHeries

- FAOSTAT − Food

  홈페이지: apps.fao.org/page/collections?subset＝FoodQua-lity

- FisHERS

홈페이지:(www.fao.org/fi/statist/fisoft/fisHers.asp

- FisHSTAT

  홈페이지: www.fao.org/fi/statist/fisoft/fisHplus.asp

- Foris

  홈페이지: www.fao.org/forestry/foris/webview/forestry2/
  index.jsp?siteId = 1141&langId = 1

- INPhO

  홈페이지: www.fao.org/inpho

- PAAT Information System

  www.fao.org/PAAT/html/home.htm

- TERRASTAT

  홈페이지: www.fao.org/ag/agl/agll/terrastat

- FAO David Lubin Memorial Library

  홈페이지: www.fao.org/library/_info_services/IndexEN.htm

- FAOLEX

  홈페이지: http://faolex.fao.org/faolex/index.htm

- World Health Organization(WHO)

  홈페이지: www.who.int

- The WHO/FAO Acrylamide in Food Network

  홈페이지: www.acrylamide − food.org

- WHO Information Sources

  홈페이지: www.who.int/home/info.html

- WHO Library

  홈페이지: www.who.int/hlt

- WHO Virtual Reference Desk

홈페이지: www.who.int/hlt/virtuallibrary/EnglisH/virtuallib.htm
- WHO Statistical Information System(WHOSis)
  홈페이지: www.who.int/whosis
- Codex Alimentarius
  홈페이지: www.fao.org/waicent/faoinfo/economic/esn/codex
- GFSA Food Additives Database
  홈페이지: wwww.codexalimentarius.net/gsfaonline/additives/
  search.html
- the EU Acrylamide Research Database
  홈페이지: www.ifst.org/acreu2_3.xls
- EU Community Research and Development Information
  Service(CORDis) and Databases
  홈페이지: www.cordis.lu/en/home.html
- the EU "Informall" Food Allergens Database
  홈페이지: http://foodallergens.ifr.ac.uk
- United Nations University
  홈페이지: www.unu.edu/hq/rector_office/unu－system.htm
- International Standards Organization(isO)
  홈페이지: www.iso.ch
- International Standards Organization(isO), World Trade
  Organization
- (WTO) and World Trade
  홈페이지: www.iso.ch/wtotbt/wtotbt.htm
- World Trade Organization
  홈페이지: www.wto.org

- World Trade Organization(WTO) Agreement on Technical Barriers to Trade
  홈페이지: www.wto.org/wto/legal/finalact.htm
- World Trade Organization(WTO) SPS Information Management System
  홈페이지: spsims.wto.org/
- USDA Nutrient Database for Standard Reference, Nutrient Data Laboratory Home Page
  홈페이지: www.nal.usda.gov/fnic/foodcomp
- Organization for Economic Co−Operation and Development(OECD) Biotech Database
  홈페이지: webdomino1.oecd.org/ehs/bioprod.nsf
- Gene Files A Database
  홈페이지: www.genefiles.org
- Protein Sequence Database(SWisS−PROT)
  홈페이지: us.expasy.org/sprot/sprot−top.html
- Kyoto Encyclopedia of Genes and Genomes(KEGG)
  홈페이지: www.genome.ad.jp/kegg
- Protein Data Bank(PDB)
  홈페이지: www.rcsb.org/pdb
- Physical Properties of Food Database
  홈페이지: www.nelfood.com

4) 출판물(Publications & Reviews)

2008년 7월 현재 웹페이지상에 제공되고 있는 출판물 안내는
다음과 같다.

- *Sustainable Development at Risk Ignoring the Past Joseph
  H. Hulse*, by Robert D. Reichert, Industrial Research
  Assistance Program, National Research Council of Canada,
  Ottawa, Canada

IUHPE

International Union for Health Promotion and Education
국제보건증진및교육연맹

1 기구

1) 소재지

소재국가   프랑스
주   소   IUHPE/UIPES 42 Boulevard de la Liberation
           93203 Saint‑Denis Cedex, France
전   화   +33 1 48 13 71 20
팩   스   +33 1 48 09 17 67
전자우편   iuhpe@iuhpe.org
홈페이지   http://www.iuhpe.org/

2) 성격

국제보건증진및교육연맹(IUHPE)은 전 세계적으로 보건을 증진
시키고 국가 간 보건평등 성취에 기여하기 위한 글로벌 네트워
크의 앞서 가는 기관이다.

3) 설립연혁

IUHPE는 반세기의 역사를 지닌다. 본 연맹은 다양한 회원들로부터 양질의 활동을 벌이며 지식기반을 증진시킬 수 있는 기록유지시스템을 형성하고 보건증진의 효과성을 증가시키기 위해 활동하고 있다.

4) 비전 및 임무

IUHPE의 임무는 전 세계 보건을 촉진하고 국가 간 보건평등을 실현시키고자 하는 데에 있다.

① 보건홍보

② 효과적 건강 증진에 관한 지식개발 및 보건교육개발

③ 정책 및 실제적 효과성 증가

④ 건강 증진 및 보건교육을 위한 역량 강화

5) 조직

IUHPE는 지역사무소를 중심으로 활동한다. 본 연맹의 활동은 세계보건기구, 유네스코, 유니세프, 그 외 정부 간 기구 및 비정부기구 등과의 긴밀한 협동하에 이루어지고 있다.

6) 회원

① 평회원(Trustee Members)

평회원은 건강 증진 및 보건교육을 담당하는 국가단위의 기구들로 이루어진다. 해당 회원기구들은 다음과 같다.

- 오스왈도 크루즈 재단, 대중보건 국립학교(Oswaldo Cruz

Foundation, National School of Public Health), 브라질
(Brazil)

- 건강캐나다(Health Canada), 캐나다(Canada)
- 보건개발국(Health Development Agency), 영국 잉글랜
  드(England, U.K.)
- 보건교육 및 증진센터(Centre for Health Education and
  Promotion), 에스토니아(Estonia)
- 건강 증진센터(Centre for Health Promotion), 핀란드(Finland)
- 프랑스보건교육및예방국가연구소(French National Institute
  for Prevention and Health Education), 프랑스(France)
- 보건개발국가연구소(National Institute for Health and Development), 헝가리(Hungary)
- 보건국 보건증진팀(Health Promotion Unit, Department
  of Health), 아일랜드(Irelan)
- 하트파일(Heartfile), 파키스탄(Pakistan)
- 보건복지부(Ministry of Health and Social Services), 캐
  나다 퀘벡(Quebec, Canada)
- 보건부 보건증진국(Department of Health Promotion, Ministry of Health), 스페인(Spain)
- 건강 증진 및 질병 예방연구소(Institute for Health Promotion and Disease Prevention), 네덜란드(the Netherlands)
- 질병 관리 및 예방센터(Centers for Disease Control and
  Prevention), 미국(United States)
- 웨일스국가의회 건강 증진부(Health Promotion Division,

National Assembly for Wales), 영국 웨일스(Wales, U.K.)
- 스위스건강 증진(Health Promotion Switzerland), 스위스-
  (Switzerland)

② 기관회원(Institutional Members)
기관회원은 건강 증진 및 보건교육과 관련하여 하나 또는
그 이상의 분야에 대한 연구 등에 관여하는 국제, 국가, 지
역 단위의 기구들로 구성된다.

③ 개인회원(Individual Members)
개인회원은 IUHPE의 사명, 목표 및 목적을 지지하는 개인
들로 구성된다.

④ 학생회원(Students Members)
학생들은 특별회원가로 회원가입이 가능하며, 미래의 건강
증진에 영향을 주고자 하는 젊은 전문가들과 다른 학생들과
의 글로벌네트워크(www.isecn.org)에 가입할 수 있다.

7) 주요 행사

- 호주건강 증진학교협회국가콘퍼런스(Australian Health Promoting Schools Association National Conference), 2008년 4
  월 2일~4일, 호주
  홈페이지: www.sapmea.asn.au/ahpsa2008
- 제9회 북유럽 대중보건 콘퍼런스(9th Nordic Public Health

Conference), 2008년 6월 11일~13일, 스웨덴

홈페이지: www.fhi.se/nordfolkhalsa2008

- 2008 행동영향에 관한 통합적 마케팅 커뮤니케이션 여름훈
  련프로그램(2008 Summer Training Programme on Integrated Marketing Communication for behavioral Impact), 2008
  년 7월 7일~26일, 미국

  홈페이지: http://steinhardt.nyu.edu/imc/
- 2008 유럽 여름학교(European Summer School 2008), 2008
  년 7월 14일~25일, 노르웨이

  홈페이지: www.etc－summerschool.eu
- 2008 대중보건의회(2008 Public Health Congress), 2008년
  7월 23일~25일, 미국

  홈페이지: www.publichealthcongress.com
- 세계사회마케팅콘퍼런스(World Social Marketing Conference),
  2008년 9월 29일~30일, 영국

  홈페이지: http://www.tcp－events.co.uk/wsmc

8) 관련 기관

다음은 IUHPE의 관련 기관에 대한 연락처이다.

① 세계보건기구(World Health Organization)

　　주 소: World Health Organization Avenue Appia 20 CH

　　　　－1211 Geneva 27 Switzerland

　　전 화: ＋41 22 791 2111

　　팩 수: ＋41 22 791 3111

Telex: 415 416

Telegraph: UNisANTE GENEVA

전자우편(일반): info@who.int

전자우편(문서): library@who.int

전자우편(출판물) publications@who.int

홈페이지: http://www.who.int

[지역사무소]

- 아프리카지역사무소(AFRO: WHO Regional Office for Africa)

  홈페이지: http://www.whoafr.org

- 미국/미국지역보건기구(PAHO: WHO Regional Office for the Americas/Pan American Health Organization)

  홈페이지: http://www.paho.org/

- 동부지중해지역사무소(EMRO: WHO Regional Office for the Eastern Mediterranean)

  홈페이지: http://www.who.sci.eg

- 유럽지역사무소(EURO: WHO Regional Office for Europe)

  홈페이지: http://www.who.dk

- 동남아시아지역사무소(SEARO: WHO Regional Office for South - East Asia)

  홈페이지: http://www.whoseas.org

- 서태평양지역사무소(WPRO: WHO Regional Office for the Western Pacific)

  홈페이지: http://www.who.org.ph/

② 유니세프(UNICEF)

　주 소: UNICEF 3 United Nations Plaza New York New
　　　　York 10017 USA

　전 화: +1 212 326 7000

　팩 스: +1 212 887 7465

　전자우편: netmaster@unicef.org

　홈페이지: http://www.unicef.org

③ 유네스코(UNESCO)

　주 소: UNESCO 7, Place de Fontenoy 75007 Paris France

　전 화: +33 1 46 68 10 00

　팩 스: +33 1 45 67 16 90

　홈페이지: http://www.unesco.org

④ 유엔하비타트(UN‑HABITAT)

　주 소: UN‑HABITAT P.O. Box 30030, GPO, Nairobi,
　　　　00100, Kenya

　전 화: (254‑20) 7621234(교환)/7 623120(정보서비스팀)

　팩 스: (254‑20) 7624266/7624267/7624264/7623477/624060

　전자우편: infohabitat@unhabitat.org

　홈페이지: http://www.unhabitat.org/

⑤ 유럽의회(European Commission)

　주 소 European Commission Euroforum Building Rue
　　　　Robert Stumper L‑2929 Luxembourg

전　화: +352 4301 32 719

팩　스: +352 4301 34 511

전자우편: sanco－mailbox@cec.eu.int

홈페이지: http://europa.eu.int/comm/dg05/phealth/index_ph.htm

⑥ 국제교육(Education International)

　　주 소: Education International 155 Blvd. Emile

　　　　　 Jacqmain(8) 1210 Brussels, belgium

　　전 화: +32 2 224 0611

　　팩 스: +32 2 224 0606

　　전자우편: educint@ei－ie.org

　　홈페이지: www.ei－ie.org

② 정보원

1) 정보원배포정책

IUHPE의 정보원은 'Publications'와 'Links'로 나뉜다. 발간 자료(Publications)는 저널, 비디오, 특별보고서로 나뉘어 있다.

2) 발간 자료(Publications)

① 저널(Journals)

모든 저널들은 온라인상으로의 무료열람은 불가능하고, 직접 구독 문의를 해야 한다. 아래의 모든 저널들은 IUHPE

의 공식적인 저널들이다.

- *Promotion & Education – P&E*
- *Health Promotion International – HPI*
- *Health Education Research – HER*
- *Reviews of Health Promotion and Education online –*
  RHPEO, 전자저널

② 비디오(Video)

비디오 자료는 구매양식을 작성하여 구매신청을 하거나 jcadinu@iuhpe.org로 이메일 문의 후 구매할 수 있다. 구매 가능한 목록은 다음과 같다.

[Alain Dubuc]

- *La Santé Sous Observation* – 25 Minutes – 2000 – N° Pour Commander: V – 418

[Alexandre berlin]

- *Health and the European Community* – 34 Minutes – 1998 – N° Ref: V – 428
- *La Santé et la Communauté Européenne* – 30 Minutes – 1998 – N° Ref: V – 415

[David McQueen]

- *A View from the CDC* – 25 Minutes – 1999 – N° Ref: V – 437

[Felix Gutzwiller]

- *the Swiss Health Care System* - 25 Minutes - 1998 - N°
  Ref: V - 432

[Fred Paccaud]

- *Réformes des Systèmes de Santé et Aide Aux Pays en
  Voie de Développement* - 25 Minutes - 1998 - N° Ref:
  V - 423

[Heather MacLean]

- *Women's Health* - 26 Minutes - 1998 - N° Ref: V - 435

[Ilona Kickbusch]

- *the Future of Public Health* - 27 Minutes - 1997 - N°
  Ref: V - 434
- *Le Futur de la Santé Publique* - 27 Minutes - 1997 -
  N° Ref: V - 421

[Irving Rootman]

- *Evaluation and Health Promotion* - 22 Minutes - 1997
  - N° Ref: V - 440
- *Evaluation et Promotion de la Santé* - 22 Minutes -
  1997 - N° Ref: V - 426

[Jean Rochon]

- *Going from Words to Action* − 34 Minutes − 1997 − N° Ref: V − 43
- *De la Parole à L'action* − 34 Minutes − 1997 − N° Ref: V − 424

[Jean − Pierre Deschamps]

- *Poverty and Health* − 23 Minutes − 1997 − N° Ref: V − 430
- *Pauvreté et Santé* − 25 Minutes − 1997 − N° Ref: V − 417

[Lawrence Green]

- *the Logic of Health Promotion in North America* − 28 Minutes − 1999 − N° Ref: V − 431

[Lucien Abenhaim]

- *Toward a New Public Health* − 28 Minutes − 2000 − N° Ref: V − 427
- *Vers Une Nouvelle Santé Publique* − 26 Minutes − 2000 − N° Ref: V − 414

[Marc Danzon]

- *How Transferable Are Health Care Systems?* − 24 Minutes − 1998 − N° Ref: V − 429
- *Les Systèmes de Santé S'exportent − ils?* − 23 Minutes − 1998 − N° Ref: V − 416

[Michael Marmot]

- *the Whitehall Studies* − 33 Minutes − 1997 − N° Ref: V − 436
- *Les Etudes de Whitehall* − 35 Minutes − 1997 − N° Ref: V − 422

[Michel Clair]

- *Transforming Health Care Systems, the Quebec Experience* − 35 Minutes − 2001 − N° Ref: V − 444
- *Transformer les Systèmes de Santé, L'exemple du Quèbec* − 41 Minutes − 2001 − N° Ref: V − 443

[Patrice Huerre]

- *Prévention et Santé de L'adolescent* − 27 Minutes − 1998 − N° Ref: V − 420

[Spencer Hagard]

- *Revisiting the Ottawa Charter* − 29 Minutes − 1997 − N° Ref: V − 433
- *Une Relecture de la Charte d'Ottawa* − 29 Minutes − 1997 − N° Ref: V − 419

[Victor Rodwin]

- *Comparative Health Care Systems, the State of the Art* − 36 Minutes − 2000 − N° Ref: V − 438

- *L'art de Comparer les Systèmes de Santé* – 34 Minutes – 2000 – N° Ref: V – 425

③ 특별보고서(Special Reports)

IUHPE의 연구보고서 시리즈이다.

- *The Evidence of Health Promotion Effectiveness*
- *Model Legislation for Tobacco Control: A Policy Development and Legislative Drafting Manual*

3) 링크(Links)

① 관련 기관 웹사이트(Sources)

- ABRASCO – Brazilian Association of Collective Health
- ABRASCO – Brazilian Association of Collective Health
- American Public Health Association
- Atlas – A Website Database of Mental Health Resources
- Best Practices Learning Centre
- Canadian Mental Health Support Network
- Center for Health Promotion at the University of Toronto
- Center for World Indigenous Studies
- Centre for Health Promotion Studies at the University of Alberta
- Centre for International Cooperation in Health and Development Inc.
- Centre for International Health Studies

- Centre for Science and Environment
- Centre for Social Justice
- Cochrane Health Promotion and Public Health Field
- Commission on Macroeconomics and Health
- Conference of NGOs(ConGO)
- The Caledon Institute for Social Policy
- The Canadian Council for Social Development
- The Communication Initiative
- ETR Associates
- EuroHealthNet
- European Multilingual Thesaurus on Health Promotion
- European Network for Workplace Health Promotion
- European Training in Effective Adolescent Care and Health
- European Who's Who in Health Promotion
- Evidence in Ethnicity, Health and Diversity
- Framework Convention Alliance
- Global Directory of Health Information Resource Centers
- Global Health Calendar
- GLOBALink－The International Tobacco－Control Network
- Health Equity Network
- Health in Action
- Health Promotion Hot Links
- Health Promotion Index
- Health Promotion on the Internet

- Health Promotion Research Internet Network
- Health! Canada Online Magazine
- Healthlink Worldwide
- HealthWrights
- The Healthy Way: The European Site of Materials for Adult Health Education
- IUHPE Student and Early Career Network
- id21 Health: the New Health Research Reporting Service
- Institute for Global Communications
- Institute for Research on Public Policy
- International Alliance of Patients' Organizations
- International Institute for Health Promotion
- International Network for the Availability of Scientific Publications – Health
- International Public Health Watch
- International Society for Equity in Health
- International Union against Cancer
- Jakarta Declaration on Health Promotion into the 21st Century(1997)
- John's Hopkins University Center for Communications Programs
- Massive Effort
- Mental Health Works
- Minority Health Project
- The Mental Health Promotion Unit, Health Canada

- National Heart, Lung and Blood Institute Healthy People 2010 Gateway
- Netlinks: A Database of Internet Resources in Public Health
- Ontario Health Promotion Resource System
- Organization for Economic Co-operation and Development
- Ottawa Charter for Health Promotion(1986)
- PAHO/WHO Online Bookstore
- Population-Environment Resources
- Prevention Dividend Project
- Royal Society for the Promotion of Health
- Saving Women's Lives
- SHARED
- Society for Public Health Education
- Student Dietician WWW Gateway
- Sundsvall Statement on Supportive Environments for Health(1991)
- United Nations
- United Nations Development Programme
- United Nations Environmental Programme
- United Nations Population Fund
- WHO Health Promotion Glossary(PDF)
- WomenWatch
- Working Groups on Girls
- World Food Programme

- WWW Virtual Library: Public Health

② 연구 관련 웹사이트(Research)
- British Medical Association Library
- The Combined Health Information Database
- Directory of Electronic Health Science Journals
- Health Promotion Index – United Kingdom
- Health Promotion Researchers Internet Network
- Information Waystations & Staging Posts
- International Bibliographic Information on Dietary Supplements – Database
- International Network for the Availability of Scientific Publications
- ISI – Thompson Scientific
- Medline Plus
- MedWeb Plus
- National Center for Health Statistics – CDC, USA
- National Electronic Library for Health – NHS, UK
- Netlinks – A Database of Internet Resources for Public Health
- Netting the Evidence
- Oxford University Press
- Pub Med, National Library of Medicine
- Sage Publications
- Science Direct

IUNS

International Union of Nutritional Sciences
국제영양학연맹

① 기구

1) 소재지

소재국가	미국
주 소	International Union of Nutritional Sciences (IUNS) c/o UCLA School of Public Health Dr. Osman Galal, Secretary General P.O. Box 951772 Los Angeles, California 90095 – 1772 U.S.A.
전 화	+1 310 206 9639
팩 스	+1 310 794 1805
전자우편	info@iuns.org
홈페이지	http://www.iuns.org/

2) 성격

국제영양학연맹(IUNS)은 식량 및 영양정보와 국제친교와 관련된 활동을 하는 기구이다.

3) 설립연혁

1946년 7월 런던에서 열린 영국영양협회(British Nutrition Society)에 의한 회의에서 처음으로 IUNS에 대한 제안이 이루어졌다. 이 회의는 13개국에서 모인 22인의 연구원이 참석하였다. 2년 후인 1948년 6월에 열린 국제임시위원회(International Provisional Committee)에서 IUNS의 법령 및 세칙이 논의되었다. 또한 이 회의에서 연맹의 주요 목적이 정의되었다. 또한, 소규모의 행정위원회(Executive Committee)가 지정되었다.

그 이후로 IUNS는 지속적으로 발전해 왔다. 의회뿐 아니라 다른 중요한 활동들이 장기적인 계획과 효율적인 행정을 바탕으로 개발되었다. 연맹의 업무는 총회(General Assembly)에 의해 주도되며, 총회는 IUNS의 최상위 조직으로 활동한다.

4) 비전 및 임무

① 글로벌단계에서의 국제협력을 통한 영양학, 연구, 개발 성취 촉진
② 현대커뮤니케이션기술을 이용한 영양학에 관한 정보의 배포 및 영양학자들 간의 커뮤니케이션과 협동 장려

5) 조직

본 연맹은 협의회(Council)와 회원기관들이 주요 조직을 이루고 있으며, 임명의원회(Nominating Committee) 및 외부그룹대표단(Representatives to External Groups)으로 이루어져 있다.

6) 대책본부(Task forces)

2002년 3월 일본 오사카에서 열린 IUNS 협의회에서, 연맹위원
회 및 대책본부에 대한 검토작업이 이루어졌으며, 생산적이거
나 효과적이지 못한 기능들에 대한 감사가 이루어졌다. 감사의
결과, 위원회의 해산이 결정되었고, 대책본부는 아직 완결되지
않은 아젠다에 한하여 그 기능을 지속하기로 하였다.
재정적인 문제에 의하여 대책본부의 업무수행은 전자적인 수단
을 이용하고 있다.

7) 주요 행사

제25회 신체활동 및 운동연구 국제협의회(25th International
Council for Physical Activity & Fitness Research)
- 행사기간: 2008년 9월 2일~4일
- 행사장소: 웡케리(Wong Kerlee) 국제콘퍼런스센터, 미국 캘리
  포니아
- 행사내용: http://www.llu.edu/llu/sph/cpe/icpafr.html

8) 협력기관

다음은 IUNS의 협력기관이다.
- 아시아태평양 임상영양학협회(APCNS: Asia Pacific
  Clinical Nutrition Society)
  홈페이지: http://www.apcns.org
- 유럽영양학학회(EANS: European Academy of Nutritional

Sciences)

전자우편: secretariat@eans.net

- 아프리카영양학협회연합(FANUS: Federation of African Nutrition Societies)

  홈페이지: http://www.africanutrition.org/

- 아시아영양학협회연합(FANS: Federation of Asian Nutrition Societies)

  홈페이지: http://www.fans‑web.org

- 유럽영양학협회연합(FENS: Federation of European Nutrition Societies)

  홈페이지: http://www.fensweb.org/

- 국제영양학협회(ICDA: International Confederation of Dietetic Associations)

  홈페이지: http://www.internationaldietetics.org

- 요오드결핍장애관리 국제협의회(ICCIDD: International Council for Control of Iodine Deficiency Disorders)

  홈페이지: http://www.iccidd.org

- 국제영양성빈혈증자문그룹(INACG: International Nutritional Anemia Consultative Group)

  홈페이지: http://inacg.ilsi.org/

- 국제비만대책기구(IOTF: International Obesity Task force)

  홈페이지: http://www.iotf.org

- 임상영양에 관한 국제심포지엄(isCN: International Symposium on Clinical Nutrition)

  전자우편: mark.wahlqvist@adm.monash.edu.au

- 국제아연영양자문기구(IZiNCG: International Zinc Nutrition Consultative Group)
  홈페이지: www.izincg.org
- 멕시코영양학협회연합(Mexican Federation of Societies of Nutrition)
  전자우편: svillalp@insp.mx
- 미량원소포럼(the Micronutrient forum)
  홈페이지: www.micronutrientforum.org
- 중앙아시아및북아프리카영양학협회(MENANA: Middle East and North Africa Nutrition Association)
  전자우편: azzagohar@redakamel.com
- 영양에관한협력행정위원회(ACC/SCN: Administrative Committee on Coordination/Sub-Committee on Nutrition)
  홈페이지: http://www.unsystem.org/scn
- 유엔식량기구(FAO: Food and Agriculture Organization of the United Nations)
  홈페이지: http://www.fao.org
- 국제원자력기구(IAEA: International Atomic Energy Agency)
  홈페이지: http://www-naweb.iaea.org/nahu/nahres/default.shtm
- 국제식량학기술기구(IUFoST: International Union of Food Science & Technology)
  홈페이지: http://www.iufost.org
- 유엔아동기금(UNICEF: United Nations Children's Fund)
  전자우편: dalnwick@unicef.org
- 유네스코(UNESCO: United Nations Educational, Scientific

and Cultural Organization)

홈페이지: http://www.unesco-nairobi.org.efa.asp

- 유엔대학식량및영양프로그램(UNU: UNU Food and Nutrition Program, United Nations University)

    홈페이지: http://www.unu.edu/capacitybuilding/foodnutrition/-cornell.html

- 세계보건기구(WHO: World Health Organization)

    홈페이지: http://www.who.int/nutrition/en/

② 정보원

1) 정보원배포정책

IUNS의 정보원은 'Features'와 'Nutrition Journals'에서 찾아볼 수 있다. 'Features'를 통해서 IUNS의 연구논문 및 보고서의 PDF를 통한 무료열람이 가능하다.

2) 연구논문 및 보고서(Features)

- *IUNS 2007 Summary Report to the International Nutrition Community*
- *Effective International Action against Undernutrition: Why has It Proven So Difficult and What can de Done to Accelerate Progress?*
- *A Personal View. Food Companies and Nutrition for Better*

Health

- *Do We Believe Derek's Motives for Taking His New Job at PepsiCo?*
- *International Workshop on Leadership Skills in Nutritional Sciences*
- *Indigenous Peoples' Food Systems and Nutrition*
- *Prevention and Control of Malnutrition. By Ann Ashworth*
- *INFOODS, the International Network of Food Data Systems, Activity Report, 2006 – 2007*
- *Report on Activities of the Task Force on the "Nutrition in Transition."*
- *Metrological Concepts for Enhancing the Reliability of Food and Nutritional Measurements*
- *Stopping the Rot in Nutrition Science*
- *Nutrition Solutions to Major Health Problems of Pre – School Children. How to Optimize Growth and Development?*
- *Standing Committee on Nutrition*
- *Innocenti Declaration – On the Protection, Promotion and Support of Breastfeeding*
- *Joint IUNS/World Health Policy Forum Initiative on the New Nutrition Science*
- *Report on Activities of the Task Force on "Diet Nutrition and Long – Term Health."*
- *Report on Activities of the Task Force on "School Children*

Nutrition and Health."

- *Report on Activities of the Task Force on "Technologies and Nutrition." INFOODS, the International Network of Food Data Systems, Activity Report, 2003－2005Indigenous Peoples' Food Systems and Nutrition*

- *Treatment, and Prevention of HIV Disease in Women, Infants, and Children*

- *World Health Organization Consultation on Nutrition and HIV/AIDS in Africa, Durban, South Africa, 10－13 April 2005. Participant's Statement*

- *Minutes of the Meeting of the IUNS Task Force on "Evidence Based Nutrition."*

- *Letter Written by Dr. Mark Wahlqvist Regarding "Free Sugars and Human Health: Sufficient Evidence for Action?"*

- *Enhancing Human Capital in Sub－Saharan Africa in Food Science and Technology Through Distance Education*

- *Requirements for Healthy Nutrition: Integrating Food Sustainability, Food Variety and Health*

- *Statement on Benefits and Risks of Genetically Modified Foods for Human Health and Nutrition*

- *Sciences for Food Security(CSFS), Scoping Workshop on Future Activities of ICSU on Food Security*

- *17th International Congress of Nutrition, 2001 Final Report*

- *Summary of the Scientific Evidence on the Nature and*

Determinants of Child Development and Their Implications for Programmatic Interventions with Young Children.
- *The Global Challenge of Obesity and the International Obesity Task force*
- *Considerations in Defining a Research Agenda to Address Food and Nutrition Problems in Developing Countries*
- *Food Safety Training for Nutritionists*
- *U.S. National Committee to the International Union for Nutritional Sciences Global Survey*
- *International Union of Nutritional Sciences(IUNS): An Overview*

3) 영양학 저널(Nutrition Journals)

IUNS는 다음과 같은 영양학에 관한 저널로의 링크를 제공하고 있다.
- *African Journal of Food, Agriculture, Nutrition and Development(AJFand)(formerly African Journal of Food & Nutrition Sciences −AJFNS)*
- *American Journal of Clinical Nutrition, the(AJCN)*
- *Annals of Nutrition & Metabolism*
- *Applied Physiology, Nutrition, and Metabolism*
- *Asia Pacific Journal of Clinical Nutrition(APJCN)*
- *British Journal of Nutrition*
- *European Journal of Clinical Nutrition(EJCN)*

- *Food and Agricultural Immunology*
- *Food and Nutrition Bulletin*
- *Journal of Nutrition, the*
- *Journal of the American College of Nutrition(JACN)*
- *Nutrition Research Reviews*
- *Pan American Health Organization's Publications Program most Recent Title, "Nutrition and an Active Life: From Knowledge to Action."*
- *Proceedings of the Nutrition Society*
- *Public Health Nutrition*

MFI

Malaria Foundation International

국제말라리아재단

① 기구

1) 소재지

주　　소	Malaria Foundation International 2120 Spencers Way, Stone Mountain, GA 30087
전자우편	Donations@malaria.org
홈페이지	http://www.malaria.org/

2) 설립연혁

국제말라리아재단(MFI)은 1992년에 설립된 비영리기구로서 말라리아 퇴치에 앞장서고 있다. MFI의 현 웹사이트는 1995년에 설계되어 말라리아를 퇴치하는 데 도움이 되는 주요 정보를 제공해 오고 있다. MFI는 많은 개인 및 단체와 함께 파트너십을 이루어 활동하고 있다. 또한 MFI는 말라리아 퇴치를 위한 방법 및 적용에 대한 단기 및 장기간 개발 프로그램의 인식, 교육, 연구, 리더십을 지지해 오고 있다.

3) 설립목적

MFI는 말라리아로 인해 생긴 건강, 경제, 사회 문제들에 대한 해결책의 개발 및 이행을 촉진시키는 데에 그 목적을 두고 있다.

4) 조직

MFI의 위원회는 크게 다음의 다섯 가지로 나뉜다.
① 국제자문위원회(International Advisory Board)
② 과학자문위원회(Scientific Advisory Board)
③ 경영자문위원회(Business Advisory Board)
④ 미국신탁위원회(MFI, USA Board of Trustees)
⑤ 영국신탁위원회(MFI, UK Board of Trustees)

5) 주요 사업

다음과 같은 사업을 중심으로 활동한다.
① 글로벌 커뮤니케이션 및 네트워킹
② 말라리아 연구
③ 교육
④ 말라리아 제어를 위한 리더십

6) 프로젝트

MFI는 파트너십을 바탕으로 다음과 같은 프로젝트를 수행해왔다.
- SYAHD – Nigeria Project

- Rwanda Village Concept Project
- Play Soccer Malawi
- The Goals of the End Malaria – Blue Ribbon Clubs in India
- A life Saved – A Child's Story
- ADWR Project in India
- A.V.I.D. Students Join End Malaria – Blue Ribbon Campaign
- End Malaria – Blue Ribbon Campaign
- Malaria Awards Ceremony 2007
- Paltalk Malaria Business Leadership Conference 2006
- Emory Student Leaders against Malaria
- Student Leaders against Malaria
- Pilot Program Successes
- Student Leaders in Atlanta – Georgia
- The Emory Southern Sudan Project
- Joy for Kids
- Partnership for Social Sciences in Malaria Control(PSSMC)
- Other MFI Supported Project Pioneers
- MFI Past Projects

② 정보원

1) 정보배포정책

MFI의 정보원은 'News'에서 찾아볼 수 있다. 'News'에서는 말라리아 및 건강 관련 정보를 직접 정리해 놓거나 관련 기관의 웹사이트로의 링크를 제공하고 있다.

2) 정보 자료

① News

최근의 대표적인 목록은 다음과 같다.

[아프리카 내 말라리아 관련 보도 자료]

- *Uganda: 300 March against Malaria* – Staff Writers, 05 Nov 2007, New Vision
- *Rwanda: Spraying Campaign is Having Its Impact* – Sam Ruburica, 01 Nov 2007, Focus Media(Kigali)
- *Insecticide Spraying a Must against Malaria* – Naomi Schwarz, 29 Oct 2007, Voice of America
- *West Africa: New Approach to Malaria Recommended* – None, 24 Oct 2007, UN Integrated Regional Information Networks
- *Nigeria: U.S. to Support Four States, FCT against Malaria* – Hassan Karofi, 23 Oct 2007, Daily Trust
- *Rewards and Supervision Cut Child Malaria Deaths – Study* – Staff Writers, 22 Oct 2007, Reuters Africa

- *Gates Fights to Eradicate Malaria* ─ Ruthie Ackerman, 19 Oct 2007, Forbes
- *Defeating an Ancient Killer* ─ Michel Kazatchkine & Tim Ziemer, 17 Oct 2007, Seattle Times
- *Newest Malaria Medicine May be Losing Potency in Asia, WHO Says* ─ Jason Gale & John Lauerman, 17 Oct 2007, Bloomberg
- *A Potential Breakthrough in Malaria Prevention* ─ Gilbert Ross, 17 Oct 2007, American Council on Science and Health
- *Mozal Wins War against Mozambique Mozzies* ─ Xolile Bhengu, 16 Oct 2007, the Times
- *China Plans to Build 10 Anti ─ Malaria Centers in Africa This Year* ─ None, 15 Oct 2007, People's Daily
- *Junk Science: DDT Backlash Continues* ─ Steven Milloy, 12 Oct 2007, Fox News
- *World Bank's 2 ─ Year Report on Special Anti ─ Malarial Project Says Success Brings Expansion* ─ Associated Press, 12 Oct 2007, International Herald Tribune
- *Lutheran World Relief Receives USAID Grant to Combat Malaria in Tanzania* ─ None, 12 Oct 2007, Lutheran World Relief
- *Battle over Bednets* ─ April Harding, 11 Oct 2007, Center for Global Development
- *Episcopal Relief and Development Awarded $1.5 Million*

Grant for Malaria Program – Staff Writers, 11 Oct 2007, Episcopal Life online

- *USAID Announces First Malaria Grants* – Douglas Mpuga, 08 Oct 2007, Voice of America
- *Mwakyusa: Govt Set to Build Malaria Drugs Factory* – Charlotte Schubert, 05 Oct 2007, IPPMedia
- *Tanzania for Indoor DDT Spraying Next Year in Fight against Malaria* – Njonanje Samwel, 02 Oct 2007, IPPMedia
- *Berlin Meeting Raises 9.7 Bln Dollars for AIDS, TB, Malaria* – None, 27 Sep 2007, Agence France Presse
- *Africa Germ, Asian Insect Meet in Italy, Spur Disease* – Jason Gale, 25 Sep 2007, Bloomberg
- *Zambia: U.S. Donates Insecticides* – Staff Writers, 14 Sep 2007, Times of Zambia
- *Uganda: Malaria – 320 Die Daily* – Yasiin Mugerwa, 13 Sep 2007, Monitor(Kampala)
- *Researchers Launch Global Malaria Tracking Network* – Staff Writers, 06 Sep 2007, ABC News Australia
- *Tanzania: Protectionism in Trade a Barrier to Prosperity* – Alec Van Gelder, 06 Sep 2007, New Vision
- *Tilapia FisH Can Pose Danger to Ecosystems* – Warea Orapa, 05 Sep 2007, SciDev.Net
- *Malaria Nets, the Latest Fashion Accessory?* – Winter Miller, 05 Sep 2007 , New York Times

- *Ranbaxy to Become First Indian Pharma to Launch NCE Globally* – Anil Joseph, 05 Sep 2007, Hindustan Times
- *Malawi: Talking Malaria* – Staff Writers, 04 Sep 2007, the Chronicle Newspaper(Lilongwe)

[글로벌 건강보고서 최근 자료]

- *HIV/TB Co – Epidemic Rapidly Spreading in Sub – Saharan Africa*, Report Says – 2007 – 11 – 02
- *Immigrants with TB not Likely to Spread Disease in New Countries*, Study Says – 2007 – 11 – 02
- *Guardian Examines Role of Deforestation, Climate Change in Resurgence of Malaria in Peruvian Amazon* – 2007 – 11 – 01
- *Global Fund Should Focus on 'Wider Factors' Involved in Fighting Diseases*, Editorial Says – 2007 – 11 – 02
- *IRIN News Examines Relationship between HIV/AIDS, Food Shortages in Southern* Africa – 2007 – 11 – 02
- *HIV Prevalence in Zimbabwe Decreases to 15.6%, Health Official Says* – 2007 – 11 – 02

[건강 관련 웹사이트의 보도 자료 페이지]

- Emerging Infectious Diseases Journal – Centers for Disease Control and Prevention
  홈페이지: http://www.cdc.gov/ncidod/EID/index.htm
- United States Agency for International Development

홈페이지: http://www.usaid.gov/our_work/global_health/
home/News/enewsletter/index.html

- Bulletin of the World Health Organization
  홈페이지: (http://www.usaid.gov/our_work/global_health/
  home/News/enewsletter/index.html)
- Global Health Council
  홈페이지: (http://www.usaid.gov/our_work/global_health/
  home/News/enewsletter/index.html)

MSF

Medecins Sans Frontiers

국경없는의사회

① 기구

1) 소재지

소재국가

주 소	Rue de Lausanne 78 CP 116, 1211, Geneva 21 SWITZERL
전 화	+41 22 849 84 00
팩 스	+41 22 849 84 04
전자우편	webmaster@msf.org
홈페이지	http://www.msf.org/

2) 설립연혁

국경없는의사회(MSF)는 1968년 나이지리아 비아프라 내전에 파견된 프랑스 적십자사 소속 베르나르 쿠시네(bernard Kouchner)를 비롯한 의사와 언론인 12명이 1971년 파리에서 '중립·공평·자원'의 3대 원칙과 '정치·종교·경제적 권력으로부터의 자유'라는 가치 아래, 전쟁·기아·질병·자연재해

등으로 고통받는 세계 각 지역의 주민들을 구호하기 위하여 설립한 국제 민간 비영리단체로서 정치, 경제, 종교적 권력으로부터 일체의 구속을 받지 않는다.

3) 설립목적

전쟁, 내란, 전염병 또는 자연재해로 고통받는 지구촌 모든 사람에게 긴급의료구호를 제공하는 것이 MSF의 설립목적이다.

4) 주요 사업

응급구호를 요하는 지역과 전쟁피해지역에서 기본적인 치료, 수술, 병원과 진료소의 복구, 영양보급 및 공중위생프로그램 운영, 의료요원 교육을 제공한다. 현재까지 MSF 구호활동의 도움을 받았거나 받고 있는 국가는 세계 70여 개국에 이른다.

② 정보원

1) 정보배포정책

MSF의 정보원은 'Content'의 'Advocacy', 'Publications' 그리고 'Press Release'에서 찾아볼 수 있다. 'Advocacy'에서는 MSF와 관련된 보도 자료 및 단편 자료들을 제공하고 있으며, 'Publications'에서는 MSF의 출판물을 열람할 수 있다. 단, 'Publications'에 있는 자료는 모두 'Advocacy'에서도 제공된다.

'Press Release'에서는 동영상 보도 자료를 찾아볼 수 있다.

2) 정보 자료

① Advocacy/Publications

대표적인 열람가능 자료는 다음과 같다.

- *Right to Health Care for Vulnerable Migrants* - 11/09/2007
- *Yet Another Arrogant Move? MSF's Stance on Its Relationship with the Rest of the International Aid System* - 03/09/2007
- *Somalia: Reaching out* - 13/08/2007
- *Chad's Rainy Season, with Ongoing Violence and Displacement, Brings the Health Situation Closer to Emergency Levels* - 30/07/2007
- *Lampedusa Shipwrecks - and the Number of Victims Continues to Increase* - 12/07/2007
- *Continuing Violence in Darfur Traps Hundreds of Thousands and Leaves Millions Dependent on Aid for their Survival* - 25/06/2007
- *Voices from Somalia: Stories of People Who Fled MogadisHu* - 11/06/2007
- *The Rohingyas in Bangladesh: 'There's No Happiness in This Place'* - 04/06/2007
- *MSF Response to: 'Thailand Violates Drug Patents for*

Emergency Relief to Development – 09/02/2007

- *MSF Mobile Clinics Serve Indonesia's Flooded Capital, Jakarta* – 09/02/2007
- *Stepping up Assistance to Displaced in Southeast Chad Amid Deteriorating Security* – 07/02/2007
- *From Classrooms to Jungle Sites – Health Care and Trauma Counselling in Malaysia's Grey Zones* – 06/02/2007
- *One Koro of Millet to Feed 13 Mouths – Displaced in Eastern Chad* – 05/02/2007
- *Responding to Iraq's Emergency* – 04/02/2007
- *Somalia: The Need for Independent Humanitarian Aid* – 19/01/2007
- *Overcoming the Gaps in TB Drug Development – 'No Time to Wait' Conference Statement* – 12/01/2007
- *North – East Kenya: Rift Valley Fever Claims Dozens of Lives Following Floods* – 05/01/2007
- *As MSF Returns to Somali Flood Area, All Now Depends on Security and Access* – 02/01/2007
- *Aceh, Indonesia – Two Years after the Tsunami* – 29/12/2006
- *What Displaced and Refugees Face in Chad* – 19/12/2006
- *MSF Welcomes Move to Overcome Patent on AIDS Drug in Thailand* – 30/11/2006
- *Chad: Caring for Refugees and Displaced Amid Deteriorating Security* – 23/11/2006
- *Deteriorating Situation in the Central African Republic*

- 22/11/2006

- *Thousands Displaced after Fresh Violence Hits Villages in Southeast Chad* - 21/11/2006
- *Darfur, Sudan: 'A Crisis of Human Suffering'* - 14/11/2006
- *Who is Really Feeling the Pressure over Darfur?* - 14/11/2006
- *One Year after the Earthquake in Kashmir - Interview with Fasil Tezera, MSF Head of Mission in Pakistan* - 10/10/2006
- *Childbirth Often Means Death in Haiti* - 02/10/2006
- *Malaria House Calls in Sierra Leone* - 25/09/2006
- *What Impact Does the Security Situation Have on MSF Work in Darfur* - 17/09/2006
- *Insecurity Remains the Dominant Context for MSF Work in Darfur, Sudan* - 14/09/2006
- *As Novartis Challenges India's Patent Law, MSF Warns Access to Medicines is Under Threat* - 12/09/2006
- *In the Darfur Trap* - 11/09/2006
- *Call for Moratorium on Trade Provisions That Threaten Access to Medicines or Treatment Programmes* - 17/08/2006
- *From Darfur: Adam's Song* - 12/08/2006
- *MSF Disappointed by the Verdict in Court Case about the Killing of Five of Its Staff in Afghanistan in 2004* - 09/08/2006
- *Relief Goods are Reaching Lebanon with Difficulties* -

31/07/2006

- *Although the Displaced Remain after the Kashmir Earthquake, Aid Falters* – 28/07/2006
- *Humanitarian Needs Remain as DRC Election Approaches* – 28/07/2006
- *Flooding in Somalia: Disease in the Wake of Devastation* – 12/07/2006
- *First MSF Teams to Indonesia Earthquake* – 28/05/2006
- *BBC Video: Cholera in Angola* – 18/05/2006
- *Neglected Drugs Continue their 30 Year Record* – 12/05/2006
- *Living in Fear: Colombia's Cycle of Violence* – 27/04/2006
- *MSF Launches New Health Care Project in Galgaduud, Somalia* – 03/04/2006
- *In Luanda, Angola, the First Cholera Outbreak in Ten Years is Now Spreading to Other Areas* – 31/03/2006
- *DRC Measles Vaccination Campaign Ends* – *Numbers Fall but Coverage is Complete* – 29/03/2006
- *Peru's Lurigancho Prison Project: Five Years Working with People forgotten before they Were Dead* – 22/03/2006
- *Nigeria's Food Crisis was Scarcely Visible* – *But Thousands of Children Were Starving* – 27/02/2006
- *Darfur, Sudan: 'The Chronic Insecurity Has Led us to Redefine and Step up Our Activities'* – 16/02/2006
- *Running for their Lives* – *Repeated Civilian Displacement*

- *in Central Katanga, DRC* − 09/02/2006
- *MSF Role in Haiti, January 2006* − 19/01/2006
- *BBC World: Doctors on the Frontline* − 16/01/2006
- *Cholera Outbreak May be one of Largest in Zambia's History* − 10/01/2006
- *MSF Looks Back on Its Lebanon Emergency Response* − 09/01/2006
- *Angola's Cholera Outbreak* − *'Unless Something is Done about Water and Sanitation, We'll Have Another Epidemic on Our Hands Here within One or Two Years'* − 06/01/2006
- *Asian Tsunami: One Year on, Health Watch Remains a Key MSF Concern* − 28/12/2005
- *Mental Health Care in Banda Aceh: Violence Paired with Natural Disaster* − 28/12/2005
- *Mental Health Care Grows in Strength and Experience Caring for Tsunami Survivors* − 28/12/2005
- *Haiti's Cité Soleil: Treating Bullet Wounds and Delivering Babies* − 27/12/2005
- *Forgotten People of the Balkans* − 23/12/2005
- *Nolist* − *Surviving AIDS and TB in South Africa* − 22/12/-2005
- *One Year after the Indian Ocean Tsunami Disaster* − 20/12/2005
- *Indonesia* − *Tsunami One Year Review* − 20/12/2005

- *India － Tsunami One Year Operations Review* － 20/12/2005
- *Thailand － Tsunami One Year Operations Review* － 20/-12/2005
- *Myanmar － Tsunami One Year Operations Review* － 20/-12/2005
- *Use of Tsunami Funds* － 20/12/2005
- *Sri Lanka － One Year Operational Review* － 20/12/2005
- *Revisit Prudence Radebe － South Africa and AIDS Treatment* － 20/12/2005
- *Inflatable Hospital Increases Aid in Pakistan Earthquake Region* － 19/12/2005
- *Monsoon Rains and Floods Hit Tsunami － Affected Area in Tamil Nadu, India* － 16/12/2005
- *Two MSF Colleagues Killed in Airline Crash in Nigeria* － 14/12/2005
- *Activity Report 2005* － 05/12/2005
- *2005: The Year in Review* － 05/12/2005
- *MSF's Principles and Identity － the Challenges Ahead* － 05/12/2005
- *A Simple Yet Crucial Demand: Ensuring That Crimes against Humanitarian Workers* － 05/12/2005
- *Lessons Learned: 'Chagas Disease, an Invisible Threat in Nicaragua'* － 07/09/2005
- *Know More about Chagas Disease* － 07/09/2005
- *Chagas Treatment: Far from Ideal* － 07/09/2005

- *Chagas Disease: Lack of Access to Medicines* – 07/09/- 2005
- *Crushing Burden of Rape: Sexual Violence in Darfur, Sudan* – 03/08/2005
- *JUNE 20, WORLD REFUGEE DAY: Migrating Women and Children are Most Vulnerable to Sexual Violence* – 20/06/2005
- *Now That the Dust Has Settled: The Consequences of the New Indian Patents Act* – 01/04/2005
- *Are Sources of Affordable Generic Medicines Drying up?* – 15/03/2005
- *A Guide to the Post – 2005 World: TRIPS, R&D and Access to Medicines* – 25/02/2005
- *Will the Lifeline of Affordable Medicines for Poor Countries be Cut?* – 25/02/2005
- *Asian Tsunami: Overview of MSF Activities in India, Thailand, Myanmar and Malaysia* – 31/01/2005
- *Trauma of Chechnya's Ongoing War on Internally Displaced People* – 13/09/2004
- *Running out of Breath: TB Day 2004* – 24/03/2004
- *The Role of Civil Society in Protecting Public Health over Commercial Interests: Lessons from Thailand* – 13/02/2004
- *DOHA DERAILED: Enduring Myths* – 10/09/2003
- *Big Pharma Puts Block on Cheap Drug Imports* –

03/08/2003

- *Ten Years of Conflict, Violence and Human Suffering* − 19/11/2002
- *Colombia: Assisting Civilian Victims of Increasing Violence* − 02/11/2002
- *Ten Years With the Moscow Homeless − Any Reason to Celebrate?* − 23/05/2002
- *Palestinian Authority: Medical and Psychological Care for People in Distress* − 13/12/2001
- *Report Shows Near Empty Pipeline of Drugs for Diseases of the World's Poor* − 09/10/2001
- *Bringing the Pharmaceuticals Industry to Its Senses* − 04/09/2001

MWIA

Medical Women' International Association

국제여의사협회

① 기구

1) 소재지

소재국가 　캐나다

주　　소 　Medical Women's International Association
Secretary‐General, Shelley Ross M.D. 7555
Morley Drive, Burnaby, B.C. CANADA V5E
3Y2

전　　화 　＋1 604 439 8993

팩　　스 　＋1 604 439 8994

전자우편

홈페이지 　http://www.mwia.net/

2) 성격

국제여의사협회(MWIA)는 국제비정부기구로서 전 세계 5개 대
륙의 여의사들을 대표한다.

3) 설립연혁

본 협회는 1919년에 설립된 가장 오래된 국제수준의 전문기구 중 하나이다. 본 협회는 비정치적이며 비영리적 기구로 여의사들의 의문점과 공동의 관심사를 토론할 수 있는 포럼의 필요성에 의해 설립되었다.

대부분의 의과대학에서 적어도 50% 정도를 이루고 있는 여의사들은 여전히 의사로는 소수집단에 속하고 있다. 의사 세계에서 여성이 점점 많아짐으로써 이 문제에 대한 새로운 이슈가 떠오르고 그에 따라 본 협회도 생겨나게 되었다.

4) 조직

MWIA는 총 8개의 지리적 지역권으로 나뉘며, 각각의 지역은 그 지역의 부위원장(Vice‒President)에 의한 경영위원회(Executive Committee)에 의해 관리된다. 7개의 지역은 다음과 같다.

북부유럽(Northern Europe), 중부유럽(Central Europe), 남부유럽(Southern Europe), 북미(North America), 남미(Latin America), 아프리카(Near East and Africa), 중앙아시아(Central Asia), 서태평양(Western Pacific)

5) 회원

MWIA는 전 세계 90개국을 대표하는 회원협회의 모체이다. 회원들은 각기 다른 문화적 배경과 의료전통 및 문제 등을 포럼

을 통해 공유한다. MWIA의 회원은 준국가협회, 개인회원, 은
퇴회원, 명예회원으로 나뉜다. 회원국의 분류는 다음과 같다.

① 제휴국가협회(Affiliated National Associations)
덴마크(Denmark), 핀란드(Finland), 노르웨이(Norway), 스웨
덴(Sweden), 영국(United Kingdom), 아이슬란드(Iceland)

② 중부유럽(Central Europe)
오스트리아(Austria), 불가리아(Bulgaria), 조지아(Georgia),
독일(Germany), 헝가리(Hungary), 폴란드(Poland), 루마니아
(Rumania), 스위스(Switzerland)

③ 남부유럽(Southern Europe)
벨기에(belgium), 프랑스(France), 그리스(Greece), 이스라엘
(israel), 이태리(Italy)

④ 북미(North America)
캐나다(Canada), 미국(United States of America)

⑤ 남미(Latin America)
아르헨티나(Argentina), 볼리비아(Bolivia), 브라질(Brazil),
콜롬비아(Colombia), 멕시코(Mexico), 파나마(Panama), 페루
(Peru)

⑥ 아프리카(Near East and Africa)

카메룬(Cameroon), 이집트(Egypt), 가나(Ghana), 나이지리아(Nigeria), 시에라리온(Sierra Leone), 탄자니아(Tanzania), 우간다(Uganda), 잠비아(Zambia)

⑦ 중앙아시아(Central Asia)

인도(India), 태국(Thailand)

⑧ 서태평양(Near East and Asia)

호주(Australia), 일본(Japan), 한국(Republic of Korea), 필리핀(Philippines), 대만(Taiwan ROC)

⑨ 개인회원의 국적분포

알바니아(Albania), 아르마니아(Armenia), 보스니아(Bosnia Herzegovina), 불가리아(Bulgaria), 부룬디(Burundi), 차드(Chad), 코스타리카(Costa Rica), 크로아티아(Croatia), 콩고민주공화국(Dem. Rep. of Congo), 에스토니아(Estonia), 에티오피아(Ethiopia), 기니(Guinea), 인도네시아(Indonesia), 이란(Iran), 이라크(Iraq), 아일랜드(Ireland), 요르단(Jordan), 코소보(Kosovo), 라트비아(Latvia), 리투아니아(Lithuania), 말레이시아(Malaysia), 말리(Mali), 몽고(Mongolia), 네덜란드(Netherlands), 뉴질랜드(New Zealand), 북마리아나제도(Northern Mariana islands), 파키스탄(Pakistan), 러시아(Russia), 르완다(Rwanda), 사우디아라비아(Saudi – Arabia), 남아공(South Africa), 스페인(Spain), 스리랑카(Sri Lanka),

수단(Sudan), 스와질란드(Swaziland), 탄자니아(Tanzania), 통가(tonga), 튀니지(Tunisia), 터키(Turkey), 아랍에미리트(United Arab Emirates), 우크라이나(Ukraine), 우즈베키스탄(Uzbekistan), 베네수엘라(Venezuela), 유고슬라비아(Yugoslavia), 짐바브웨(Zimbabwe)

6) 주요 활동

국제의회 및 총회는 3년마다 열리게 되어 있다. 의회에서는 정해진 주제에 관한 논문이 제출되고 있으며, 총회는 행정정책에 대한 결정을 내린다. MWIA는 또한 장학사업을 통해 회원들의 석·박사 교육을 지원하고 있다. 본 협회는 유엔의 경제사회이사회(Economic and Social Council)의 자문단에 속해 있으며 또한 세계보건기구와 공식적인 관계를 맺고 있다. MWIA의 많은 활동들은 주로 국가단계에서 국가협회들을 통해 이루어지고 있다. 예를 들어, 의료서비스, 과학콘퍼런스, 강의 등이 국가활동에 포함된다.

7) 주요 프로젝트

① 엄마에게서 자녀로 전염되는 에이즈 예방
② 보건에 있어서의 젠더주류화
③ 약품의 여성화
④ 사춘기 성 정체성

8) 국제활동

본 협회는 1950년 초반부터 비정부기구로서 유엔의 활동에 활발히 참여해 오고 있다. 오늘날의 MWIA는 국제보건기구와의 공식적인 활동을 함께 하고 있으며 유니세프의 면역프로그램(Immunization Programmes)에도 참여하고 있다. MWIA는 뉴욕과 제네바에 있는 세 개의 유엔센터에 참여하고 있으며 국제의학기구협의회(CIOMS: Council for International Organizations of Medical Sciences)에 활발히 참여하고 있다.

9) 관련 기관

다음은 MWIA의 관련 기관 및 기관 웹사이트이다.
- 세계보건기구(WHO: World Health Organization)
  홈페이지: http://www.who.int
- 유엔(UN: United Nations)
  홈페이지: http://www.un.org
- 세계의학협회(WMA: World Medical Association)
  홈페이지: http://www.wma.net
- 유엔 NGO 위원회(ConGO: UN Committee of NGO's)
  홈페이지: http://www.ngocongo.org/
- 국제의학기구협의회(CIOMS: Council for International Organizations of Medical Sciences)
  홈페이지: http://www.cioms.ch
- 유럽여성로비(EWL: European Women's Lobby)
  홈페이지: http://www.womenlobby.org

- 건강웹(HealthWeb)

  홈페이지: http://www.healthweb.org

- Terre — des — Femmes

  홈페이지: http://www.terre — des — femmes.de

- 여성전자뉴스(Women's eNews)

  홈페이지: http://www.womensenews.org

- 유엔여성지위향상국(DAW: United Nations Division for the Advancement of Women)

  홈페이지: http://www.un.org/womenwatch/daw/cedaw

- 유엔여성개발기금(UNIFEM: United Nations Development Fund for Women)

  홈페이지: http://www.un.org

- 유니세프(UNICEF: Unite Nations Children Fund)

  홈페이지: http://www.unifem.org

② 정보원

1) 정보원배포정책

MWIA의 정보원은 'MWIA Publications', 'News' 그리고 'Links'에서 찾아볼 수 있다. 출판물은 안내서, 뉴스레터, 의회보고서, 총회보고서로 나뉜다. 대부분의 자료는 PDF로 무료열람이 가능하다.

2) 출판물(Publications)

① 안내서(Manuals)

- *Training Manual on Gender Mainstreaming in Health*
- *Training Manual for Adolescent Sexuality*

② 뉴스레터(Newsletter)

WMIA의 뉴스레터의 공식적인 명칭은 '업데이트(Update)'이며, 1년에 3-4차례 발간된다. 뉴스레터 목록의 예는 다음과 같다.

- *Update 20*
- *Update 21*
- *Update 22*
- *Update 23*
- *Update 24*
- *Update 25*
- *Update 26*
- *Update 28*
- *Update 29*
- *Update 30*
- *Update 31 September 2007*
- *Update 32*
- *Update 34*
- *MWIA March 2008 update*

③ 의회보고서(Congress Reports)

- *Congress Report Sydney 2001*
- *Congress Report Tokyo 2004*
- *Congress Program 2004*

④ 총회보고서(Annual Reports)

- *Annual Report 2003 - 2004*
- *Annual Report 2004 - 2005*

3) 보도 자료(News)

웹페이지지상에 가장 최근 보도 자료를 한 편씩 제공하고 있다. 2008년 7월 현재, 2007년 8월 업데이트된 내용의 보도 자료가 올라와 있다.

- Communique at the End of the 27th Congress of Medical Women's International Association Held in Accra, Ghana from 31st July to 4th August 2007

4) 링크(Links)

- World Health Organization(WHO)
- United Nations(UN)
- World Medical Association(WMA)
- UN Committee of NGO's(ConGO)
- UN Economic and Social Counsel(ECOSOC)
- Commission on the Status of Women(CSW)

- Council for International Organizations of Medical Sciences (CIOMS)
- European Women's Lobby(EWL)
- HealthWeb
- Terre − des − Femmes
- Women's eNews
- United Nations Division for the Advancement of Women (DAW)
- United Nations Development Fund for Women(UNIFEM)
- Unite Nations Children Fund(UNICEF)

OxHA

Oxford Health Alliance
옥스퍼드보건연맹

① 기구

1) 소재지

소재국가	영국
주　　소	1st Floor 28 Margaret Street London W1W 8RZ United Kingdom
전　　화	+44 20 7637 4330
팩　　스	+44 20 7637 4336
전자우편	stig.pramming@oxha.org
홈페이지	http://www.oxha.org/

2) 성격

옥스퍼드보건연맹(OxHA)은 만성질병의 국제적 영향을 감소시키고 예방하기 위한 기구이다.

3) 설립연혁

OxHA는 2003년 옥스퍼드대학교와 노보노르디스크사(Novo

Nordisk A/S) 간의 파트너십으로 형성되었다. 많은 관계자들이
질병의 원인과 해결방법에 연관되어 노력을 지속하고 있다.
OxHA의 최초 참가자들은 2003년 12월의 옥스퍼드 비전 2020
회의에서 처음으로 그 뜻을 같이 하였다. OxHA는 2005년 초
반 참가자들의 참여 여부를 넓히기 위해서 그 이름을 지금의
OxHA로 바꾸게 되었다. OxHA는 그 후 잉글랜드와 웨일스의
자선위원회(Charity Commission)에 등록되었다.

4) 비전 및 임무

OxHA는 질병에 대한 인식을 높이고 주요 정책입안가들을 교
육하여 예방 가능한 질병에 대한 대책을 강구하는 데에 그 목
적을 두고 있다.

5) 조직

OxHA의 자문위원회(Advisory Board)는 만성질병 예방 전문가
들로 구성되어 있다. 이 위원회는 OxHA의 노력을 강화하고
연맹 활동의 효과를 극대화하기 위해 구성되었다.

6) 아시아태평양지역센터(Asia‑Pacific Regional Centre)

OxHA의 아시아태평양지역센터는 시드니대학교의 호주보건정
책연구소(Australian Health Policy Institute)에 위치하고 있다.
이 지역센터는 2006년에 설립되었으며 건강하고 지속 가능한
커뮤니티(Healthy and Sustainable Communities)와 같은 세미

나를 주최하고 있다.

7) 신온라인네트워크(New Online Network)

OxHA는 만성질병을 예방하는 데 기여하고 이 질병들의 심각한 결과에 대한 인식을 높이는 데 전념하고 있는 전문가 및 활동가들의 새로운 온라인 네트워크를 구축하였다. 이 네트워크는 OxHA의 새로운 웹사이트인 www.3FOUR50.com의 일부로 구성되었다.

3FOUR50의 이용을 위해서는 웹사이트의 회원가입이 필요하다. 또는 info@oxha.org로 회원가입신청 이메일을 보낼 수도 있다.

② 정보원

1) 정보원배포정책

OxHA의 정보원은 'Knowledge'에서 찾아볼 수 있다. '지식(Knowledge)' 부분은 다시 관련 주제에 대한 '배경설명(Backgrounders)'과 '출판물(Publications)'로 나뉘어 정보를 제공하고 있다.

2) 출판물(Publications)

대부분의 자료는 PDF 또는 웹페이지지상에서 원문 무료열람이 가능하다.

- *FTC: Marketing Food to Children*

- *SciDev.Net on Chronic Diseases*
- *Health Systems of China and India*
- *Ambitions for Health*
- *3FOUR50 Flyer*
- *Healthy Eating Toolkit*
- *Food and the Environment*
- *OxHA Workplace Health Programme*
- *Inequalities in Young People's Health*
- *Health Inequalities: Progress and Next Steps*
- *Cycling: Getting Australia Moving*
- *Our Cities, Our Health, Our Future*
- *Social Determinants of Health: Primer to Action*
- *Sydney Principles(Article)*
- *NICE: Physical Activity in the Workplace*
- *Worldwide Variability in Physical Inactivity*
- *World Health Statistics 2008*
- *Eldis: Health Reporter, May 08: Chronic Disease*
- *Eldis Web Resource on Chronic Disease*
- *Diabetes Voice－Special issue*
- *WHO: Implementing Global Strategy*
- *Health, Place and Nature－Powerpoint*
- *Health, Place and Nature*
- *Low Income Groups and Behaviour Change*
- *CIH Introductory Booklet*
- *An Economic Framework*

- *LGA Written Evidence, March 2008*
- *NIOSH 'Worklife' Consultation*
- *Urban Health and Healthy Weights*
- *Working for a Healthier Tomorrow*
- *Healthy Cities − Framing the Issue*
- *Andreasen Presentation OxHA Summit 08*
- *Sydney Resolution*
- *Nutbeam Presentation OxHA Summit 08*
- *Adshead Presentation Summit '08*
- *McKee Presentation Summit 08*
- *Finegood Healthy Food Presentation Summit 08*
- *Matthews Presentation Summit 08*
- *Chapman Presentation OxHA Summit 08*

3) 배경설명(Backgrounders)

만성질병 예방에 대한 간략한 설명을 제공한다.

- Prevention Works Poster
- OxHA Note to Prime Minister's Office
- Three Risk Factors: Fact Pack
- The Costs of Chronic Disease
- Risk Factor: Tobacco
- Risk Factor: Physical Activity
- Human Rights and Health
- Risk Factor: Diet

PMNCH

Partnership for Maternal, Newborn and Child Health

산모, 신생아, 아동건강파트너십

① 기구

1) 소재지

주　　소　the Partnership for Maternal, Newborn and Child Health Secretariat Hosted by the World Health Organization 20 Avenue Appia, 1211 Geneva 27 Switzerland

전　　화　＋41 22 791 2595

팩　　스　＋41 22 791 5854

전자우편　pmnch@who.int

홈페이지　http://www.who.int/pmnch/en/

2) 설립연혁

산모, 신생아, 아동건강파트너십(PMNCH)은 2005년 9월에 시작된 글로벌 건강 파트너십(the Partnership)에 산모, 신생아, 아동건강(MNCH: Maternal, Newborn and Child Health) 커뮤니티가 더해져 총 180여 회원연합을 바탕으로 여성, 신생아, 아동이 건강한 상태에서 살 수 있도록 하기 위해 설립된 조직이다.

3) 설립목적

PMNCH는 산모, 신생아 그리고 아동의 건강을 증진시키고 올바르게 유지하기 위한 투자에 그 목적이 있다. 약 60여 개의 큰 부담을 지고 있는 국가들의 50%가 5년 안에 새천년목표(MDGs)의 4항과 5항을 달성할 수 있도록 지원한다.

4) 조직

PMNCH는 총 4개의 업무그룹(Working Group)을 운영한다.
① 국가지원 업무그룹(Country Support Working Group)
   국가에서 행해지는 업무를 지원한다.
② 홍보 업무그룹(Advocacy Working Group)
   산모, 신생아, 아동건강과 관련한 내용을 국제적으로 그리고 국가적으로 전파하는 역할을 한다.
③ 효과적 중재 업무그룹(Effective Interventions Working Group)
   국가단계에서의 건강과 관련한 중재를 효과적으로 수행하기 위한 전략 및 도구를 촉진·이행하는 역할을 한다.
④ 감독 및 평가 업무그룹(Monitoring & Evaluation Working Group)
   주요 국가에서의 프로그램 이행과 관련한 자원분배 및 진보평가를 담당한다.

5) 주요 사업

PMNCH의 4개 업무그룹이 관여하는 활동이 PMNCH의 주요 사업의 주축을 이룬다.

② 정보원

1) 정보배포정책

PMNCH의 정보원은 'Health Resources'와 'Media Center', 그리고 'Partnership Information'에서 찾아볼 수 있다. 정보원을 통해 건강 관련 정보, 보도 자료, 유용사이트 링크 등을 온라인 상에서 무료로 열람할 수 있다.

2) 정보 자료

① Health Resources

주제별로 출판물 및 관련 사이트의 링크를 제공한다.

[산모건강]

- 출판물
  - *Skilled Care During Childbirth: Policy Brief*
  - *Working Together for Better Health*
  - *Reducing Maternal Deaths: Evidence and Action [pdf 850kb]*
  - *The Lancet Maternal Series*
  - *Maternal Mortality Update 2004: Delivering into Good Hands, UNFPA*

- 관련 웹사이트
  - Averting Maternal Death and Disability(AMDD)
  - Family Care International
  - Initiative for Maternal Mortality Programme Assessment/University of Aberdeen(IMMPACT)
  - International Association for Maternal and Neonatal Health(IAMNEH)
  - National Institute of Child Health and Human Development(NICHD)
  - UNFPA Resources on Safe Motherhood
  - USAID－Maternal and Child Health
  - The White Ribbon Alliance for Safe Motherhood
  - WHO－Maternal Health
  - WHO－Pregnancy
  - Women and Children First
  - Women's Global Health Imperative

[아동건강]
- 출판물
  - *Tracking Progress in Child Survival: Countdown to 2015*
  - *UNICEF(2007), the State of the World's Children US Agency for International Development(2006), Tracking Official Development Assistance for Child Health: Challenges and Prospects*

- 관련 웹사이트
    - Basic Support for Institutionalizing Child Survival
    - International Pediatric Association(IPA)
    - The Task Force for Child Survival and Development
    - United Nations Children's Found(UNICEF)
    - US Coalition for Child Survival
    - USAID – Maternal and Child Health
    - WHO – Child and Adolescent Health and Development
    - WHO – Child Health
    - WHO – Millennium Development Goal 4

[신생아건강]
- 출판물
    - *Opportunities for Africa's Newborns: Practical Data, Policy and Programmatic Support for Newborn Care in Africa*
    - *Skilled Care During Childbirth: Policy Brief*
    - *Tracking Pprogress in Child Survival: Countdown to 2015*
    - *The Lancet Newborn, Child and Maternal Survival Series, 2005*

- 관련 웹사이트
    - Council of International Neonatal Nurses(COINN)
    - Enfants du Monde, Switzerland
    - Institute of Child Health, International Perinatal Care Unit
    - International Pediatric Association(IPA)
    - National Institute of Child Health and Human Development(NICHD)
    - Save the Children, Saving Newborn Lives Initiative
    - Lancet Series – Executive Summary on Neonatal Survival [pdf 160kb]
    - WHO – Millennium Development Goal 4

[새천년개발목표 4 & 5]

- 출판물
    - *Millennium Project(2006), Public Choices, Private Decisions: Sexual and Reproductive Health and the Millennium Development Goals*
    - *Millennium Project(2005), Who's Got the Power? Transforming Health Systems for Women and Children*
    - *United Nations(2007), the Millenium Development Goals Report, 2005*
    - *United Nations(2006), the Millennium Development Goals Report, 2006*

- *United Nations(2005), the Millennium Development Goals Report, 2007*
- *World Health Organization(2005), Health and the Millennium Development Goals*

② Media Center

보도 자료를 열람할 수 있다. 대표적인 목록은 다음과 같다.

- *Global Drive to Improve Maternal and Child Health Launched at Clinton Global Initiative,* New York 26 September 2007
- *Partnership Member Appointed a Federal Minister of Health, Nigeria,* 27 July 2007, Lagos/Geneva
- *Safe Blood for Safe Motherhood,* 14 June 2007, Geneva
- *Global Health Conference,* 30 May 2007, Washington D.C.
- *60th World Health Assembly,* 15 May 2007, Geneva
- *Partners' Forum Meeting,* 17 April 2007, Dar es Salaam, Tanzania
- *Quick Wins Versus Strengthening Health Systems,* 16 June 2006, London
- *Ex-Prime Minister of Norway Urges the Delegates at the World Health Assembly to Take Immediate Action to Save 11 Million Maternal, Newborn and Child Lives Each Year,* 24 May 2006 Geneva
- *Dr. Francisco Songane, Former Mozambican Health*

Minister – Named New Director of the Partnership for Maternal, Newborn & Child Health, 13 December 2005, London

- *Countdown to 2015: Tracking Progress in Child Survival,* 13 December 2005, London

③ Partnership Information

PMNCH의 기본지식이 되는 자료를 찾아볼 수 있다.

- Ten – Year Strategy
- Conceptual and Institutional Framework(CI&F)
- International Conference on Population and Development (ICPD)
- Fourth World Conference on Women(FWCW)
- UN Millennium Development Goals
- The Delhi Declaration
- 2007 Partners' forum, Dar Es Salaam, Tanzania

ProCOR

Conference on Cardiovascular Health

심장혈관의료콘퍼런스

1 기구

1) 소재지

소재국가	미국
주 소	Lown Cardiovascular Research Foundation 21 Longwood Ave, Brookline, MA 02446
전 화	+1 617 732 1318
팩 스	+1 617 734 5763
전자우편	info@procor.org
홈페이지	http://www.procor.org/

2) 성격

심장혈관의료콘퍼런스(ProCOR)는 이메일과 웹사이트를 기반으로 한 전자콘퍼런스로서, 개발도상국의 심장혈관질병을 알리는 역할을 하고 있다.

3) 비전 및 임무

ProCOR은 활동적인 국제적 포럼을 형성하여 의료관리자와 연구원, 대중보건 인력들 그리고 일반대중이 시기적절한 정보를 공유하고 새로운 대중보건 문제에 관한 인식을 고취하고자 한다.

① 예방의 효과성에 관한 교육의 필요성 강조

② 고비용 기술 시대에 있어서 심장학이 나아가야 할 방향에 대한 국제적 대화 촉진

③ 글로벌 대화를 도모하기 위한 시기적절한 관련 정보 및 의견으로의 공헌

4) 조직

ProCOR은 뛰어난 자문위원회에 의해 도움을 받고 있으며, 이 자문위원회는 국제적으로 인정받고 있는 기관에서 일하고 있는 회원들로 구성된다.

5) 여성심장건강(Women's Heart Health)

여성심장건강 부문은 심장혈관 질환을 앓고 있는 개발도상국의 여성들에 대한 대화를 촉진시키기 위해 형성되었다. 이러한 대화를 촉진함으로써 특히 여성들에게 효과적인 영향을 기대하고 있다.

6) Ashanti - ProCor Project

이 프로젝트는 2007년 6월과 7월 두 달간 여러 번의 인터뷰, 회

의, 이벤트를 통해 가나의 쿠마시(Kumasi)와 아크라(Accra)에서
공식적으로 시작되었다. 이 프로젝트는 ProCOR과 미국에 기반
을 둔 NGO 기관들, 그리고 몇몇 병원의 심장혈관계 의사들과의
공동협력에 의해 개발된 4년간의 프로젝트이다.

7) 협력기관

다음은 ProCOR이 제공하는 관련 기관이다.
- 흡연규제연맹(Framework Convention Alliance for Tobacco Control)
  홈페이지: www.fctc.org
- 글로벌신체활동연맹(Global Alliance for Physical Activity)
  홈페이지: www.globalpa.org.uk
- 건강연구글로벌포럼(Global forum for Health Research)
  홈페이지: www.globalforumhealth.org
- 글로벌링크(GLOBALink)
  홈페이지: www.globalink.org
- 글로벌지식파트너십(Global Knowledge Partnership)
  홈페이지: www.globalknowledge.org
- 흡연규제글로벌파트너십(Global Partnerships for Tobacco Control)
  홈페이지: www.essentialaction.org/Tobacco
- 국제당뇨병연합(International Diabetes Federation)
  홈페이지: www.idf.org
- 국제흡연반대여성네트워크(International Network of Women

against Tobacco)

홈페이지: www.inwat.org

- 국제비만대책본부(International Obesity Task force)

  홈페이지: www.iotf.org

- 국제 신체활동 및 환경 네트워크(International Physical Activity and the Environment Network)

  홈페이지: www.ipenproject.org

- 국제심장연구협회(International Society for Heart Research)

  홈페이지: www.isHrworld.org

- 국제고혈압협회(International Society of Hypertension)

  홈페이지: www.isH-world.com

- 건강 증진 및 교육 국제연맹(International Union for Health Promotion and Education)

  홈페이지: www.iuhpe.org

- 국경 없는 도서관원(Librarians without Borders)

  홈페이지: www.lwb-online.org

- 옥스퍼드건강연맹(Oxford Health Alliance)

  홈페이지: www.oxha.org

- 세계보건기구(WHO: World Health Organization)

  홈페이지: www.who.int

- 세계심장연합(World Heart Federation)

  홈페이지: www.worldheart.org

- 세계고혈압리그(World Hypertension League)

  홈페이지: www.worldhypertensionleague.org

② 정보원

1) 정보원배포정책

ProCOR의 정보원은 'Journal Club'에서 찾아볼 수 있다. 저널은 연도별 및 주제별 브라우징이 가능하며 기본적인 정보와 원본논문을 제공하는 웹페이지로의 링크를 제공하고 있다.

2) 저널

최근 저널 논문의 대표적인 예는 다음과 같다.

- *Screening for Type 2 Diabetes Mellitus in Adults: US Preventive Services Task Force Recommendation Statement*
- *The Risk of Dying by Age, Sex, and Smoking Status in the United States: Putting Health Risks in Context*
- *Nurse-Coordinated Multidisciplinary, Family-Based Cardiovascular Disease Prevention Programme(EUROACTIon) for Patients with Coronary Heart Disease and Asymptomatic Individuals at High Risk of Cardiovascular Disease: A Paired, Cluster-Randomised Controlled Trial*
- *Active and Passive Smoking and Depression among Japanese Workers*
- *Perception of ischaemic Heart Disease, Knowledge of and Attitude to Reduction of Its Risk Factors*
- *Erectile Dysfunction Predicts Coronary Heart Disease in Type 2 Diabetes*

- *Admission of Hypertensive Patients at the University of Benin Teaching Hospital, Nigeria*
- *Adherence to Mediterranean Diet and Risk of Developing Diabetes: Prospective Cohort Study*
- *The Long – Term Effect of Lifestyle Interventions to Prevent Diabetes in the China Da Qing Diabetes Prevention Study: A 20 – Year Follow – up Study*
- *Impact of Body Mass Index on Incident Hypertension and Diabetes in Chinese Asians, American Whites, and American Blacks*
- *Relation of Central Adiposity and Body Mass Index to the Development of Diabetes in the Diabetes Prevention Program*
- *Patterns of Coronary Heart Disease Mortality over the 20th Century in England and Wales: Possible Plateaus in the Rate of Decline*
- *Different Strategies for Screening and Prevention of Type 2 Diabetes in Adults: Cost Effectiveness Analysis*
- *Effect of a Pediatric Practice – Based Smoking Prevention and Cessation Intervention for Adolescents: A Randomized, Controlled Trial*
- *Treatment and Outcomes of Acute Coronary Syndromes in India(CREATE): A Prospective Analysis of Registry Data*
- *Global Burden of Blood – Pressure – Related Disease, 2001*
- *Risk Factors Associated with Uncontrolled Hypertension:*

Findings from the Baseline CARMEN Survey in Cienfuegos, Cuba

- *Diabetic Retinopathy and Risk of Heart Failure*
- *The Impact of a Smoking Ban on Hospital Admissions for Coronary Heart Disease*
- *Trends in Fruit and Vegetable Consumption among US Men and Women, 1994 – 2005*
- *Has the Risk for Coronary Heart Disease Changed among US Adults?*
- *Risk Factors for Myocardial Infarction in Women and Men: Insights from the INTERHEART Study*
- *CARMELA: Assessment of Cardiovascular Risk in Seven Latin American Cities*
- *Addressing Stroke Signs and Symptoms Through Public Education: The Stroke Heroes Act FAST Campaign*
- *Exposure to Environmental Tobacco Smoke in the Non-smoking Population of Cambodia*
- *Egg Consumption in Relation to Cardiovascular Disease and Mortality: The Physicians' Health Study*
- *Benefit of Low – Fat over Low – Carbohydrate Diet on Endothelial Health in Obesity*
- *Nutrition and Cardiovascular Disease*
- *The Association of Smoking and Cardiovascular Disease in a Population with Low Cholesterol Levels: A Study of 648,346 Men from the Korean National Health System*

Prospective Cohort Study

- *Smoking Reduction Fails to Improve Clinical and Biological Markers of Cardiac Disease: A Randomized Controlled Trial*

- *Perceptions, Knowledge and Beliefs about Prevention of Cardiovascular Diseases in Villa Nueva, Guatemala*

- *Secondhand Smoke Exposure among Women and Children: Evidence from 31 Countries*

- *Spectrum of Heart Disease and Risk Factors in a Black Urban Population in South Africa(the Heart of Soweto Study): A Cohort Study*

- *Effects of Age, Time Period, and Birth Cohort on the Prevalence of Diabetes and Obesity in Korean Men*

- *Cholesterol, Diabetes and Major Cardiovascular Diseases in the Asia − Pacific Region*

- *Prospective Observational Study of Acute Coronary Syndromes in China: Practice Patterns and Outcomes*

- *Dietary Phosphorus and Blood Pressure: International Study of Macro − and Micro − Nutrients and Blood Pressure*

- *Body Mass Index, Blood Pressure, and Mortality From Stroke, A Nationally Representative Prospective Study of 212,000 Chinese Men*

- *Effect of the Italian Smoking Ban on Population Rates of Acute Coronary Events*

- *Pulse Hypertension: A New Component of the Metabolic*

Syndrome in Elderly Women?

- *Epidemiological Transition of Stroke in China: Twenty − one − Year Observational Study from the Sino − MonICA − beijing Project*

- *Metabolic Effects of Weight Loss on a Very − Low − Carbohydrate Diet Compared with an isocaloric High − Carbohydrate Diet in Abdominally Obese Subjects*

- *Effectiveness of the Diabetes Education and Self Management for Ongoing and Newly Diagnosed(DESMonD) Programme for People with Newly Diagnosed Type 2 Diabetes: Cluster Randomised Controlled Trial*

- *Secondhand Smoke Exposure in Public Places in Guatemala: Comparison with Other Latin American Countries*

- *Salt Intake is Related to Soft Drink Consumption in Children and Adolescents: A Link to Obesity?*

- *Perceptions of Nigerian University Students about the Influence of Cigarette Advertisement on Smoking Habit: A Quantitative Analysis*

- *How Much of the Recent Decline in the Incidence of Myocardial Infarction in British Men can be Explained by Changes in Cardiovascular Risk Factors?: Evidence From a Prospective Population − Based Study*

- *A Nationally Representative Case − Control Study of Smoking and Death in India*

- *Duration of Breast − Feeding and the Incidence of Type 2*

TDR

UNICEF – UNDP – World Bank – WHO Special Programme
or Research and Training in Tropical Diseases
**열대병에 관한 연구 및 교육을 위한 유니세프, 유엔개발프로그램,
세계은행, 세계보건기구 합동 특별 프로그램**

① 기구

1) 소재지

주 소	Communications Unit Special Programme for Research & Training in Tropical Diseases (TDR) World Health Organization 1211 Geneva 27, SWITZERLand
전 화	+41 22 791 3725
팩 스	+41 22 791 4854
전자우편	tdr@who.int
홈페이지	http://www.who.int/tdr/index.html

2) 설립연혁

열대병에 관한 연구 및 교육을 위한 유니세프, 유엔개발프로그
램, 세계은행, 세계보건기구 합동 특별 프로그램(TDR)은 독립
적인 과학적 협동형태의 글로벌 프로그램이다. TDR은 세계 주

요 전염병을 퇴치하기 위한 협력, 지원, 노력을 위해 1975년 유니세프, 유엔개발프로그램, 세계은행, 세계보건기구의 공동후원으로 설립되었다.

3) 설립목적

① 연구 및 개발
② 교육 및 개발능력 강화

4) 조직

TDR은 2004년 11월 과학적인 운영을 강화하기 위해 새로운 조직시스템을 도입하였다. 이 새로운 시스템하에서 TDR은 다음과 같은 5개의 영역으로 나뉘어 운영되고 있다.

① 연구 및 방법 도입(IRM: Implementation Research and Methods)
② 상품개발 및 평가(PDE: Product Development and Evaluation)
③ 전략적 발견연구(SDR: Strategic and Discovery Research)
④ 연구 능력 강화(RCS: Research Capability Strengthening)
⑤ 말라리아에 관한 다자적 이니셔티브(MIM: Multilateral Initiative on Malaria)

② 정보원

1) 정보배포정책

TDR의 정보원은 'Research Results' 및 'Publications'에서 찾아볼 수 있다. 'Research Results'에서는 연구결과보고서를 제공하고 있으며, 'Publications'에서는 출판물 및 TDR의 뉴스레터를 열람할 수 있다.

2) 정보 자료

① 연구결과보고서
다음과 같은 보고서 열람이 가능하다.

- *Director's Report on 2006 Activities*
- *Project Reports: final Report Series*
- *Progress 2003 - 2004*
- *Progress 2001 - 2002*
- *Progress 1999 - 2000*
- *Progress 1997 - 1998*

[Disease Watch]

- *Tuberculosis*
- *LeisHmaniasis*
- *Soil - Transmitted Helminthiasis*
- *Chlamydia*
- *Syphilis*

- *Dengue*
- *Malaria*
- *Human African Trypanosomiasis*
- *SARS*
- *Schistosomiasis*
- *Onchocerciasis*
- *Leprosy*
- *Chagas Disease*

② 출판물

TDR의 출판물은 연도별 또는 질병분류별로 나뉘어 브라우
징이 가능하다. 대표적인 최근의 목록은 다음과 같다.

[Publications]

- *Report of the Expert Consultation on Immunotherapeutic Interventions for Tuberculosis*
- *Equitable Access to Health Care and Infectious Disease Control: Concepts, Measurement and Interventions*
- *Tropical Disease Research: Progress 2005－2006*
- *Neglected Diseases: A Human Rights Analysis*
- *Applied Social Sciences for Public Health(ASSPH): Higher Degree Training for Implementation Research on Tropical Diseases*
- *Making a Difference－30 Years of Research and Capacity Building in Tropical Diseases*
- *Scientific Working Group Report on Dengue*

- *Effective Project Planning and Evaluation in Biomedical Research - TRAINER'S MANUALS*
- *Ethical Challenges in Study Design and Informed Consent for Health Research in Resource - Poor Settings*
- *Lessons Learned in Home Management of Malaria*
- *Scientific Working Group on Tuberculosis*
- *Scientific Working Group on Schistosomiasis*
- *Partnerships for Malaria Control: Engaging the formal and Informal Private Sectors*
- *The Fourth External Review: Final Reports*
- *The Use of Rapid Syphilis Tests*
- *Diagnostics for Tuberculosis - Global Demand and Market Potential*
- *TDR Summary Report 2004 - 2005 in Arabic*
- *TDR Informe Resumido de las Actividades de 2004 - 2005*
- *Multicountry Study of Aedes Aegypti Pupal Productivity Survey Methodology*
- *Gender and Tuberculosis: Cross - Site Analysis and Implications of a Multi - Country Study in Bangladesh, India, Malawi, and Colombia*
- *TDR: Health Research That Makes a Difference*
- *TDR Summary Report 2004 - 2005*
- *Handbook: Quality Practices in Basic Biomedical Research*
- *Scientific Working Group on Lymphatic Filariasis*

- *TDR Quality Information in Field Research*
- *TDR Effective Project Planning and Evaluation in Biomedical Research – PARTICIPANTS' GUIDE*
- *TDR Approved Programme Budget 2006 – 2007*
- *Strategic Initiative for Developing Capacity in Ethical Review(SIDCER)*
- *Operational Guidance: Information Needed to Support Clinical Trials of Herbal Products*
- *Operational Guidelines for the EstablisHment and Functioning of Data and Safety Monitoring Boards*
- *Tropical Disease Research: Progress 2003 – 2004*
- *Dengue Diagnostics: Proceedings of an International Workshop*
- *The Gender Agenda in the Control of Tropical Diseases: A Review of Current Evidence*
- *Strategic Review of Traps and Targets for Tsetse and African Trypanosomiasis Control*
- *Research Instruments and Guidelines for Infectious Diseases Developed and PublisHed*
- *Research Instruments and Guidelines for Infectious Diseases Produced by Scientists from Disease Endemic Countries [DECs]*
- *Research Instruments and Guidelines for Infectious Diseases Developed and PublisHed*
- *Research Instruments and Guidelines for Infectious*

Diseases   Produced   by   Scientists   from   Disease Endemic Countries [DECs]

[Newsletter]

- *On the Making and Writing of History*
- *Making a Difference: 30 Years of Research and Capacity Building in Tropical Diseases*
- *How Implementation Research Helped Drive Policy Change*
- *Open Access Database Spurs Drug Target Research*
- *TB－HAART Study Begins*
- *Health Research Project Management*
- *Expanding Clinical Trials in Developing Countries*
- *Giving a Voice to Health Researchers in Disease Endemic Countries*
- *Artemisinin－Combination Therapies(ACTs) Used Effectively in Home Management of Malaria*
- *MIM/TDR Task Force Holds Consultation and Meeting on Malaria Research Capacity Strengthening in Africa*
- *TDR and PAHO Convene Experts to Review Procedures for Testing Chagas Disease Drug Candidates*
- *Helminth Drug Initiative Moves into Action*
- *South－East Asia Advisory Committee Meets In Memoriam*

UNAIDS
United Nations Programme on HIV/AIDS
유엔에이즈계획

① 기구

1) 소재지

주　　소　　UNAIDS20, avenue AppiaCH－1211 Geneva 27, Switzerland

전　　화　　＋ 41　22　791　3666

팩　　스　　＋ 41　22　791　4187

전자우편　　unaids@unaids.org

홈페이지　　http://www.unaids.org/en/default.asp

2) 설립연혁

UNAIDS은 각 국가들의 에이즈 관리 및 예방사업을 돕기 위해 1996년 1월 창설된 유엔 산하 에이즈 전담기구이다. 1990년 중반에 이르러 에이즈의 확산이 심각해지면서 전문적인 유엔 기구의 필요성이 대두되었다. 이에 6개 유엔기구가 함께 에이즈 프로그램을 실시하게 되었는데, 초기에 참여한 6개 기구는 UNICEF, UNDP, UNFPA, UNESCO, WHO, WB였으며 최근에 UNDCP가 새롭게 참여하여 총 7개 기구가 함께하는 프로그램이 되었다. 전 세계적으로 약 155개국을 상대로 활동하며, 132개의 UNAIDS 담당 사무소가 있다.

3) 설립목적

UNAIDS는 HIV와 AIDS에 대한 대응책을 강화하고, 지원하는 사명을 가지고 있다. 여기에는 HIV의 확산을 막는 한편, 보균자들의 생활을 보호 · 지원하고, 개개인과 집단의 HIV에 대한 방어능력을 키우는 등의 임무가 포함되어 있다.

4) 주요 사업

UNAIDS는 각 국가에 에이즈에 대한 신속한 정보를 제공하고 있으며 HIV 확산 방지와 감염이나 그로 인한 피해자를 위해 지원활동 등을 한다. 더욱 효과적이며 조직적인 국제적 대응책 마련을 위한 UNAIDS의 주요 사업은 다음과 같다.

① AIDS의 효과적인 대응책에 대한 인식 고취(Leadership and Advocacy for Effective Action on the Epidemic)

② AIDS 예방을 위한 전략 정보 및 기술 지원(Strategic Information and Technical Support to Guide Efforts against AIDS Worldwide)

③ AIDS 발생과 대응 상황 추적, 감시 및 평가(Tracking, Monitoring and Evaluation of the Epidemic and of Responses to it)

④ 시민 사회의 참여와 전략적 파트너십 개발(Civil Society

Engagement and the Development of Strategic Partnerships)

⑤ 효과적인 대응책 수립을 위한 재원 마련(Mobilization of Resources to Support an Effective Response)

② 정보원

1) 정보배포정책

UNAIDS의 정보원은 HIV/AIDS에 관한 다양한 주제를 다루고 있다. 거의 모든 정보원이 온라인상으로 이용 가능하며 검색방법은 다음과 같다.

① 주제 분야별 훑어보기: 페이지 오른쪽 상단에 있는 키워드 검색 기능을 통해 주제, 나라/지역, 출판

② 기관별 검색: 오른쪽 상단에 위치한 상세 검색 기능('How to Order UNAIDS Publications'란에 나와 있는 전체 출판물 목록 참고)

2) 정보 자료

① Resource

메인 메뉴 중 'Resources'를 클릭하면 'Epidemiology', 'Publications', 'Fast Facts about AIDS', 'Questions & Answers', 'Terminology'의 항목이 나타난다.

- Epistemology

유행/전염병학이라는 뜻의 항목명처럼 HIV/AIDS에 대

한 전반적인 정보를 다루고 있으며 다양한 정보원을 보
유하고 있다.

- *AIDS Epidemic Update*
  HIV/AIDS에 대한 최신 정보를 알려 주는 연속간행
  물이다. 현재 2004년판이 홈페이지에 제공되어 있다.
- *Global Summary of the HIV and AIDS Epidemic in
  2004*
  HIV/AIDS의 세계 분포 등 통계 수치를 명료하게
  정리해 놓은 DPT 형식의 정보원이다.
- *Report on the Global AIDS Epidemic*
  연 2회 간행되는 나라별 HIV/AIDS 현황 자료이다.
- *Epidemiological Fact Sheets on HIV/AIDS and Sexually Transmitted Infections*
  최신 HIV/AIDS 발생 사례 및 빈발 지역 등에 대한
  자료를 정리해 놓았다. 제목을 클릭하면, 원문뿐 아
  니라 2004년에 갱신된 'Epidemiological Fact Sheet'
  를 나라별로 선택하여 볼 수 있다. 이 외에도 화면 오
  른쪽의 'In This Section' 메뉴를 보면, 다양한 정보원
  이 나와 있다.
- 'Epidemiological Databases'
  HIV/AIDS와 관련된 데이터베이스를 소개하고 있다.
  Global HIV/AIDS Online Database(UNAIDS/World
  Health Organization); World Population Prospects;
  The 2004 Revision Population Database(United Nations
  Population Division); HIV/AIDS Surveillance Data

Base(United States Bureau of the Census); HIV/AIDS Survey Indicators Database(MEASURE DHS+MACRO International); Global HIV/AIDS Training Materials Database(Centers for Disease Control and Prevention) 등의 데이터베이스가 링크되어 있다. 특히 첫 번째 Global HIV/AIDS online Database는 'Interactive Mapping' 같은 시각장치가 잘 구비되어 있어서 세계지도를 보면 한눈에 HIV/AIDS 현황을 파악할 수 있다. 'Data Query' 등 정보검색 기능도 세세하게 준비되어 있다.

- 'Epistemology Slide Search'
  PPT 슬라이드 형식의 정보원 검색 기능을 제공한다. 지도, 통계표 등의 자료가 많이 있다. 키워드, 출판 날짜, 나라, 지역별로 검색이 가능하다.

- 'Recent Epidemiological Publications'
  최근 'Epistemology' 관련 출판물 목록이다. 제목과 간단한 소개말이 나와 있으며, 제목을 클릭하면 원문을 볼 수 있다.

- 'In This Section'
  하단에 Links 메뉴에는 'Epidemiological Fact Sheet by Country'라는 항목이 있다. WHO와 UNAIDS가 공동 제공하는 나라별 HIV/AIDS 현황 자료이다. 역시 제목을 클릭하면 나라별로 선별해서 'Fact Sheets'를 볼 수 있게 링크되어 있다.

- Publications

  UNAIDS 출판물의 검색 방법은 위의 정보정책에서 언급했다. 화면 오른쪽 'In This Section' 메뉴에 나와 있듯이 UNAIDS 출판물은 다음과 같이 분류된다.

  - Latest Publications

    2005년 현재 최근 출판물 목록이다. 2004년 목록은 별도로 링크되어 있다. 전체 목록은 'How to Order UNAIDS Publications'란에 나와 있다.

  - Corporate Publications

    UNAIDS의 법인출판물 목록이다. 제목을 클릭하면 전문 보기 창이 나타난다.

  - Best Practice Collection

    Best Practice Collection은 UNAIDS가 효과성, 윤리적 타당성, 관련성, 효율성, 그리고 지속성의 기준에 따라 성공적인 AIDS 대응책을 선정하여 문헌화한 100여 권 규모의 'Best Practice' 출판물을 말한다. 여기에는 AIDS 교육을 장려하고, 경험을 나누고, HIV/AIDS 예방을 위해 노력하는 사람들을 지원하는 내용의 정보원들이 포함된다. 'Best Practice Collection'란의 'In This Section' 메뉴에 보면, 'Best Practice Publications'가 있다. 해당 페이지에 'Browse the Complete List of Titles in the best Practice Collection'을 클릭하면 'best Practice Collection'의 전 목록을 확인할 수 있으며 원문을 다운받을 수 있다.

  - Publications on the Follow up to the UN Special

Session on HIV/AIDS

'실천선언(Declaration of Commitment)' 이후 국제
사회의 AIDS 확산을 막고 현존하는 감염인구를 보호
하려는 구체적인 실천 노력에 대한 정보 자료들을 모
아 놓았다. 현재까지 간행된 연속간행물목록이 나와
있으며, 제목을 클릭하면 전문 보기 창이 나타난다.

- How to Order UNAIDS Publications

  'Best Practice Collection'을 포함한 UNAIDS 출판
  물의 전체 목록과 무료 원문 다운로드가 제공되며,
  인쇄본 주문 시에는 unaids@unaids.org의 주소로
  'Information Centre'에 연락하면 된다. 자세한 주문
  방법과 우편주소 역시 게재되어 있다.

• Fast Facts about UNAIDS

아래의 다섯 분야에 대한 정보가 Q&A의 형식으로 제공
되어 있다.

- General Information about HIV and AIDS
- Transmission
- Prevention
- Care
- Testing
- Myths

• Questions & Answers

위의 'Fast Facts about UNAIDS'가 일반대중을 위한
알기 쉽고 개괄적인 정보 제공란이라면, 'Questions &
Answers'는 HIV/AIDS의 정의, 파급력, UNAIDS의 역

할과 사명 등에 대한 더욱 자세하고 전문적인 정보를
제공한다. 아래의 세 항목으로 나뉘어 있다.

- Q&A Ⅰ: International Programmes, Initiatives and
  Funding Issues
- Q&A Ⅱ: Basic Facts about the HIV/AIDS Epidemic
  and Its Impact
- Q&A Ⅲ: Selected Issues: Prevention and Care

각 항목을 클릭하면 새 창을 통해 자세한 내용을 볼 수
있으며 전문을 다운로드할 수도 있다.

• Terminology

- Glossary of HIV/AIDS - Related Terms

  일부 HIV/AIDS 관련 용어들은 HIV 감염자들에게
  부정적인 의미를 내포하는 경우가 있다. 이 용어집은
  HIV/AIDS 관련 용어들을 총정리해 놓았으며 부정적
  의미를 내포한 용어들을 알려 주고 대체 용어를 제
  시하고 있다.

- UNAIDS Terminology Database

  UNAIDS Terminology Database는 영어, 불어, 러시
  아어, 스페인어로 제공되며 현재 사용 여부나 선호도
  에 근거해 HIV/AIDS 용어와 관련된 혼란을 해소하
  고자 만들어졌다. UNAIDS 구조와 관련된 용어, UN
  기관이나 프로그램명, 국제회의 등의 관련 용어, 그
  리고 HIV/AIDS 관련 의학용어, 기관명 등을 실었다.
  지금도 계속 갱신되고 있다.

• 각 메뉴를 클릭하면 이용할 수 있다. ‘Glossary of

HIV/AIDS – Related Terms'는 알파벳 순서로 정리되어 있으며, 'UNAIDS Terminology Database'는 전체 목록 보기나 용어 검색이 가능하다.

② Media

메인메뉴 중 'Resource' 밑에 위치한 'Media'에는 언론 관련 정보원들이 있다. Media 중에서 정보원이 담긴 항목들을 소개하면 아래와 같다.

- Press Releases

  날짜순으로 나열된 보도 자료 목록이 제공되어 있다. 제목을 클릭하면 원문을 볼 수 있다.

- Fact Sheets

  Q&A, 표, 그래프, 각국의 HIV/AIDS 관련 지표 등을 담은 'Fact Sheet'들이 날짜순으로 정리되어 있다. 제목을 클릭하면 원문을 볼 수 있다.

- Recent News

  최근 소식들을 간단히 요약해 놓았다. 'Press Release'를 클릭하면 해당 보도 자료로 이동한다.

WHF
World Heart Federation
세계심장연합

① 기구

1) 소재지

소재국가	스위스
주 소	World Heart Federation, 7, rue des Battoirs 1205 Geneva, Switzerland
전 화	+41 22 807 03 20
팩 스	+41 22 807 03 39
전자우편	admin@worldheart.org
홈페이지	http://www.worldheart.org/

2) 성격

세계심장연합(WHF)는 모든 심장계 질병과 관련된 내용을 다루는 스위스연방 시민법에 의거한 공식협회이다.

3) 설립연혁

WHF는 원래 1978년 국제심장학사회(ISC: International Society

of Cardiology)와 국제심장학협회(ICF: International Cardiology Federation)가 합쳐져 국제심장학사회협회(ISFC: International Society and Federation of Cardiology)라는 명칭으로 만들어졌다. 그 후 1998년 ISFC는 지금의 세계심장협회로 명칭이 변경되었다.

ISC는 1946년 전문과학기구로서 국가심장학사회 회원들로 구성되어 설립되었다. ICF는 1970년 전 세계 심장재단으로서 국제연구, 전문교육, 대중교육, 커뮤니티 프로그램 등을 지원하는 목적으로 설립되었다.

1996년 유네스코(UNESCO)와 세계보건기구(WHO) 간의 협정에 의해 WHF는 류마티성 열과 심장질환 방지와 같은 각기 다른 프로젝트에 참여하게 되었다. 합동프로젝트는 현재도 계속 진행 중에 있다. WHF는 현재 WHO에 의해 인정받는 심장질환 방지 분야에서 앞서가는 NGO 협력기관이다. 1998년 위원회에 의해 기존의 ISFC가 현재의 WHF로 변경되었다.

4) 비전 및 임무

심장질환 방지 및 통제를 통해 개발도상국의 국민들이 좀 더 길고 나은 삶을 이룰 수 있도록 하는 사명을 지닌다.

5) 조직

WHF의 조직은 크게 위원회(Board)를 기준으로 구성되어 있다.
① 과학자문위원회(SAB: Scientific Advisory Board)
과학자문위원회는 적절한 의학 및 과학지식이 세계심장협회

의 노력을 뒷받침하여 심장질환 및 발작의 영향을 감소시킬 수 있도록 한다. 이 위원회의 역할은 세계심장협회의 사명을 지원하는 데에 있다.

과학자문위원회는 이 위원회의 과학협의회(Scientific Councils), 전문가패널, 심장혈관 세계의회 과학프로그램위원회(Scientific Programme Committee of the World Congress of Cardiology) 그리고 대륙회원협회(Continental Member Society) 총회의 공동 후원을 통해 세계심장협회의 임무를 완수하는 책임이 있다. 이들 각각은 사명을 중심으로 한 활동 완수를 지원하는 데에 다방면적인 노력을 제공하고 있다.

② 재단자문위원회(Foundations Advisory Board)

재단자문위원회는 세계심장협회의 홍보 및 건강촉진활동에 긴밀히 관여하고 있다. 이 위원회의 임무는 공공정책 및 대중교육 개발 및 촉진에 있다. 또한 이 위원회는 국가심장재단의 기금마련사업 및 심장병방지프로그램을 지원한다. 재단자문위원회는 새로운 국가 및 지역재단의 설립을 지원하기도 한다.

6) 회원

세계심장연합는 회원제로 운영되는 기관으로서 심장 관련 의료커뮤니티와 대중보건커뮤니티가 함께한다. 세계심장협회는 전 세계 약 100개국의 총 197개의 회원기관으로 구성된다.

① 국가회원

심장 관련 국가사회 또는 국가심장재단으로 이루어진다.

② 대륙회원

대륙사회 또는 재단으로 구성되며 유럽, 북미 및 중남미, 아시아 태평양지역 그리고 아프리카 지역의 국가그룹으로 이루어진다.

③ 준국가회원

심장질환 및 발작의 방지 및 통제와 관련되는 업무를 지원하는 국가사회 또는 세계심장질환과 비슷한 목적을 가지고 있는 기관으로 이루어진다.

④ 준국제회원

독립적인 법인기관으로서 심장질환 및 발작의 방지 및 통제와 관련된 활동을 하는 기관들로 구성된다.

⑤ 준개인회원

국가회원이 불가능한 국가의 국민으로서 세계심장협회의 회원 자격을 원하는 개인들로 이루어진다.

7) 파트너십

특정화된 목표의 성취를 위한 공동협력 및 책임에 의해 형성된 개인 또는 그룹 간 관계를 지향하는 파트너십은 둘 또는 그 이상의 협력자들 간의 합의에 의해 이루어진 공동의 관심그룹이라 할 수 있다. 세계심장협회는 협력을 바탕으로 한 활동이야말로 인식을 증가시키고 심장 관련 질병을 방지하는 노력을 확대할 수 있다고 믿는다. 이에, 세계심장협회는 다양한 기관들과의 파트너십을 개발해 왔다. 세계심장협회는 일반적인 대중보건, 심장 관련 질병, 흡연통제, 신체활동 그리고 아동 미디어 및 교육활동과 관련한 활동에 있어서 다른 기관들과 협력관계에 있다.

8) 주요 시범 사업

① 세계 심장의 날(World Heart Day)
② 세사미 워크숍(Sesame Workshop)
③ 중국 - 격차 줄이기(China - Bridging the Gap)

9) 협력기관

다음은 세계심장연합이 제공하는 관련 기관이다.
- 클린턴 글로벌 이니셔티브(CGI: Clinton Global Initiative)
  홈페이지: www.clintonglobalinitiative.org
- 프레임워크 컨벤션 연맹(Framework Convention Alliance)
  홈페이지: http://www.fctc.org/
- 비만방지 및 관련 만성질병을 위한 글로벌 연합(the Global Alliance for the Prevention of Obesity and Related Chronic Disease)
  홈페이지: www.preventionalliance.net

- 글로벌 금연 파트너십(Global Smokefree Partnership)

  홈페이지: http://www.globalsmokefree.com/gsp/

- 옥스퍼드 건강연맹(Oxford Health Alliance)

  홈페이지: http://www.oxha.org/

- 세사미워크숍(Sesame Workshop)

  홈페이지: http://www.sesameworkshop.org/

- 유럽축구협회단체(UEFA: Union of European Football Associations)

  홈페이지: http://www.uefa.com/

- 개발과 평화를 위한 유엔 스포츠(United Nations Sport for Development and Peace)

  홈페이지: http://www.un.org/themes/sport/

- 유네스코(UNESCO: United Nations Educational, Scientific and Cultural Organization)

  홈페이지: http://portal.unesco.org/en/ev.php－URL_ID＝2900 8-&URL_ DO＝DO_toPIC&URL_SECTIon＝201.html

- 세계경제포럼(the World Economic forum－WEF)

  홈페이지: http://www.weforum.org/en/index.htm

- 세계보건기구(World Health Organization－WHO)

  홈페이지: http://www.who.int/en/

② 정보원

1) 정보원배포정책

WHF의 정보원은 'Publications'와 'Press'에서 찾아볼 수 있다. 발간 자료(Publications)는 저널, 보고서, 서적 그리고 뉴스레터로 나뉘어 제공된다.

2) 보도 자료(Press)

WHF의 보도 자료는 영어, 스페인어, 프랑스어로 제공된다. 언어별 그리고 연도별 구분 브라우징이 가능하다. 영어로 제공되는 2008년 보도 자료는 다음과 같다.

- 09.06.2008 *Know Your Risk! – World Heart Day 2008, Sunday 28th September*
- 21.05.2008 *World Heart Federation Appoints Sidney Csmith JR as President Elect and Susanne Volqvartz as Vice President Elect from January 2010*
- 19.05.2008 *Fuster Joins Forces with Sachs to Fight Poverty*
- 18.05.2008 *Hypertension Treatment in Elderly Patients over 80 Years of Age Reduces Mortality by 21%*
- 18.05.2008 *New Strategies for the Prevention of Obesity and a Sedentary Lifestyle in Chldren*
- 18.05.2008 *Stress at Work Increases the Progression of Arteriosclerosis*
- 18.05.2008 *Passive Smoking: 30 Minutes is Enough to*

Cause Observable Changes in the Arteries

- 13.05.2008 *Science and Prevention at the World Congress of Cardiology*
- 07.03.2008 *Global Launch of First International Women's Heart Health Advocacy drive*
- 20.02.2008 *World Heart Federation Urges Geneva to Vote for Smoking Ban*

3) 발간 자료(Publications)

① 저널

WHF은 방지와 통제저널*(Prevention and Control Journal)*과 자연임상실험심장혈관약 *저널(Nature Clinical Practice Cardiovascular Medicine Journal)*을 발간하고 있다.

② 보고서

WHF가 제공하는 보고서는 WHF의 자체보고서라기보다는 관련 기관들의 관련 자료를 담고 있는 보고서라 할 수 있다. 최근목록은 다음과 같다.

- *Preventing Chronic Diseases −A Vital Investment*
- *The SuRF(Surveillance Risk Factors) Reports*
- *World Health Reports*

③ 서적

2008년 6월 현재 웹페이지상에 소개되고 있는 서적은 다음과 같다.

- *A Race against Time*
- *Avoiding Heart Attacks and Stroke*
- *The Atlas of Heart Disease and Stroke*

④ 뉴스레터

이메일 신청을 통해 직접 본인의 이메일로 WHF의 뉴스레터를 받아 볼 수 있다. 최근 3년 동안 발간된 뉴스레터는 다음과 같다.

- April/May 2008
- February/March 2008
- December 2007/January 2008
- October/November 2007
- August/September 2007
- June/July 2007
- April/May 2007
- February/March 2007
- December 2006/January 2007
- October/November 2006

WHL

World Hypertension League

세계고혈압연맹

① 기구

1) 소재지

소재국가	캐나다
주　　소	Dr. Arun Chockalingam Secretary General Blusson Hall－11016 Faculty of Health Sciences Simon Fraser University 8888 University Drive Burnaby, BC V5A 1S6, Canada
전　　화	＋1 778 782 6952
팩　　스	＋1 778 782 5927
전자우편	whlsec@sfu.ca
홈페이지	http://www.worldhypertensionleague.org/Pages/Home.aspx

2) 성격

세계고혈압연맹(WHL)은 국제고혈압협회(isH: International Society of Hypertension)의 한 부서이며 세계보건기구(WHO)와

공식적인 협력관계에 있는 기구이다.

3) 설립연혁

고혈압이 전 세계적인 문제라는 것은 1950년대 및 1960년대부터 알려진 사실이다. 많은 연구들이 1964년 isH의 설립 이래로 발달해 왔으며, isH 의회는 연구정보의 교환을 강조해 왔다. 그러나 고혈압 환자들로의 실제적인 적용은 연구발달의 수준에는 훨씬 뒤지고 있었다. 고혈압 관리라는 의미가 1970년대에 들어서 WHO 및 미국 국가고혈압교육프로그램(U.S. National High Blood Pressure Education Program)에 의해 널리 퍼지게 되었다. 고혈압 방지와 관련된 많은 국가연맹들이 유럽 국가들에서 생겨나게 되었다. 1975년 유럽연맹에 대한 아이디어가 제안되었고, 1977년 고혈압유럽연맹에 대한 제안이 이루어졌다. 1982년 WHO와 국제녹십자(International Green Cross)에 의해 고혈압연맹의 더 큰 의미의 협회가 확실하게 정의되었다. 1983년 세계고혈압연맹(WHL)의 형성이 진행되었으며 1984년 WHL은 비로소 비영리국제기구로서 제네바에서 등록되었다. 2007년 현재 총 85개의 회원기구와 1개의 후원회원이 WHL에서 활동하고 있다.

4) 비전 및 임무

WHL은 전 세계 인구의 혈관 고혈압의 방지 및 관리를 증진시키기 위해 활동한다.

5) 회원

WHL은 1984년 1월 4일 15개의 유럽연맹 회원을 토대로 스위스에서 법인으로 시작한 기구로서 2007년 현재 85개의 글로벌 회원연맹과 1개의 후원회원기구로 이루어져 있다. 회원연맹의 지역별 구분은 아프리카 및 중동, 아시아, 호주, 유럽, 북미, 그리고 남미로 이루어진다.

6) 관련 기관

① 국제기구(International Organizations)
* 국제고혈압협회(International Society of Hypertension)
* 유럽고혈압연맹(European Society of Hypertension)
* 미대륙간고혈압연맹(Inter‒American Society of Hypertension)
* 세계보건기구(World Health Organization)
* 심장혈관질병(Cardiovascular Diseases)
* 건강인터네트워크/연구(Health InterNetwork/Access to Research)
* 세계심장연합(World Heart Federation)

② 미국(USA)
* 미국심장협회(American Heart Association)
* 고혈압정보(High Blood Pressure Information)
* 미국고혈압협회(American Society of Hypertension)
* 미국심장협회 고혈압연구협의회(Council for High Blood

Pressure Research‑American Heart Association)
- 고혈압네트워크(Hypertension Network)
- 국가심장폐혈연구소(National Heart, Lung and Blood Institute)
- 혈압 낮추는 방법(Your Guide to Lowering Blood Pressure)
- 당뇨, 소화, 신장 질병 국가연구소(National Institute of Diabetes & Digestive & Kidney Diseases)
- 메릴랜드대학교 의료시스템(University of Maryland Medical System)
- 메릴랜드대학교 의과대학 심장센터(University of Maryland Medicine Maryland Heart Center)
- 메릴랜드대학교 의과대학 심장건강안내(University of Maryland Medicine Heart Health Guide)
- 메릴랜드대학교 의과대학 특별기획‑고혈압: 조용한 살인을 멈추는 방법(University of Maryland Medicine Feature Story: "High Blood Pressure: Tips to Stop the Silent Killer")

③ 과학문헌(Scientific Literature)
- 뉴잉글랜드고혈압연구의학저널*(New England Journal of Medicine Hypertension Research)*

② 정보원

1) 정보원배포정책

WHL의 정보원은 'Newsletter', 'In Focus' 그리고 'Links'에서 찾아볼 수 있다. 'In Focus'에서는 WHL의 성명서 및 선언문을 열람할 수 있다.

2) 뉴스레터(Newsletter)

최근 뉴스레터(Current Newsletter)는 PDF로 열람이 가능하고, 그 이전의 뉴스레터들은 뉴스레터기록관(Archived issues)을 통해서 찾아볼 수 있다. 기록관 저장 뉴스레터 역시 PDF로 무료 열람이 가능하다.

3) In Focus

[성명서(Statements)]

- *Alcohol and Hypertension: Implications for Management*
- *Physical Exercise in the Management of Hypertension: Consensus Statement by the World Hypertension League*
- *Can Non-Pharmacological Interventions Reduce Doses of Drugs Needed for the Treatment of Hypertension?*

[WHL 선언문(1995 WHL Ottawa Declaration)]

- *Hypertension Control in the World: An Agenda for the Coming Decade*

4) 링크(Links)

[국제기구(International Organizations)]
- International Society of Hypertension
- European Society of Hypertension
- Inter-American Society of Hypertension
- World Health Organization
- Cardiovascular Diseases
- Health InterNetwork/Access to Research
- World Heart Federation

[미국(USA)]
- American Heart Association
- High Blood Pressure Information
- American Society of Hypertension
- Council for High Blood Pressure Research-American Heart Association
- Hypertension Network
- National Heart, Lung and Blood Institute
  홈페이지: www.nhlbi.nih.gov/hbp/hbp/whathbp.htm
- Your Guide to Lowering Blood Pressure
- National Institute of Diabetes & Digestive & Kidney Diseases
- University of Maryland Medical System
- University of Maryland Medicine Maryland Heart Center

- University of Maryland Medicine Heart Health Guide
- University of Maryland Medicine Feature Story: "High Blood Pressure: Tips to Stop the Silent Killer"

[과학문헌(Scientific Literature)]
- *New England Journal of Medicine Hypertension Research*

[후원기관(Supporting and Funding Bodies)]
- Omron

WHO

World Health Organization

세계보건기구

① 기구

1) 소재지

주   소   Avenue Appia 20 1211 Geneva 27, Switzerland
전   화   + 41 22 791 2111
팩   스   + 41 22 791 3111
전자우편   info@who.int
홈페이지   http://www.who.int/

2) 설립연혁

세계보건기구(WHO)는 제2차 세계대전에 존재하였던 국제공공
위생사무소(Office of International Public Hygiene), 국제연맹
보건기구(League of Nations Health Organization) 및 UNRRA-
(UN Relief and Rehabilitation Agency) 보건국의 제반 임무를
계승받은 기구로서, 1948년 4월 7일 61개 회원국이 WHO헌장
에 대한 비준을 함으로써 정식 발족하였는데, 이후부터 4월 7
일을 세계보건의 날로 정해 기념식을 거행하고 있다. 제1차

WHO총회는 1948년 6월 24일 제네바에서 개최되었으며 이에 앞서 조직되었던 WHO임시위원회는 같은 해 9월 1일자로 해체되었다.

3) 설립목적 및 기능

WHO에서는 세계 인류가 신체적·정신적으로 최고의 건강수준에 도달하는 것을 목적으로 활동한다. 이를 위해 중앙검역소 업무와 연구 자료 제공, 유행성 질병 및 전염병 대책 후원, 회원국의 공중보건 관련 행정 강화와 확장 지원 등의 일을 맡아 본다. 헌장에서 건강은, 육체적·정신적·사회적으로 완전히 행복한 상태를 말하며, 단순히 질병에 관한 것만을 지칭하는 것이 아니라고 정의한다. WHO는 국제보건사업의 지도적·조정적 기구의 성격을 띠며, 주요 사업은 본부 사무국을 중심으로 한 중앙기술사업과 각 지역 사무국을 중심으로 한 각국에 대한 기술원조로 나뉜다.

4) 회원

UN 가입 국가는 WHO의 헌장을 받아들임으로써 회원이 될 수 있다. 총 192개국이 회원으로 등록되어 있다.

5) 한국과의 관계

① 가입
 • 1949년 8월 17일

- 집행이사국 4연임 중(1960∼1963, 1984∼1987, 1995∼ 1998, 2001∼2004)

② 우리 인사 고위직 진출현황
- 한상태 박사, 서태평양지역 사무처장 역임(1989∼1994, 1994∼1999)
- 이종욱 박사, 2003년 7월 21일 제6대 WHO 사무총장으로 취임
- 이 외 WHO 본부 및 서태평양지역 사무처에 6명(P-5급) 진출

③ WHO 주한 대표부
- 1965년 상주대표부 설치
- 1999년 4월 30일 동 대표부 폐쇄
- 한국의 OECD 가입에 따라 2000년부터 연락사무소(Country Liaison Office)로 대체

④ 우리나라의 분담금
- 우리의 의무 분담금(Assessed Contribution) 비율은 2004∼2005년의 경우 1.8213%로 회원국 중 제10위

2 정보원

1) 온라인 서점

WHO 온라인 서점에서 1948년부터 발행된 WHO의 간행물과 그 외의 자료(뉴스, 간행물목록, 구독정보, 무료정보)를 볼 수 있고 구매도 가능하다(URL: http://www.who.int/bookorders/).

2) 유료 정기간행물(정기구독 가능)

- *Bulletin of the World Health Organization*
- *Weekly Epidemiological Record*
- *Pan American Journal of Public Health*
- *WHO Drug Information*
- *Eastern Mediterranean Health Journal*

3) 무료 정기간행물

- *World Health Report*
- *Weekly Epidemiological Record*(매주 금요일 배포)

4) 도서관

WHO는 기탁도서관 제도를 시행 중이며 각 회원국에 최소 1개의 기탁도서관이 있다.

5) 한국 내 기탁도서관

① 고려대학교

주   소   서울특별시 성북구 안암동 5가 1번지(136 – 701)

전   화   02 3290 1486, 1492

전자우편   libweb@korea.ac.kr

홈페이지   http://www.library.korea.ac.kr/index.jsp

자료유형	기증자료	
단행본	1533종	1603책
연간물	25종	781책
CD – ROM	4종	8책

WHPA

World Health Professions Alliance

국제의료전문직연맹

① 기구

1) 소재지

주 소	the World Health Profession Alliance(WHPA) 3 Place Jean Marteau, 1201 Geneva, Switzerland
전 화	+41 22 908 0100
팩 스	+41 22 908 0101
전자우편	whpa@icn.ch
홈페이지	http://www.whpa.org/

2) 설립연혁

국제의료전문직연맹(WHPA)은 1999년 국제적으로 건강문제를 고려하는 전 세계의 의사, 간호사, 약사들을 대표하는 기관으로 설립되었다. 2005년에 WHPA는 치과의들도 이 연맹의 일원으로 받아들였다. WHPA는 현재 세계적으로 약 23만 명 이상의 의료직 종사자들의 주요 지식을 총망라하는 기관이 되었다. WHPA는 또한 정부, 정책입안가, 세계보건기구 등과 협력하여 활동하기도 한다.

3) 회원

다음과 같은 회원기관을 두고 있다.

① 국제간호사협의회(ICN: International Council of Nurses)
   홈페이지: www.icn.ch

② 국제약사회(FIP: International Pharmaceutical Federation)
   홈페이지: www.fip.org

③ 세계치과협회(FDI: FDI World Dental Federation)
   홈페이지: www.fdiworldental.org

④ 세계의료협회(WMA: World Medical Association)
   홈페이지: www.wma.net

4) 주요 사업

WHPA는 다음의 이슈와 관련된 활동을 한다.

① 인권으로서의 건강

② 환자안전

③ HIV/AIDS

④ 국제흡연관리(Global Tobacco Control)

② 정보원

1) 정보배포정책

WHPA의 정보원은 'Press Releases', 'Joint Statement', 'Fact Sheet', 그리고 'Links'로 나뉜다. WHPA 관련 보도 자료나 회원기관들과 공동으로 발표한 성명성, 관련 단체 웹사이트로의 링크 등을 열람할 수 있다.

2) 정보 자료

① Press Releases

WHPA가 제공하는 보도내용이다. 대표적인 목록은 다음과 같다.

- 14 December 2006. *WMA and ICN Plead to Drop Death Sentences against Doctors and Nurses after New Scientific Evidence*
- 29 May 2006. *World Health Professionals Urge FIFA to Make the Wold Cup 2006 Smokefree WHPA Open Letter to FIFA*
- 7 April 2006. *World Health Professions Alliance Commends the Essential Contribution of Health Care Workers Worldwide*
- 22 August 2005. *World Health Professions Alliance Expands to Include Dentists*
- *31 May 2005. Health Professions Worldwide Are Key*

in Tobacco Control

- *2 March 2005. World's Health Professions Celebrate Adoption of Global Anti－Tobacco Treaty*
- *19 January 2005. Health Professionals and Patients Announce Historic Partnership*
- *12 July 2004. Health Professionals Call for More Research and Development of Medicines and Vaccines and the Optimization of Pharmacotherapy*
- *07 June 2004. International Health Professional Poll Puts Heart Disease, Obesity and Cancer As top Health Problems*
- *16 May 2004. Health Professionals issue a Wake up Call on AIDS*
- *27 May 2003. the World Health Professions Alliance Urges Taiwan's Acceptance to the WHO as an Observer*
- *28 February 2003. Main Health Professions Say Stronger Government Action against Tobacco is a Must*
- *04 November 2002. Poor Health Choices are Robbing Years of Life Worldwide Says WHPA*
- *29 April 2002. Health Professionals Call for Priority on Patient Safety*
- *15 April 2002. WHPA Expresses Concern That Health Professionals are being Prevented from Reaching Those in Need of Care*
- *7 January 2002. Nurses, Doctors and Pharmacists Join in Condemning Human Cloning*

- *9 May 2001. Slaying of Red Cross Workers Condemned by World Health Professions Alliance*
- *26 March 2001. Antibiotic Resistance is a Global Public Health Threat Calling for Urgent International Action*
- *27 November 2000. the Nurses, Pharmacists and Physicians of the World Plead for India to Utilise only Iodised Salt*
- *17 July 2000. Health Professions Speak out against the Confusing Messages Regarding HIV/AIDS*
- *12 May 2000. Physicians, Nurses and Pharmacists Announce a New Global Alliance for Improved Health*

② Joint Statements
- Joint Statement from the International Council of Nurses and the World Medical Association Re: Libya Verdict for Bulgarian Nurses and Palestinian Doctor－14 December 2006
- Resolution on HIV/AIDS－16 May 2004
- Promotion and Protection of Human Rights
- Joint Statement on Mental Health－15 May 2001
- Proposal for a UN Special Rapporteur on the Integrity and Independence of Health Professionals－April 2000
- ICN Joins Other Health Professionals Calling for a Tobacco Free World on World No Tobacco Day 1999 －31 May 1999

③ Fact Sheets

- Patient Safety: Medication Use in the Ageing Population
- Patient Safety
- Antimicrobial Resistance－World Health Professions Alliance
- Iodine Deficiency

④ Links

WHPA는 다음과 같은 기관과 협력관계에 있다.

- International Council of Nurses(ICN)
- International Labour Organization－Health Services
- International Pharmaceutical Federation(FIP)
- Office of the High Commissioner for Human Rights
- UNHCR
- UNCTAD
- UN Division for the Advancement of Women
- UNESCO
- UNICEF
- UNICEF International Child Development Centre
- WHO
- World Bank(WB)
- World Dental Federation(FDI)
- World Medical Association(WMA)

WMA

World Medical Association
세계의료협회

① 기구

1) 소재지

주 소	13, ch. du Levant, CIB－Bâtiment A 01210 Ferney－Voltaire, France
전 화	＋33 4 50 40 75 75
팩 스	＋33 4 50 40 59 37
전자우편	wma@wma.net
홈페이지	http://www.wma.net/e/

2) 설립연혁

세계의료협회(WMA)는 전 세계 의사들을 대표하는 국제기구이
다. WMA는 1947년 9월 17일에 설립되었다. 이날은 설립일이
기도 하지만 27명의 서로 다른 국가에서 온 회원들이 최초로
모인 제1회 총회가 열린 날이기도 하다. WMA는 의사들의 독
립성을 보장하고 윤리행동의 가능한 기준을 세우기 위해 설립
되었다.

3) 설립목적

WMA의 설립목적은 의학교육, 의료과학, 의료예술, 의학윤리에 관한 가장 높은 국제표준을 달성하고자 기여하는 데에 있다.

4) 조직

WMA의 의사결정기관은 총회이며 총회는 1년에 한 차례 소집된다. 총회는 각 국가회원협회의 사절단, 운영진, WMA 협의회 구성원, 그리고 협회회원 대표들로 구성된다. 총회는 WMA 협의회를 선출하게 되는데, 2년에 한 차례 아프리카, 아시아, 유럽, 남미, 북미 그리고 태평양의 6개 지역 대표들이 선출된다. 협의회의 회장은 WMA 협의회에 의해서 2년마다 바뀌게 된다. 협의회 회장은 전체 WMA의 정치적 수장 역할을 담당한다.

5) 회원

WMA의 회원은 정회원과 준회원으로 나뉜다. 정회원은 각 국가의 국가의사협회를 대표하는 기관이 대부분이다. 준회원은 개인회원을 말한다.

6) 주요 사업

WMA는 다음의 영역과 관련된 활동을 한다.
① 건강과 관련된 인권
② 의학교육

③ 의료서비스를 위한 인적 자원 계획

④ 환자안전

⑤ 흡연관리 및 예방접종 등의 대중건강정책 및 프로젝트

⑥ 새로운 의료협회를 위한 민주주의 구축

⑦ 리더십과 직업 개발

⑧ 의사권리와 환자권리 홍보

⑨ 직업적 건강과 안전

그 외에 WMA는 포럼을 개최하는 등 전 세계 의사들이 정보를 공유할 수 있도록 하기 위해 노력한다.

② 정보원

1) 정보배포정책

WMA의 정보원은 'Press Releases' 및 'Publications'와 'Links'로 나뉜다. 'Press Release'에서는 WMA의 보도 자료, 저널에 실린 논문 그리고 뉴스레터를 무료로 온라인 열람이 가능하다. 'Publications'에서는 WMA의 출판물을 열람할 수 있으며 'Links'에서는 관련 웹사이트의 목록을 찾아볼 수 있다.

2) 정보 자료

① Press Releases

[WMA 최신 보도 자료]

2004년 이후의 보도 자료를 열람할 수 있다. 열람 가능한

목록은 다음과 같다.

- 8 October 2007. *World Medical Association General Assembly*
- 8 October 2007. *Doctors Urged to Document Cases of torture*
- 6 October 2007. *World Medical Association Reviewing Declaration of Helsinki*
- 5 October 2007. *New WMA President Highlights* Physicians' Obligations to Respect Human Life
- 5 October 2007. *Chinese Medical Association Reaches Agreement with World Medical Association against Transplantation of Prisoners' Organs*
- 23 August 2007. *World Medical Association Launches on Line Medical Ethics Course for Physicians*
- 24 July 2007. *ICN and WMA Welcome the Release of Bulgarian Nurses and Palestinian Physician*
- 14 May 2007. *World Medical Association Council Meeting*
- 11 May 2007. *World Medical Association Urges Support for Doctors Facing Pressure on Torture*
- 10 May 2007. *American Family Physician becomes Chair of the World Medical Association*
- 21 March 2007. *New Online Tuberculosis Course for Physicians Piloted by World Medical Association*
- 19 December 2006. *World Medical Association and International Council Of Nurses Appalled at Libyan Death*

Sentences

- 12 December 2006. *Self Governance of Medical Profession Threatened*
- 8 December 2006. *WMA and ICN Plead to Drop Death Sentences*
- 16 October 2006. *WMA General Assembly*
- 16 October 2006. *WMA Condemns All forced Feeding*
- 14 October 2006. *Governments Urged to Issue Scientifically Proven Messages on Preventing HIV/AIDS*
- 13 October 2006. *New WMA President Urges Global Action to Fight Lifestyle Diseases*
- 19 September 2006. *WMA Annual General Assembly*
- 26 June 2006. *New Online Tuberculosis Course for Physicians to be Piloted by World Medical Association*
- 30 May 2006. *WMA Urges Politicians and Actors to Set an Example by Stopping Smoking*
- 22 May 2006. *World Medical Association Demands China Stops Using Prisoners for Organ Transplants*
- 22 May 2006. *World Medical Association Clarifies Its Ethical Advice to Physicians on Torture*
- 20 May 2006. *World Medical Association Calls for Taiwan to be Given Observer Status at World Health Assembly*
- 21 March 2006. *Nobel Peace Laureates and Representatives of 20 Million Health Care Providers Call on Governments to Fund the Scale up of Human Resources Need-*

ed to Fight TB

- 26 January 2006. *World Medical Association Secretary General Awarded Honorary Degree*
- 26 December 2005. *Nurses and Physicians Welcome Libyan Court's Decision to Reverse Death Sentences*
- 7 December 2005. *Physicians Support International Human Rights Day by Condemning Stigma of Mental Illness*
- 17 October 2005. *World Medical Association General Assembly*
- 17 October 2005. *Genetic Testing Advised for Those at Risk of Disease*
- 16 October 2005. *Physicians Propose Far Reaching Measures to Reduce the Global Impact of Alcohol on Health*
- 14 October 2005. *All Physicians Should be Kept Informed on Avian Flu Threat, Says WMA*
- 14 October 2005. *Health Care Dumbed Bown to Lowest Common Denominator of Cost, Warns President of World Medical Association*
- 26 September 2005. *WMA Annual General Assembly*
- 22 August 2005. *World Health Professions Alliance Expands to Include Dentists*
- 16 May 2005. *World Medical Association Council meeting*
- 15 May 2005. *World Medical Association Calls to End*

to Taiwan's Exclusion From Receipt of Health Information

- 15 May 2005. *Physicians' Leaders Urge World Health Organization to Take Action on Medical Migration*
- 18 April 2005. *World Medical Association Council*
- 26 January 2005. *Physicians and Lawyers Learn to Collaborate on Detecting Evidence of Torture*
- 19 January 2005. *Health Professionals and Patients Announce Historic Partnership*
- 18 January 2005. *New Manual Launched to Help Physicians Facing Ethical Challenges*
- 6 January 2005. *National Medical Associations Quick to Join Global Relief Effort*
- 27 December 2004. *World Medical Association Urges Physicians to Aid Earthquake Disaster Victims*
- 18 November 2004. *Physicians for Human Rights Moves to Cambridge; Artists and Activists will Collaborate in New Space*
- 28 October 2004. *World Medical Association Launches Search for the World's Most Caring Physicians*
- 11 October 2004. *Clarification on Declaration of Helsinki*
- 11 October 2004. *New WMA Secretary General Appointed*
- 10 October 2004. *Plea for Every Human to Have Access to Safe Drinking Water*
- 9 October 2004. *Physicians' Ethical Duty in Times of*

Armed Conflict Reiterated

- 9 October 2004. *WMA Issues New Guidelines on the Relationship between Physicians and Commercial Enterprises*

- 9 October 2004. *Physicians and Patients Urged to Fight Barriers to Quality Patient Care*

- 7 September 2004. *AMA, WMA and Others Unite to Celebrate Global Medical Ethics Day*

- 27 August 2004. *WMA General Assembly*

- 27 July 2004. *WMA: Letter sent to the British Prime Minister*

- 24 June 2004. *World's Physicians Make Final Plea for Tobacco Control Treaty*

- 12 June 2004. *Physicians Should Report Acts of Torture, Says WMA President*

- 9 June 2004. *Governments Should Pay More Attention to Children's Health Rights, Says WMA*

- 7 June 2004. *International Health Professional Poll Puts Heart Disease, Obesity and Cancer As Top Health Problems*

- 17 May 2004. *World Medical Association Council Meeting*

- 16 May 2004. *Health Professionals Issue a Wake up Call on AIDS*

- 15 May 2004. *WMA Appeals to Libya to Lift Death Sentences*

- 15 May 2004. *WMA Calls for Greater Physician Involvement in Preparing for Health Emergencies*
- 24 April 2004. *World Medical Association "Appalled" at Oral Mutilation in Parts of Africa*
- 13 April 2004. *Historic Gathering of Key Health Professions*
- 06 April 2004. *WMA Regrets Maltese Government's Decision to Delay No Smoking Ban*
- 23 March 2004. *World Medical Association Pleads for Doctors and Dentists Imprisoned in Cuba*
- 27 February 2004. *Help Urged for Universities in Developing Countries*
- 30 January 2004. *WMA Work Group Seeks Further Advice on Declaration of Helsinki*
- 12 January 2004. *WMA Leader Urges Further Action to Combat Violence*

[WMA 기록관]

1996년부터 2003년 사이의 보도 자료를 열람할 수 있다. 대표적인 목록은 다음과 같다.

- 30 December 2003. *Young Doctors Should Work in Poorer Nations, Says WMA President*
- 17 December 2003. *Urgent Need for New Drugs in Sub Saharan Africa, Says WMA President*
- 29 October 2003. *Developed World Warned to Avoid*

Complacency over SARS

- 10 October 2003. *WMA Leaders in Talks on Implementing New Guidelines for Torture Documentation*
- 15 September 2003. *World Medical Association General Assembly*
- 15 September 2003. *Action Urged to Improve Response to World Health Epidemics*
- 14 September 2003. *WMA to Continue Discussion on Declaration of Helsinki*
- 13 September 2003. *Physicians Urged to Denounce Acts of Torture*
- 13 September 2003. *New WMA President Condemns Ill Treatment of Children*
- 12 September 2003. *Quality of Medical Education at Risk from Growing Number of Medical Schools*
- 11 September 2003. *Patients becoming More Empowered, New Study Finds − Embargo: 00:01 Hrs, 11 September 2003*
- 4 August 2003. *Physicians and Dentists Join Forces to Help their Patients in the Battle against Tobacco*
- 30 June 2003. *World Medical Association Appoints New Head Of Medical Ethics*
- 30 June 2003. *Global Communication Network for Physicians and Other Health Professionals*
- 26 June 2003. *Declaration on Tobacco Free Initiative*

by Physicians

- 26 June 2003. *Message by Secretary −General Kofi Annan for the International Day in Support of Victims of torture*
- 26 June 2003. *United Nations International Day in Support of Victims of Torture*
- 23 June 2003. *Physicians Under Threat, Warns WMA President*
- 20 May 2003. *World Medical Association 164th Council Meeting*
- 19 May 2003. *Health Ministers Urged to Stand Firm on Tobacco Action*
- 18 May 2003. *the Law and Medical Ethics*
- 18 May 2003. *Global Network for Physicians Should be Developed, Says WMA*
- 16 May 2003. *World Medical Association Urges Taiwan's Acceptance to the Who As An Observer*
- 15 May 2003. *New Plans to Detect torture Announced*
- 24 April 2003. *Newark, N.J., forum Focuses on Medical, Pharmaceutical Ethics*
- 28 January 2003. *Dr Jong Wook Lee Nominated to be WHO Director −General*

[의학저널 논문]

- *News from the International Alliance of Patients'*

Organizations(IAPO) July 2003

[뉴스레터]

- *Policy Statement and Guidelines for Patient Involvement in Health Policy. IAPO May 2005*
- *Nurses for Patient Safety: Targeting Counterfeit and Substandard Medicines − The International Council of Nurses* May 2005
- *"Prevent" the Newsletter of the Global Campaign for Violence Prevention*
- *Global Campaign for Violence Prevention* April 2005
- *International Alliance of Patient's Organizations IAPO April 2005*
- *Important News from IAPO IAPO April 2005*
- *News from the IRCT IRCT March 2005*
- *First Ever Global Patients Congress*
- *IAPO Manifesto for Patient − Centred Healthcare Tops the Agenda IAPO 23 February 2005*
- *International Alliance of Patients' Organizations(IAPO). IAPO 1 February 2005*
- *Plant − made Pharmaceuticals Show Promise for Disease Treatment − IAPO 11 January 2005*
- *Royal College of Psychiatrists' Press Release: Cognitive Behaviour Therapy and Coping with Trauma 11 January 2005*

- *Priority Medicines Project – IAPO 19 November 2004*
- *International Alliance of Patients' Organizations(IAPO) IAPO 26 July 2004*
- *IAPO(International Alliance of Patients Organizations) Press Release IAPO 7 July 2004*
- *News from International Alliance of Patients' Organizations(IAPO) IAPO June 2004*
- *Health in the Enlarged EU CPME Info – Standing Committee of European Doctors 17 May 2004*
- *News from International Alliance of Patients' Organizations(IAPO) IAPO April 2004*
- *News from International Alliance of Patients' Organizations(IAPO) IAPO February 2004*
- *News from the IRCT IRCT September 2003*
- *International Training on Refugees Health IFMSA – International Federation of Medical Students Association September 2003*

② Publications

WMA의 저널 및 정기간행물을 PDF로 다운받아 열람할 수 있다.

[WMA 저널]

- *WMJ* 01 2007
- *WMJ* 02 2007
- *WMJ* 03 2007

- *WMJ* 01 2006
- *WMJ* 02 2006
- *WMJ* 03 2006
- *WMJ* 04 2006
- *WMJ* 01 2005
- *WMJ* 02 2005
- *WMJ* 03 2005
- *WMJ* 04 2005
- *WMJ* 01 2004
- *WMJ* 02 2004
- *WMJ* 03 2004
- *WMJ* 04 2004

[WMA 정기간행물]
- *Exhibitions & Conferences* 2001 – 2002
- *Global Healthcare* 2002
- *Global Healthcare* 2001
- *Global Healthcare* 2000

③ Links
WMA가 제공하는 기관의 웹사이트 링크 목록은 다음과 같다.
[WMA와 공식적인 관계에 있는 기관들]
- Comité Permanent des Médecins Européens(CPME)
- International Labour Office(ILO)
- World Health Organization(WHO)

- WHO Tobacco Free Initiative
- WHO European Partnership Project to Reduce Tobacco Dependence and the Society for Research on Nicotine and Tobacco(SRNT)

[WMA의 자문기관들]
- Council of Europe
- United Nations Economic and Social Council(ECOSOC)

[WMA의 협력기관들]
- American Association for the Advancement of Science (AAAS) AAAS Science and Human Rights Program
- Amnesty International(AI) International Secretariat
- Commonwealth Medical Association(CMA)
- Confederation of Medical Associations in Asia and Oceania(CMAAO) Japan Medical Association
- Confederaciòn Médica Latino Americana y del Caribe (ConFEMEL)
- Council for International Organizations of Medical Sciences(CIOMS)
- Guidlines International Network
- International Alliance of Patients' Organizations
- International Committee of the Red Cross(ICRC)
- International Council of Nurses(ICN)
- International Federation of Clinical Chemistry(IFCC)

- International Federation of Medical Students' Associations (IFMSA)
- International Federation of Pharmaceutical Manufacturers Associations(IFPMA)
- International Hospital Federation(IHF)
- International Medical Informatics Association(IMIA)
- International Pharmaceutical Federation(FIP)
- International Rehabilitation Council for Torture Victims (IRCT)
- International Social Security Association(isSA)
- International Union of the Medical Press(IUMP)
- Medical Women's International Association(MWIA)
- Pan American Health Organization(PAHO)
- Physicians against Land Mines(PALM) Center for International Rehabilitation
- Rehabilitation International(RI)
- Union Médicale Balkanique(UMB)
- World Confederation for Physical therapy(WCPT)
- World Dental Federation(FDI)
- World Federation for Medical Education(WFME) Faculty of Health Sciences
- The Panum Institute
- World Psychiatric Association(WPA)
- World Self-Medication Industry(WSMI)

참고문헌

한명규. 2003. 최신 공중보건학. 서울: 도서출판신정.

이인모. 2001. 최신 공중보건학. 서울: 계축문화사.

방두연 외. 2008. 공중보건학. 파주: 동화기술

이용성 외. 2005. 공중보건학. 서울: 동화기술.

약 어 표

ACQUIRE Project	Access, Quality, and Use in Reproductive Health Project 모자보건프로젝트
AED - SATELLIFE	Center for Health Information and Technology 의료정보기술센터
FCTC	Framework Convention Alliance for Tobacco Control 흡연규제협약연합
FDIWDF	FDI World Dental Federation FDI 세계치과연합
FENS	Federation of European Nutrition Societies 유럽영양학협회연합
FIP	International Pharmaceutical Federation 국제약학연합
GFHR	Global Forum for Health Research 세계보건연구포럼
GHC	Global Health Council 세계건강협의회
GWA	Gender and Water Alliance 젠더와물동맹기구
HINARI	Health InterNetwork Access to Research Initiative 연구이니셔티브를위한건강네트워크
HMN	Health Metrics Network 의료메트릭스네트워크

HN TPO	HealthNet TPO TPO 건강네트
IAPO	International Alliance of Patients' Organizations 국제환자기구동맹
IASO	International Association for the Study of Obesity 국제비만연구협회
ICDA	International Confederation of Dietetic Associations 국제식이성협회연합
ICN	International Council of Nurses 국제간호사협의회
IDF	International Diabetes Federation 국제당뇨병연맹
IFICF	International Food Information Council Foundation 국제식량정보협의회재단
IFMSA	InternationL Federation of Medical Students' Associations 국제의대생협회연합
IFPMA	International Federation of Pharmaceutical Manufactueres & Associations 국제약업단체연합회
INRUD	International Network for the Rational Use of Drugs 합리적약물복용을위한국제네트워크

INWAT	International Network of Women against Tobacco 국제흡연반대여성네트워크
IPA	International Pediatric Association 국제소아협회
IRC	International Water and Sanitation Center 국제물위생센터
IRC RCM	International Red Cross and Red Crescent Movement 국제적십자사
isH	International Society of Hypertension 국제고혈압연합
ISID	International Society for Infectious Diseases 국제전염성질병협회
IUATLD	International Union against Tuberculous and Lung Disease 국제결핵및폐질병퇴치연맹
IUFoST	International Union of Food Science & Technology 국제식량과학기술연합
IUHPE	International Union for Health Promotion and Education 국제보건증진및교육연맹
IUNS	International Union of Nutritional Sciences 국제영양학연맹

MFI	Malaria Foundation International
	국제말라리아재단
MSF	Medecins Sans Frontiers
	국경없는의사회
MWIA	Medical Women' International Association
	국제여의사협회
OxHA	Oxford Health Alliance
	옥스퍼드보건연맹
PMNCH	Partnership for Maternal, Newborn and Child Health
	산모, 신생아, 아동건강파트너십
ProCOR	Conference on Cardiovascular Health
	심장혈관의료콘퍼런스
TDR	UNICEF－UNDP－World Bank－WHO Special Programme or Research and Training in Tropical Diseases
	열대병에 관한 연구 및 교육을 위한 유니세프, 유엔개발프로그램, 세계은행, 세계보건기구 합동 특별 프로그램
UNAIDS	United Nations Programme on HIV/AIDS
	유엔에이즈계획
WHF	World Heart Federation
	세계심장연합
WHL	World Hypertension League
	세계고혈압연맹

WHO	World Health Organization
	세계보건기구
WHPA	World Health Professions Alliance
	국제의료전문직연맹
WMA	World Medical Association
	세계의료협회

국문색인

영문색인

· 저자 ·

노영희
(魯榮姬)

•약 력•

연세대학교 문헌정보학과 정보학 박사
한국과학기술연구원(KIST) 자료실 연구원
한국정보공학(KIES) 정보검색엔진개발팀 팀장
이화여대 국제정보센터 자료실장
현) 건국대학교 문헌정보학과 교수
　　교육인적자원부 대학도서관 정책자문위원
　　DLS 표준관리위원회 위원

•주요 저서 및 논문•

「개념기반 검색을 위한 시소러스 관계의 효과적 활용방안에 관한 연구」
「주제별 분산 지식베이스에 의한 개념기반 정보검색 시스템의 성능향상에 관한 연구」
「A Study on Automatic Text Categorization of Internet Documents」
「A Study on the Estimation of Performance of Concept Based Information Retrieval Model Using the Web」
「기계학습 기반 피드백 과정을 통한 SDI 시스템의 성능향상에 관한 연구」
「문헌정보학 교육과정의 특성화된 프로그램 개발 및 활용에 관한 연구」
『디지털콘텐츠의 이해』
『인문과학과 예술의 핵심 지식정보원』
『경제학의 핵심 지식정보원』
『2009 한국문헌정보학 교과과정』
『개념기반 정보검색 기법』

외 다수

홍현진
(洪賢珍)

•약 력•

연세대학교 문과대학 문헌정보학과(학사)
University of Michigan in Ann Arbor 문헌정보학과(석사)
연세대학교 대학원 문헌정보학과(박사)
대우경제연구소 정보자료실 실장
한국도서관협회 기획위원
국립중앙도서관 장서개발위원
문화관광부 문화기반시설 평가위원
현) 정보관리학회 편집위원
　　교육인적자원부 대학도서관 정책자문위원
　　문화관광부 국가도서관정책 자문위원
　　전남대학교 사회과학대학 부학장
　　전남대학교 사회과학대학 문헌정보학과 교수

•주요 저서 및 논문•

「우리나라 공공도서관에 대한 평가지표 연구」
「웹 기반 데이터베이스의 품질평가 기준 개발에 관한 연구」
「국가문헌센터 건립 최적화 연구」
「A Study on Possible Ways to Improve Policy Information Services and Demand Survey Analysis」

「도서관의 정보서비스 품질평가 연구에 관한 고찰」
「정책정보통합서비스시스템 구축 모형에 관한 연구」
『문헌정보학의 연구방법론』
『한국도서관기준』
『국제기구 지식정보원의 이해와 활용』
『경제관련 국제기구 지식정보원』
『도서관 조직의 혁신과 변화논리』

도서관 경영정책과 정보서비스 분야에 약 50여 편의 논문을 발표함

국제기구 지식정보원 시리즈 ❽

건강보건관련 국제기구 지식정보원

초판인쇄 | 2009년 7월 31일
초판발행 | 2009년 7월 31일

지은이 | 홍현진·노영희
펴낸이 | 채종준
펴낸곳 | 한국학술정보㈜
주 소 | 경기도 파주시 교하읍 문발리 파주출판문화정보산업단지 513-5
전 화 | 031) 908-3181(대표)
팩 스 | 031) 908-3189
홈페이지 | http://www.kstudy.com
E-mail | 출판사업부 publish@kstudy.com

등 록 | 제일산-115호(2000. 6. 19)
가 격 | 39,000원

ISBN   978-89-268-   Paper Book)
        978-89-268-0233-5 98060(e-Book)